COAL BURNING FREIGHT ENGINE

Rogers L. & M. Works

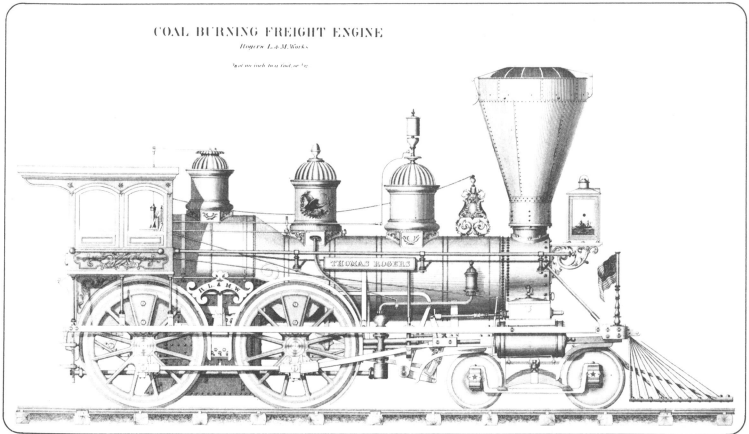

Mr. Lincoln's Military Railroads

Mr. Lincoln's Military Railroads

A Pictorial History of United States Civil War Railroads

BY ROY MEREDITH AND ARTHUR MEREDITH

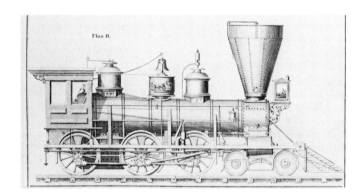

W.W. Norton & Company
New York   London

Books by Roy Meredith

Mr. Lincoln's Camera: Matthew B. Brady

The Face of Robert E. Lee

Mr. Lincoln's Contemporaries

The American Wars

Storm Over Sumter

This Was Andersonville

Mr. Lincoln's General: U. S. Grant

The World of Matthew Brady

People You Will Never Meet

Copyright © 1979 by W. W. Norton & Company, Inc. Published simultaneously in Canada by George J. McLeod Limited, Toronto. Printed in the United States of America.

All Rights Reserved

FIRST EDITION

Library of Congress Cataloging in Publication Data

Meredith, Roy, 1908–
    Mr. Lincoln's military railroads.

    Includes index.
    1. United States—History—Civil War, 1861–1865—Transportation. 2. Military railroads—United States—History. I. Meredith, Arthur, 1931–   joint author.
II. Title.
E491.M5 1978   973.7′8   78–26056
ISBN 0–393–05703–8

Book design by Dennis J. Grastorf
Typefaces used are Caledonia and Koster
Set by The Fuller Organization, Inc.
Printed and bound by the Murray Printing Company

1 2 3 4 5 6 7 8 9 0

Dedicated to my late son,
Arthur, who conceived
the idea for the present book.

Contents

The Baltimore & Ohio's *Thatcher Perkins*, No. 117.

Star of the Baltimore & Ohio's locomotive roster, and named after its designer and builder, Thatcher Perkins, No. 117 is a classic example of steam motive power of the Civil War period. Her 4–6–0 wheel arrangement and sleek lines make this engine one of the most beautifully designed of her day.

Introduction

WHEN CONFEDERATE RAIDERS destroyed a section of his rail supply line during General Sherman's advance into Georgia in 1864, thereby temporarily cutting off his army's food supply, Sherman told his soldiers: "The quicker you build the railroad, the quicker you'll get something to eat!"

Thus, in one sentence, General Sherman unintentionally summed up how vitally important the U.S. Military Railroads system had become to the North's successful prosecution of the war. At the same time, the "war is hell" soldier unwittingly underlined the importance of the dedicated railroad men who directed, managed, operated, built—and rebuilt—the badly damaged lines in record time under crushing wartime difficulties.

For the most part, these railroad men—engineers, trainmen, firemen, track builders, car builders, locomotive mechanics, and the like—remain unknown to this day, men who risked their lives under the same battle conditions as the soldiers in uniform.

When the war began it was almost automatic, though momentarily unanticipated, that the larger eastern railroads would be called into government military service in response to President Lincoln's call for volunteers to transport those troops from the eastern, midwestern, and western states, to the staging area at Washington, D.C., that was totally unprepared to receive them.

It was a new situation that the railroads had to face, far removed from peacetime operations, but the railroads responded immediately. At times political considerations and interference, and even political chicanary, on the part of some government officials, who saw a golden opportunity to line their pockets out of the nation's distress, also added to the confusion as the North geared up for war. It was only after almost a year of political bungling and ineptitude that matters regarding the railroads in the war effort took a turn for the better as their importance began to be recognized.

The U.S. Military Railroads system was created by the Congressional Railways and Telegraphs Act of 1862, which gave President Lincoln unequivocal authority to seize any or all railroads in the nation to be employed for military purposes if those lines did not cooperate in the war effort, especially in the transport of troops and supplies to where they were needed.

Oddly enough, the South's military authorities, with the exception of General R. E. Lee, overlooked the importance of the South's existing railroads, even after Captain John B. Imboden and Stonewall Jackson spotlighted their importance in raids on the B & O line at Harper's Ferry in 1861. By the same token, it can be said that the USMRR was the "prime mover" in the North's military effort, and was more than just incidental to the successful outcome of the conflict in the North's favor.

The man responsible for making the U.S. Military Railroads a functioning instrument of war was Herman Haupt, whose genius in organization and railroad construction brought order out of chaos. By establishing strict operational regulations, and teaching "old line" army officers who did not believe in military railroads how to use them to their advantage, Haupt built the USMRR into one of the single most important nonfiring weapons in the North's arsenal.

One must bear in mind that most of the railroads of that day were single-tracked, with occasional turnouts and sidings. Operating military supply and troop trains, running in both directions at the same time, called for a managerial genius to keep those train movements from becoming hopelessly entangled, particularly when the only other means of communication was an indifferent, fragile telegraph line, cut by the enemy most of the time.

Everything Haupt, and later Daniel McCallum, established in the early operational stages of the USMRR remained in force to the end, in many cases improved upon. And it is to the credit of the USMRR and the federal government that private railroads taken over by the Union armies during a campaign in a given region were returned to their original owners when the armies moved elsewhere and the lines were no longer needed. Morever, any damage these railroads sustained during the fighting was repaired as quickly as possible by the USMRR Construction Corps, which incidently performed unheard-of feats reconstructing tracks and bridges in record time.

Mr. Lincoln's Military Railroads begins with the story of the federal government's first official train operation, bringing President-elect Abraham Lincoln to Washington, D.C., for his inauguration, and ends with the USMRR's last official function, returning President Lincoln's body to Springfield, Illinois, as the war's last casualty.

During the latter part of 1865 the USMRR, in a phasing-out process, was used to return paroled prisoners and mustered-out soldiers to their homes, as well as moving the wounded to recovery areas. Meanwhile, the repair process continued, and the lines were returned to their former owners.

After the cleanup, its postwar duties ended, the USMRR was dissolved and its military insignia removed from all rolling stock and locomotives.

The records of the U.S. Military Railroads are vast, filling many volumes. Even the report of the litigation that followed after the war, in assessing the responsibility of the federal government for war damage to the participating railroads, fills a five-hundred-page book, and is a story in itself.

Last, but certainly not least, the idea for this book was conceived by my late son, Arthur. It was his original exhaustive research on the subject, and his contacts with the various railroads—and their cheerful cooperation—that made the book possible.

Every effort has been made for accuracy in relating this story pictorially, with the gracious assistance of several good people in Maryland and Washington. Therefore, if any errors have occurred unwittingly, they are the sole responsibility of the writer.

Roy Meredith

Mr. Lincoln's Military Railroads

If other departments had been as well organized
and managed as the Military Railroads, the war chariots
would not have been so frequently off the track.
—PETER H. WATSON
Assistant Secretary of War
1861–1865

CHAPTER 1

Prelude to Conflict

In 1850 the United States was still a vast wilderness. Inland cities and towns were loosely connected by rutted wagon roads and traces. Cities located on the eastern seaboard from Maine to Florida, and on the Gulf Coast from New Orleans to Galveston, were accessible by coastwise shipping, but traveling to those same cities by overland routes required long, tedious stagecoach or horseback rides over circuitous roads, through clouds of dust in summer and quagmires of axle-deep mud or snow in spring and winter.

In the decade preceding the Civil War, America's railroads were largely an uncoordinated tangle of separate short lines less than fifty miles of length, usually serving farming or manufacturing communities. Few if any operated on daily schedules. Most were the targets of stock speculators or prey to their own directorates who fed lavishly on their revenues.

Preoccupied with personal profit, railroad promoters and operators gave little thought to long-range planning for public service. That the nation's rail lines might become vital military highways clearly never entered their minds.

As the nineteenth century passed the halfway mark, rising commercialism and the "manifest destiny" syndrome created a demand for quick, inexpensive transportation, which the federal government was incapable of providing. To add to this dilemma, the discovery of gold at Sutter's Mill in the California Sierras suddenly changed the old order of practically everything.

With each gold strike, clusters of mining towns sprang up overnight, and given names like Angel's Camp, Hangtown, Dutch Flat, and Gold Run. For each lucky miner there were thousands who failed but who still bought equipment and supplies.

To an astute eastern businessman, the bonanza lay in supplying mining equipment, food, and transportation to the California gold fields on a cash-and-carry basis. Meeting this demand was sure business, no wild gamble such as the one each prospector took. The eastern gold seeker never had to crack a rock, dig a hole, or get his feet wet rocking a cradle in a stream. He missed most of the fun, but he became rich.

The era of prosperity, which followed a decade of depression, spawned men of foresight like Marshall Owen Roberts and George Law who made fortunes buying interests in the newly organized railroads and streetcar lines. Law, for example, rose to prominence in the councils of the Mohawk & Hudson and Harlem River railroads.

Although the land grants and financing offered by Congress proved irresistible lures to many railroad promoters of questionable integrity and many miles of track were projected from nowhere to nowhere, on the whole there was more honesty of purpose than dishonesty.

During the early 1850s, the vast but rapidly filling areas of the Middle West and the West provided room and need for yet more railroad expansion. Though fairly numerous short rail lines existed between the Great Lakes and the seaboard, there were no connections between the northern and southern railroads except by steamboat on the Ohio River or ferry across the Potomac River to Alexandria, Virginia. Some combination of control and a standardization of gauges, scheduling, and equipment had to be achieved if the myriad of short, unconnected lines were to be of maximum service. Opposition to the unification of lines grew out of the national prejudice against "bigness" and monopoly. Moreover, in commercial terms the successful early railroads ran toward the proper destinations,

Railroading in the Late 1840s.

Constituent railroads in the late 1840s and 1850s were forty- or fifty-mile short lines, and single-tracked. The locomotive is the famous Pioneer of the Chicago & Northwestern Railroad. Pioneer was a 4–2–0, balloon-stacked locomotive. The wooden coach, typical of the period, has a four-wheel, two-truck arrangement, an invention of Ross Winans, a railroad mechanical engineer.

COURTESY CHICAGO & NORTHWESTERN RAILWAY.

Travel—The Way It Was Before the Railroads.

River travel was the main means of travel in the United States before the advent of the steam engine. Shown is a Mississippi River paddle-wheel steamboat passing a typical river landing and settlement.

A CURRIER AND IVES PRINT, AUTHOR'S COLLECTION.

A Three-Car Passenger Train of the Late 1840s.

A passenger train of the Louisville & Nashville Railroad crossing an iron trestle bridge over a ravine in the deep South. The L & N became a temporary part of the U.S. Military Railroads during the bloody battles for Kentucky and Tennessee.

COURTESY LOUISVILLE & NASHVILLE RAILROAD.

The *Tom Thumb.*

Designed and built by Peter Cooper in the 1830s, with the assistance of Ross Winans, Tom Thumb resembled Stephenson's Rocket.

COURTESY BALTIMORE & OHIO RAILROAD.

Early 1850 Passenger Coach.

Used extensively before and during the Civil War, this "open-end" platformed passenger coach of the Chicago & Northwestern Railway carried troops to Washington from the Midwest in 1861.

COURTESY CHICAGO & NORTHWESTERN RAILWAY.

The *Mud-Digger.*

This early B & O locomotive earned its sobriquet of "mud-digger" from its unique piston and valve motion. No mechanical beauty, the Mud-Digger was nevertheless functional.

COURTESY BALTIMORE & OHIO RAILROAD.

and for the right reasons, and their healthy financial position soon placed them in the category of "dowager railroads," a then meaning "built and operated independently without government or public aid."

The early consolidation of the New York Central Railroad was a success stemming from noncooperation and the very heavy hand of partisan politics. The Mohawk & Hudson, Utica & Schenectady, Syracuse & Utica, and Auburn & Rochester, like the rest of the nation's short lines, were operated like so many petty duchies. Insofar as joint operational cooperation between them was concerned, they might have been running on different planets. There was no physical connection between most of them, and track gauges often did not match. At most junction points, the "through" traveler had to "change cars" in order to complete his journey, since one line's cars could not operate over the tracks of the other.

The consolidation of four of New York's short

lines into the famous New York Central was accomplished through the political influence and far-sightedness of Erastus Corning, president of the Utica & Schenectady. Corning's work was accomplished with the help of Thurlow Weed, the great Whig politician called the "wizard of the Albany lobby." A power in the New York legislature, Weed knew the weaknesses of his fellow politicians and handled them accordingly, operating on the practical principle that "every man has his price." It seldom failed him.

With Weed's help, Corning got his merger in 1842 and became the New York Central's first president, a post he held until 1864. It was now possible to travel across New York State without changing trains. Many travelers, while impressed with this new, long-distance innovation, were even more astonished at the speed of the train. One traveler riding out of Albany said that he "was hurried along with rapidity . . . and in rather less than an hour reached Schenectady, a distance of sixteen miles!"

The backwoods soldier, Colonel Davy Crockett, tried a more homespun method of checking the speed of the train he happened to be riding on. "I can only judge the speed by putting my head out of the window to spit, which I did," he said, "and overtook it so quick, that it hit me smack in the face!"

Years before the New York Central merger, the

Erastus Corning

The president of the Utica & Schenectady Railroad, Corning was the prime mover in the consolidation of four New York State railroads into the New York Central in pre-Vanderbilt days. Lobbyist Thurlow Weed, "wizard of the Albany lobby," provided the heavy political clout and persuasion to accomplish the merger.

AUTHOR'S COLLECTION.

Grasshopper.

A functional locomotive of its day, it was dubbed Grasshopper for its driving-rod arrangement which resembled the long, jumping hind legs of that energetic insect.

COURTESY BALTIMORE & OHIO RAILROAD.

Thomas Swann.

A staunch Unionist, Swann, the president of the Baltimore & Ohio Railroad, used bulldozing political tactics to save his railroad from bankruptcy by establishing the important terminal at Wheeling, Virginia (now West Virginia).

AUTHOR'S COLLECTION.

Baltimore & Ohio Railroad had a difficult time trying to compete with canals such as the Lehigh Coal & Navigation Company's canal from Mauch Chunk to the Delaware River Terminal at Bristol, Pennsylvania, and the Erie Canal of New York. These canals were bringing prosperity to Philadelphia and New York, and these cities wanted no changes in the present status.

Years of discouragement and struggle ended for the B & O when Thomas Swann became its president in 1848. In the face of skepticism, looming bankruptcy, and a credit rating of nil in Baltimore, the astute Swann, with little more than just plain nerve, managed to construct the road's line as far as Wheeling, Virginia, on the Ohio River. The river terminal changed everything for the road, and the Baltimore & Ohio became one of the most important and prosperous railroads in the nation.

Swann, a staunch Unionist, could have become one of the nation's great railroad men had he chosen to do so, but he was too engrossed in politics. Later it was said that his excursion into that unsubstantial realm was accomplished by the same

bulldozing tactics he employed to save his railroad. Apparently, in Thomas Swann's case, the end had justified the means.

Meanwhile, short-line railroads, responsible for the astonishing growth of the Northwest, offered fast, direct service to northwestern markets with which the steamboats could not possibly hope to compete.

Recognizing the pressing need for a national approach to transportation the federal government initiated the era of federal subsidy. Land was granted to railroad constructors as an incentive and aid in the building of a system of railroads from Mobile, Alabama, to northern Illinois—but with stringent conditions. First, the proposed line had to be completed in ten years or all the land granted reverted back to the government. Moreover, all monies received by the state from lands already sold had to be repaid to the federal treasury. This rule applied to all grants. Grants to Pacific railroads, largely from the western territories were made directly to corporations. Heretofore government land had sold for $1.25 an acre. Coincident with the act of Congress, the price was raised to

Abraham Lincoln in 1853.

Mr. Lincoln, as he looked when he met Grenville Dodge at Council Bluffs, Iowa, where the brilliant young engineer pointed out the nation's need for a transcontinental railroad.

AUTHOR'S COLLECTION.

Railroad Bridge Construction in 1860.

Railroad expansion and construction boomed in the decade before the Civil War. Shown is a wooden truss bridge, of a type designed by Colonel Herman Haupt for the U.S. Military Railroads and prefabricated for military use. Remarkably strong, this bridge is being constructed by Chicago & Northwestern Railway.

COURTESY CHICAGO & NORTHWESTERN RAILWAY.

A Typical Train on the Chicago & Northwestern Railway in 1856.

Head-ended by a sleek, balloon-stacked 4-4-0, this train crosses a newly constructed viaduct near Alton, Illinois. The coaches are two-door baggage car and a combined passenger and baggage car.

COURTESY CHICAGO & NORTHWESTERN RAILWAY.

WANTED!
3,000 LABORERS

On the 12th Division of the

ILLINOIS CENTRAL RAILROAD

Wages, $1.25 per Day.

Fare, from New-York, only - - $4)5

By Railroad and Steamboat, to the work in the
State of Illinois.

Constant employment for two years or more
given. Good board can be obtained at two
dollars per week.

This is a rare chance for persons to go
West, being sure of permanent employment
in a healthy climate, where land can be
bought cheap, and for fertility is not surpassed
in any part of the Union.

Men with families preferred.

For further information in regard to it, call
at the Central Railroad Office,

Illinois Central Want Ad.

*Offering wages of a $1.25 a day for construction work on
the new railroad, the Illinois Central offered inducements
of a $4.50 rail fare from New York and employment for two
years.*

COURTESY ILLINOIS CENTRAL RAILROAD.

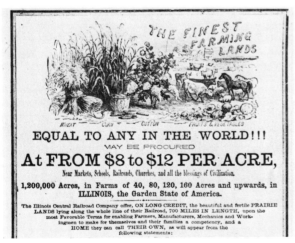

The Illinois Central Railroad's Land Department Advertisement of the 1850s and 1860s.

*Offering "long credit" to farmers, mechanics, manufacturers,
and settlers, this ad attracted thousands of people to the
Midwest, who settled on the 700-mile right-of-way.*

COURTESY ILLINOIS CENTRAL RAILROAD.

Overcoming the Union Blockade of the Gulf Coast in
1861.

*The Union naval blockade prevented steamboat travel between the terminal of the New Orleans, Opeloussas & Great
Western Railway, at Morgan City, and Texas ports.*

AUTHOR'S COLLECTION.

$2.50 an acre; but even with these advanced prices, by 1855 the government reported all the land sold.

The Illinois Central was the first carrier to take advantage of the national land grants. In the decade of prosperity before the Civil War, Senator Stephen Douglas of Illinois waged a successful campaign for the construction of the Illinois Central, and managed to get the Act of September 20, 1850, passed. It granted lands to the state for a railroad. The line was to start from the terminus of the Illinois & Michigan Canal and run to a point at or near the junction of the Ohio and Mississippi rivers, with a branch line connecting Dubuque, Iowa, with Galena and Chicago. The line had to be completed in six years, and the lands would be tax-exempt in lieu of a 5 percent cut of the gross income of the road each year to be paid into the state treasury. The line would remain a public highway, and carry mail at a price set by Congress.

After several false starts the Illinois Central got underway. Construction was pushed with such vigor that by 1856 the main line between Centralia and Dunleith, opposite Dubuque on the Mississippi River, was open to through traffic.

Under the terms of the Illinois Central charter, within six years of completion the railroad took title to 2,595,000 acres along its right of way. The company had already disposed of 1,500,000 acres, and

was offering the remaining 1,200,000 acres at prices ranging from $6.00 an acre to $25.00 an acre.

Senator Stephen Douglas and the federal government gave Illinois its central railroad; the nation got its Gulf to Galena connection; and the American people were given the transport facility for which they had been clamoring for more than a generation.

Before the end of the decade, Congress gave similar railway land grants to Alabama, Mississippi, Missouri, Iowa, Arkansas, Florida, Michigan, Wisconsin, Louisiana, Minnesota, North Dakota, and South Dakota, each receiving the same grants and stipulations as Illinois. Remarkably, in almost every instance conditions of the grants were fulfilled. Within two years, five of these states would be at war.

By 1860, approximately thirty thousand miles of railroad were in operation throughout the United States, half constructed in Ohio, Illinois, and Indiana, which led all others. The extension of the Illinois Central, and its connection to the New Orleans & Jackson and Mississippi Central railroads, provided a through line from the Gulf of Mexico to the northernmost point in Illinois.

In the twenty-five years since the advent of the *Tom Thumb*, the first steam locomotive to operate on a commercial railroad in the United States, and

"Cornfield Meet" on the C & NW in the 1850s

Head-on collisions were frequent and devastating in the early days of railroading. Lack of proper scheduling and signal systems on single-track lines were usually the cause.

COURTESY CHICAGO & NORTHWESTERN RAILWAY.

Terminal and Shops of the New Orleans, Opelousas &
Great Western Railroad at Algiers, Louisiana, 1864.

In this rare photograph of this little-known railroad in Louisiana, a train of that road and a locomotive and coach of the USMRR pose for the camera. The two high-wheeled *engines are beautiful examples of motive power of the time. Algiers shops were an important repair facility of the USMRR until 1865.* PHOTOGRAPHER UNKNOWN, COURTESY LOUISVILLE & NASHVILLE RAILROAD.

Winters Grips the Railroad

Midwestern winters were a severe experience to railroad men of the Civil War decade. This is a Rock Island locomotive, a 4–4–0, on a turntable ready to enter the round-house in the yards near Chicago. The snow-covered wood *fuel and frozen water tank indicate the extreme cold. A windmill pumps well water into the tank, the amount measured by a water gauge on the roof.* COURTESY THE ROCK ISLAND RAILROAD.

Characteristic Motive Power of Some American Railroads of the 1860s

Locomotive No. 35 of the Boston & Maine Railroad once hauled Union troops and supplies from New England to eastern bases. A 4–4–0, diamond-stacked woodburner, No. 35 sported a pair of deer's antlers on her headlight.

COURTESY BOSTON & MAINE RAILROAD.

E. P. Prentice, *a light, all-purpose 4–4–0 woodburner of the Delaware & Hudson County Railroad bore a characteristic* portrait decoration on her headlight.

COURTESY NEW HAVEN RAILROAD.

The Christopher Adams, Jr., *of the New Orleans, Opeloussas & Great Western Railroad, in 1864. Her oversize pilot truck wheels and huge sixty-three inch drivers distinguished this* 4–4–0 *woodburner. Seen at Algiers, Louisiana, Adams was captured when the road was seized and operated by USMRR and Union forces in the last year of the war.*

AUTHOR'S COLLECTION.

the laying of the first roadbed of the Baltimore & Ohio Railroad on July 4, 1828, railway construction blossomed into a masterful achievement. By 1853, the Baltimore & Ohio reached Wheeling, Virginia, and connected with Chicago over the lines of the Central Railroad of Ohio, and via the Sandusky, Mansfield & Newark and Somerset & Straitsville, with Baltimore Junction, Illinois. Rail lines radiating from Lakes Erie and Michigan tapped the Mississippi River at ten points, the Ohio River at eight. In the East, the New York Central, with a through route to Chicago and a line to Buffalo, had direct access to the Midwest's main market centers. The Pennsylvania Railroad, and its connection with the Cumberland Valley Railroad over the Allegheny Mountains to Pittsburgh and Johnstown, made it possible to travel from Washington, D.C., and Boston, to Chicago, St. Louis, and points west with few changes.

The proposed transcontinental railroad to California, linking the East and West Coasts, did not become a reality until 1863 when the Civil War was at its height; and it may have been Abraham Lincoln's trip to Council Bluffs, Iowa, by rail, stage, and steamboat in 1858, and his conversation with Grenville Dodge when he got there, that convinced Lincoln that a transcontinental railroad was badly needed to bind the nation together.

Lincoln, a strong advocate of railroad construction, had journeyed to Council Bluffs to deliver a political speech in the concert hall. There he was introduced to young Dodge, the man, it was said, who knew more about railroad construction than any three men in the country.

Later, Lincoln and young Dodge sat on a bench in the Pacific House in Council Bluffs, where Lincoln questioned the young man at length about the best route for a rail line to the Pacific Coast. "He shelled my woods completely," Dodge later recalled, "and he got all the information I had collected for Henry Farnam, my employer."

After their talk, Lincoln and Dodge walked to the

A Pioneer Railroad of the Midwest in 1850.

Railroad expansion grew very rapidly in the west in the decade before the Civil War. Shown is the first train into De Pere, Wisconsin, of the Milwaukee & Northern Railway.

The ornate, clerestory-roofed coach is a result of a decade of passenger coach improvement.

COURTESY THE MILWAUKEE ROAD.

The Chicago & Northwestern's First Suburban Train.

Arriving at Park Ridge, Illinois, this C & NW local was a forerunner of the local commuter train of the present day.

The red brick station and telegraph pole are typical of the Age of Steam.

COURTESY CHICAGO & NORTHWESTERN RAILWAY.

top of a tall hill and looked westward into the haze of the Great Plains. Dodge then pointed out to Lincoln that there was no rail line between them and the West Coast, the only railroad then in existence in California being the Sacramento Valley Railroad, twenty-two miles long. In the near future Grenville Dodge would build a great Union Pacific.

Five transcontinental railroads had been proposed to Congress, and the appropriate bills were passed by both the Senate and House, but nothing ever came of them until the rails of the Central Pacific and Union Pacific joined at Promontory Point, Utah, in 1869, when, as Bret Harte described it, "the pilots met head to head."

More significant still, in the East four railroad construction companies were throwing their tracks across the Allegheny Mountains. Although construction progressed at a rapid rate, there were more failures than successes in the building of those early lines, largely due to financing inadequate to cope with the multitude of engineering problems encountered on the nation's wilderness terrain.

The completion of the Allegheny River Bridge at Pittsburgh, and the link to Fort Wayne in 1858, enabled the Pennsylvania Railroad to solicit business for Philadelphia and its port facilities from all points in the Middle West. The Pennsylvania Railroad owed great loyalty to Philadelphia, but the road could neither pay its debts nor take advantage of its opportunities. The reason was simply that Philadelphia's port and terminal facilities were inadequate to the flow of traffic. It needed—and got—a right-of-way to New York.

At this period of transition, the nation began to experience the first symptoms of a serious political disorder. For thirty-five years the United States had been slowly becoming disunited on a question of principle—the right of individual states to maintain the institution of slavery, and the right to expand it into the Western Territories.

Aggravated by hostile, sectional attitudes of slave block members in the House and Senate, the issue at once became dangerous and explosive. The election of 1856 could have been the key to the nation's dilemma, but unfortunately for the country James Buchanan was elected on the Democratic ticket. Buchanan, a weak man, allowed the nation to drift toward war.

The election of 1860 was a far different story. The New Republican party produced a strong candidate, Abraham Lincoln of Illinois. To Southerners, Lincoln represented the devil incarnate, the "Black Republican," the symbol of aggression against their

Grenville Dodge.
Dodge met with Lincoln at Council Bluffs, Iowa, to suggest the possibility and need for a transcontinental railroad, and to discuss what it would mean to the nation when completed.
AUTHOR'S COLLECTION.

historic right, so they made their plans accordingly. If Lincoln should be elected, immediate secession would follow.

Yet, even with the outbreak of the Civil War, the lively spirit of railroad expansion never abated, nor did the enthusiasm for improving old railroads.

And so, with railroad lines connecting Washington with Chicago, New England, New York, and Philadelphia, and with the rail lines in the Middle West and Western Territories, the federal government had a built-in, twenty-thousand-mile military transportation and railway supply system ready to be called upon when needed in a national emergency. Oddly enough, Northern railroads, spreading across the eastern United States, mainly ran from east to west, with no through lines connecting the North with the South. When war came the North had more than twice the operating trackage than the South.

CHAPTER 2

Delivering a President

A COLD GRAY mist hung over the little station of the Great Western Railway at Springfield, Illinois. Even the weather reflected the somber mood of the moment. Alongside the platform a short, balloon-stacked steam locomotive of the Toledo & Wabash Railroad, coupled to a train of three special coaches and a baggage car, stood quietly by, its wispy smoke blending with the damp gray air.

On this special morning, a thousand of Springfield's citizens had assembled on the platform, long before train time, standing in the drizzle to say a fond farewell to a good friend and neighbor, Abraham Lincoln, newly elected president. Most of them had known him for more than a quarter-century. One who was missing from the crowd was William "Billy" Herndon, Lincoln's law partner and friend of many years. He remained in his office unwilling to be seen crying in public.

Inside the station, the newly elected, though not yet confirmed, chief executive of the nation waited patiently with members of his family and a party of fifteen while preparations were made for their departure on the eight o'clock for Washington. As the press of the time described it, the solemnity of the occasion was manifest in the crowd's silence, broken only by the soft, rhythmical whisperings of steam escaping from the exhaust valves of the locomotive.

Before long Mr. Lincoln, his family and party, stepped out of the doorway and walked toward the train, the legion of friends and well-wishers stepping aside quietly to allow them to pass. Many reached out to grasp his hand and wish him godspeed. Judge David Davis, Lincoln's close friend, a jolly three hundred pounds of good humor, but now more solemn than usual, followed in his path.

Among Lincoln's party was Colonel Ward Hill Lamon, perhaps the closest friend the president-elect would have in his lifetime, his towering figure resplendent in a new uniform. And there was the

Abraham Lincoln in 1861.
The president-elect as he looked when he went "to assume a task more difficult than that which devolved upon General Washington. . . ."

youthful Colonel Ephraim Elmer Ellsworth of the Chicago Zouaves, another of the president-elect's bodyguards and friends; and Colonels Edwin Sumner and David Hunter, two army officers sent by General Winfield Scott to act as guard of honor.

Mr. Lincoln reached the rear platform of the last car, climbed aboard, and paused to look at his neighbors, their heads bared in the drizzling rain. Standing quietly for a moment to collect his thoughts, he removed his hat and raised his hand for silence. Above him, the soft rain dripped off the sloping roof of the coach and ran down its sides in silvery chains. The words came slowly:

> Friends, no one who has never been placed in a like position can understand my feelings at this hour, nor the oppressive sadness I feel at this parting. For more than a quarter of a century I have lived among you, and during all that time I have received nothing but kindness at your hands. Here I have lived from my youth till now I am an old man. Here the most sacred trusts of earth were assumed; here all my children were born; and here lies one of them buried. To you, my dear friends, I owe all that I have, all that I am. . . .
>
> Today I leave you. I go to assume a task more

Colonel Ward Hill Lamon.
Lincoln's closest personal friend and bodyguard, Colonel Lamon, a towering six feet four, later became marshal of Washington City.

difficult than that which devolved upon General Washington. . . . With these few words I leave you —for how long, I know not. Friends, one and all, I bid you an affectionate farewell.

At precisely eight o'clock the brass bell of the locomotive clanged for clearance and the train rolled easily out of the station and headed eastward, leaving a sea of faces slowly receding in the distance. Thus began one of the strangest train rides in history. In less than three weeks from the day the president-elect was safely delivered to Washington, all the nation's railroads would be at war. The Northern railroads would be operating as the United States Military Railroads, under military direction.

Judge David Davis.
A close personal friend, Judge Davis, "three hundred pounds of good humor," once rode the old Eighth Circuit Court with Lincoln.

In his private car, the first coach behind the baggage car, the president-elect slipped into a seat, his newly grown beard covering the lower part of his face. Mrs. Lincoln and their boys Willie and Tad perhaps looked out the windows at the rolling countryside as the train moved on, passing little way stations where small groups of people had gathered to wave.

Inside the rattling, swaying baggage coach rode the trunks and portmanteaus holding the personal belongings, packed by the president-elect himself, all bearing the best-known address in America and written in his own hand: "A. Lincoln, The White House, Washington, D.C." A few short hours from now would be his birthday. He would be fifty-two.

Before leaving Springfield, threats of violence against Lincoln's person had been received and were treated as the mouthings of cranks. Nevertheless, the entire route was protected by guardsmen and signalmen who flagged the train around curves and over every bridge along the route.

When the train pulled into the last station stop in Illinois, Lincoln again spoke from the rear platform: "I am leaving you on an errand of national importance, attended, as you are aware, with considerable difficulties. . . ."

Indeed, he had no illusions about the difficulties he would face when he reached Washington. Intrigue and treason had taken over the nation's capital.

On February 4, the provisional government of the Confederate States was established at Montgomery, Alabama, with Jefferson Davis inaugurated as its president—and seven states announced separation from the national government.

In Charleston Harbor, South Carolina, Major Robert Anderson, and his small garrison of federal soldiers had moved secretly from Fort Moultrie into Fort Sumter in December and were now besieged and cut off from all communication from the mainland by South Carolina troops. Except for the shelling of Anderson's relief ship, *Star of the West*, neither side had been willing to commence open hostilities—neither side wanting the label of aggressor.

President James Buchanan, probably the most ineffectual chief executive the nation has ever had the misfortune to elect, wrung his hands helplessly, unable to cope with the state of his nation. The North and South were now so hopelessly divided that, for example, all trains entering South Carolina were stopped and passengers questioned as to their loyalties and the nature of business.

Meanwhile, the presidential train rolled on. With

A Three-Car Train of the Little Miami, Cleveland & Xavier Railroad.
Almost identical with the Lincoln Special, this train is *typical of the head-end and passenger equipment of 1860.*
Courtesy Rock Island Railroad.

Around the Lake Shore.

The Chicago & Northwestern Railroad's right-of-way around Lake Michigan's shorefront. The Chicago skyline can be seen *in the background. The Lincoln Special traveled this route eastward.*

AUTHOR'S COLLECTION.

Mr. Lincoln were twenty copies of his inaugural address, hidden, as it was reported, "safely in a grip-sack from prying eyes." The world watched and waited, noting the progress of the train and its very important passenger. Everything hinged upon what action the president-elect would take after he assumed office on March 4. His inaugural address contained what might be the last hope of preserving the Union without civil conflict.

Whether Mr. Lincoln would read his inaugural address in Washington depended upon how well Colonel Lamon and Colonel Ellsworth had prepared for his safety as the presidential train made its way across the cornfields and flatlands of Indiana. The party now included press correspondents, members of the legal profession, and friends of the president-elect who had once ridden the old Eighth Circuit Court, as he had done. Among them were Jesse K. Dubois and Orville Browning, who had joined the presidential party to insure Lincoln's safe arrival in Washington.

Superintendent of the railroad, James Wood, recommended by William H. Seward, had been no less careful in his efforts to afford Lincoln and his family safe conduct to the nation's capital. Wood's

rules were stringent—not to be broken by anyone: "The president-elect will, *under no circumstances,* pass through any crowd until approved by Colonel Ellsworth, charged with the safety of the president-elect." All local police and escorts were to contact Ellsworth before any arrangements were made at each stopover.

Even the train makeup had been carefully planned. The first coach carried the president-elect, Colonel Lamon, members of his suite, and two committee members. In the second coach rode two celebrated Indian fighters and two judges: Colonels Edwin Vose Sumner and David Hunter, and the Honorable N. B. Judd and David Davis of Illinois.

Colonel Ellsworth, Captain Hazzard, Lincoln's private secretary, John George Nicolay, and a single member of the escort, rode in the third coach. Mr. Lincoln's eldest son Robert, John Hay, assistant secretary to the president-elect, and two members of his escort, rode in the fourth coach. The rest of the "circular of instructions" laid down hotel accommodations, local transportation, and escort from the train to the various hotel stopovers.

The presidential escort and bodyguard was composed of some very young men for such a responsibility. Both of Lincoln's secretaries were only twenty-nine. Most colorful of all was Colonel Elmer Ellsworth, twenty-four years old, a former train newsboy, dry goods clerk, and construction worker at Hell Gate in the East River of New York. He was also a renowned athlete. Sadly, Ellsworth was destined to be shot dead in Alexandria, Virginia, shortly after his arrival in Washington.

The little Toledo & Wabash train bearing the presidential party pulled into Indianapolis at five o'clock in the afternoon, to a roaring salute of thirty-four guns. Governor Oliver P. Morton greeted Mr. Lincoln and drove him to the State House in the governor's carriage, preceded by a brass band, the mayor, and a long procession of civic officials—the police force, some troops, and a contingent of firemen. The procession moved through the crowded streets at a snail's pace. Later, Lincoln addressed a crowd of more than fifteen thousand persons from the balcony of the State House. The next morning after breakfast, Governor Morton and a couple of officers accompanied the president-elect to the station and saw him safely off to Cincinnati, where he arrived at 4:15 on the afternoon of his birthday. The reception accorded Lincoln in this city was even more impressive than the one in Indianapolis; he said, "I was overwhelmed by the magnificence of it. . . ."

Meanwhile, in Washington the electoral vote had not been announced and Lincoln had not been declared president. Moreover, it was feared the capital would be seized by secessionists. In fact, William H. Seward had written Lincoln that a plot was being hatched to take over the capital "on or before the 4th of March." But on this day, at twenty minutes past twelve, at a joint session of the Senate and House, Vice-President John C. Breckenridge, a secessionist, announced that Lincoln and Hannibal Hamlin, "having received a majority of electoral votes [were] duly elected President and Vice-President for the next four years commencing March 4th, 1861."

The presidential train now switched over to the tracks of the Little Miami Railroad to Columbus, the Ohio state capital, and that night Lincoln addressed the Ohio state legislature. At seven-thirty on the morning of February 14th, the Lincoln train made the run to Pittsburgh, with a stopover at Steubenville, where the president-elect made a short speech and took part in a parade in a drenching downpour. Later that evening the Lincoln party dined at the Monongahela House. Then came a short speech the following morning in which Lin-

coln spoke of the "artificial crisis," suggesting that "if the American people would only keep their tempers on both sides of the line," the trouble would come to an end.

Around Lake Erie to Buffalo, with a short stop at Westfield, New York, and then on toward New York City—there had been ugly rumors emanating from that great metropolis, and recent reports from Maryland were even more foreboding—the train ran over the tracks of the New York & Harlem River Railroad, through the Hudson Valley. During the final run, young Bob Lincoln was permitted to ride in the cab of the locomotive.

At three o'clock in the afternoon, the Lincoln Special chugged into the Hudson River Railroad Station at Thirteenth Street and Ninth Avenue, where Mr. Lincoln was greeted by an enormous crowd. In New York the president-elect stepped into a morass of politics, treason, and corruption. According to *Harper's Weekly*, both city and state officialdom was "composed of cormorants and thieves—novices in corruption." The lunatic fringe had taken over New York. Shortly before Lincoln's arrival Mayor Fernando Wood, a corrupt political hack, had already conspired "to turn New York into an independent city," planning to secede it from both the state and the federal union.

Despite its corrupt politicians, the metropolis was the center of everything in the Western Hemisphere. Railroads, money, trade, steamships, newspapers, music, the theater, and women's fashions went hand in hand with the world's greatest slums, miles of dilapidated, reeking tenements and dirty unpaved streets, where the crime rate soared beyond the capacity of the police department to cope with it. Such was New York City in 1861.

There were dinners, speeches, an evening at the opera for himself and Mrs. Lincoln, and then the ferry across the Hudson to Jersey City, where Lincoln was welcomed by William Dayton, attorney general of New Jersey, former U.S. senator, and the Republican party's first vice-presidential candidate. After an address from the New Jersey Senate and Assembly, Lincoln left for Philadelphia, arriving there at four o'clock in the afternoon, driving directly to the Continental Hotel on Chestnut Street.

Greeting well-wishers and friends in the hotel's parlor, Lincoln suddenly noticed John Nicolay pushing his way through the crowd, trying to get his attention. Stepping aside from the group for a moment to speak to Nicolay, Lincoln was told that his friend Norman Judd had an urgent matter to

Allan Pinkerton.

A famous Chicago detective, Allen Pinkerton uncovered the plot to assassinate President-elect Lincoln before he reached Washington.

AUTHOR'S COLLECTION.

Samuel Felton.

President of the Philadelphia, Wilmington & Baltimore Railroad, Felton rearranged Lincoln's train schedule and route from the announced schedule to frustrate plans of any would-be assassin.

AUTHOR'S COLLECTION.

discuss that could not wait. Moments later the president-elect found himself in Judd's room, where he was introduced to Allen Pinkerton, the famous Chicago detective now working as an operative for the Philadelphia, Wilmington & Baltimore Railroad to protect company property from sabotage by secessionist agitators.

Pinkerton had arrived that morning and had immediately contacted Samuel Felton, the road's president, to tell him of a conspiracy he had uncovered to assassinate Lincoln when his train passed through Baltimore. Pinkerton and Judd had met in Felton's room at the St. Louis Hotel, where the detective informed him of the threats against the president-elect's life.

In view of Pinkerton's news, Judd and Felton agreed that it would be folly to pass the president-elect through Baltimore in broad daylight according to the announced schedule, and that Lincoln should be told of the threats against his life. Since it was close to nine-thirty in the evening, there was no time to lose. Judd and Pinkerton had come directly to the Continental Hotel.

Pinkerton wasted no time in idle talk. "We have come to know, Mr. Lincoln, beyond the shadow of a doubt, that there exists a plot to assassinate you. The attempt will be made on your way through

Baltimore, day after tomorrow." Pinkerton then explained how he had uncovered the plot by posing as a secessionist. A barber named Fernandia had exposed a long knife and, waving it aloft, had exclaimed, "This hireling, Lincoln, shall never, never be president. My life is of no consequence in a cause like this, and I am willing to give it for his. . . . The North shall want another president, for Lincoln will be a corpse!"

The president-elect then questioned the detective, but his story was confirmed by both Judd and Felton. "Even Colonel Kane," said Pinkerton, "the Baltimore police chief, is in on the plot." Pinkerton urged Lincoln to leave for Washington that night. But the president-elect flatly refused, saying that he had an engagement to raise the flag at Independence Hall, and that same afternoon he would "exhibit himself" at Harrisburg. He had no intention of breaking either engagement.

To the intense relief of both Judd and Pinkerton, Lincoln agreed that after both engagements had been kept he would slip quietly away from Harrisburg that evening by any means they thought best.

Meanwhile, William H. Seward had also uncovered the plot and conspiracy in Washington, and had sent his son Frederick to Philadelphia to warn Lincoln of the "terrible snare into whose meshes he

Calvert Station of the Baltimore & Ohio Railroad.

This station figured prominently in the attempt to move Union troops into Washington, and was the focal point of secessionist activities.

COURTESY BALTIMORE & OHIO RAILROAD.

was about to run." When Frederick Seward arrived in Philadelphia and imparted the information from his father, Lincoln turned him over to Judd, who told young Seward that they already knew about the conspiracy and advised him to return to Washington, giving him just enough information to enable his father to anticipate the president-elect's arrival in the capital city.

Early on the morning of February 22, Mr. Lincoln raised the flag over Independence Hall, made a speech, and departed for Harrisburg. Enroute, Judd apprised him of the protective arrangements concluded the night before: Pinkerton, Sanford, Colonel Scott, Felton, and railroad and telegraph officials were summoned to Judd's room for final instructions, which had taken most of the night.

Sometime around six o'clock the following evening, after Lincoln had made his Harrisburg appearance, he would slip away to Jones' Hotel in company with only one member of his party. A special car and engine would be ready to receive them on a siding outside the depot. During the run to Washington all other trains were to be sidetracked until Lincoln's train had passed. Sanford was charged with the responsibility of seeing that skilled telegraph climbers stationed at key points would cut all telegraph lines, which were to be kept down until Lincoln had arrived safely in Washington.

Arrangements were then made for the president-

elect to meet Pinkerton at the West Philadelphia Station with a carriage. They would take a circuitous route through the city to the Philadelphia, Wilmington & Baltimore Station, where a special sleeping car with berths for four would be coupled to the regular midnight train to Washington. Not until the conductor had received a package marked "Important Government Dispatches," addressed to "E. J. Allen, Willards Hotel, Washington, D.C.," was the train to leave. The package would contain nothing more than old newspapers, but would be the signal that the president-elect was safely on board.

The run to Harrisburg was made in a blackout—all car lamps were turned off—and the train arrived in Harrisburg without incident.

The Harrisburg ceremonies were impressive. Mr. Lincoln was welcomed by Governor Andrew Curtin with a battalion of state militia and cannon, after which Lincoln made a speech to state legislature. It was following this public function that he discovered that the satchel containing his inaugural address had been mislaid. He had completed the address before leaving Springfield and had taken it to the *Journal* office to be set in type, under a pledge of secrecy. Copies were to be given to his friends before the inauguration. He had given the satchel to his eldest son, Bob, to hold during the Harrisburg ceremonies, and the boy had forgotten where he had left it.

Alarmed and angry, Lincoln and Ward Lamon began to search for it in the hotel baggage room. "I guess I have lost my certificate of moral character written by myself," he had said to his friend Lamon. "Bob has lost my gripsack containing my inaugural address. I want you to help me find it." After plowing through piles of luggage, a bag was spotted which looked like his own; upon being opened, however, it was found to contain a soiled shirt, a bottle of whiskey, a deck of cards, and some paper collars. "I never saw Lincoln more angry than upon this occasion," wrote Lamon long afterward, "but the liquor was of exceeding quality." At last the bag was found and Lincoln vowed it would not leave his hands until they reached Washington.

When Judd decided to inform the other members of the presidential party of the assassination plot, he summoned Colonel Sumner, Judge Davis, Ward Lamon, Major Hunter, and Captain John Pope and his bodyguard to his room for a conference. Judd opened the meeting and told them of the Baltimore conspiracy; how Pinkerton had uncovered it, its confirmation by Seward; and how they proposed to thwart the attempt by their already-planned midnight ride to Washington by way of Philadelphia. Judd finished his narrative to dead silence.

Colonel Sumner, first to break the silence, exploded with "That proceeding will be a damned piece of cowardice!" Judd regarded Sumner's remark as a "pointed hit," and replied that that aspect had already been presented to Lincoln. Throughout the meeting Judge Davis remained silent, listening carefully, weighing everything he had heard. At last he turned to Lincoln. "You personally heard the detective's story," he said. "You have heard the discussion. What is your judgment in this matter?" Lincoln thought a moment and replied, "I have thought this matter over considerably since I went over the ground with the detective last night. The appearance of Frederick Seward with warning from another source confirms my belief. Unless there are some other reasons besides fear of ridicule, I am disposed to carry out Judd's plan." That settled the matter.

One detail remained—who should accompany the president-elect "on his perilous flight"? Judd answered the question: a single man should go, and that man should be Ward Lamon.

A closed carriage was then brought to the side door of the hotel, while Lincoln hurried to his room, changed his coat and hat, and passed rapidly through the hall, out the side door, and into the carriage.

After a short drive the carriage arrived at the depot and drove into the station yard "without discovery or mishap." Except for a Mr. Lewis, general superintendent of the Pennsylvania Central Railroad, and the road's divisional superintendent, Mr. Franciscus, who had arranged for the special train, the yard was deserted. It was now ten o'clock, an hour before train time, so the president-elect, Lamon, and Pinkerton seated themselves in the carriage waiting at the depot. Mr. Kenny, an official of the Philadelphia, Wilmington & Baltimore Railroad, who was to deliver the "important parcel" to the conductor of the 10:50 train for Washington, now appeared on the scene.

It was thought unwise to stand around the station until train time, so Lincoln, Lamon, Pinkerton—with Kenny on the wagon box with the driver—drove around for the better of an hour, as Pinkerton described it, "in search of some imaginary person." Moments before the Washington train was ready to leave, the carriage pulled into the shadows of the station. Lincoln, Pinkerton, and Lamon climbed out of the carriage and walked toward the sleeping

Guarding the Lincoln Special's Route.
Union soldiers guarding the B & O's main line right-of-way into Washington against sabotage.
COURTESY BALTIMORE & OHIO RAILROAD.

car at the end of the train while Kenny delivered the important package to the conductor. Three minutes later the train was in motion.

Tickets for the entire party, procured by George Dunn, an express agent, were for the berths at the rear of the car. He insisted that the rear door be left open, "as one of the passengers is an invalid who will arrive late, and who doesn't relish the idea of being carried through the narrow passageway of the crowded car."

Mr. Lincoln stepped aboard the car through this rear door and immediately climbed into his berth, carefully closing the curtains. Lamon and Pinkerton waited for the conductor to come through the rear of the car for the tickets. Pinkerton handed the conductor the "sick man's" ticket.

During the night ride Lincoln joked and talked in soft undertones to Lamon and Pinkerton, but otherwise the rest of the car was silent. Pinkerton had stationed men at various places along the route to signal in the event of any sign of danger, and occasionally walked to the rear platform himself to check their signals, returning each time with a favorable report.

When the train pulled into Baltimore at 3:30 A.M., one of Pinkerton's men came aboard to report that all was well. Lincoln rested quietly in his berth as the car was drawn slowly through the dark streets of the city. Before long there was another pause, amid the sounds of switching cars and locomotives, as the special was hauled into the yards, but, as Pinkerton later wrote, "the passengers dozed peacefully on their shelves as if Mr. Lincoln had never been born."

Suddenly everyone in the car was awakened by the sound of a huge club being pounded against the night watchman's shanty, close to the track, as a drunk tried to awaken the sleeping watchman snoozing comfortably inside.

Before long the train sped on to Washington, running through the Baltimore suburbs without mishap, much to the relief of the apprehnsive Pinkerton and Lamon, whose worries slipped away as the miles clicked by. By six o'clock in the morning, the unfinished dome of the Capitol appeared in sight. A few moments later the train slowly rolled into the long, unsightly Washington Depot and came to a screeching, rattling stop.

Testing the Rails.
Union soldiers on a handcar, running ahead of the Lincoln Special, test the rails for breaks and sabotage to guard against derailments.

The B & O's Washington Station in 1861.
Rail end of Lincoln's night ride and secret passage into   Washington, "a city seething with treason and danger."

End of the "Night Ride" to Washington, D.C. February 1861.

Lincoln's "secret passage" arrival in Washington was a personal embarrassment, far removed from the way a president-elect should arrive at the nation's capital for his inauguration. The Baltimore Sun, *secessionist in sympathy, called it "degrading" and "the final escapade." Nevertheless, Lincoln courted danger throughout the entire journey.*

COURTESY BALTIMORE & OHIO RAILROAD ARCHIVES.

With Pinkerton leading the way, Mr. Lincoln and Lamon stepped out of the car unobserved and started down the platform, Pinkerton purposely dropping behind in the crowd of men and women who rushed toward the car. Suddenly, Lamon noticed a man in the crowd gazing at Lincoln with more than cursory interest. Standing to one side, he looked at the president-elect sharply as he passed, then reached out his hand and seized Lincoln's, at the same time shouting, "Abe, you can't play that on me!" Lamon and Pinkerton, instantly alarmed, were about to strike the stranger when Lincoln exclaimed, "Don't strike him! It is Washburne. Don't you know him?" (Seward had apparently informed Congressman Washburne of Galena of the change of plans.)

But this didn't stop Pinkerton from admonishing Washburne to keep quiet until they had all left the station. Climbing into a hack, they drove to Willard's Hotel, where Lincoln and Pinkerton entered the "Ladies Entrance" while Lamon drove around to the main entrance and sent word to the proprietor, who came out to greet his distinguished guest.

A few moments later Seward arrived and was introduced by Washburne. Seward didn't hesitate to speak in very strong terms of the danger which had been averted, and heartily applauded the wisdom of the secret passage. Such was the arrival of President-elect Abraham Lincoln into Washington City for his inauguration, a city, it was said, "seething with treason and danger."

Comments concerning the night ride came mainly from the Baltimore newspapers. which was to be expected. Said the *Baltimore Sun:* "Had we any respect for Mr. Lincoln, official or personal, as a man, or as a president-elect of the United States, his career and speeches on the way to the seat of government would have been cruelly impaired by it; but the final escapade by which he reached the capital would have utterly demolished it. . . ." Said another: "We do not believe the Presidency can ever be more degraded by any of his successors than it has by him. . . ."

After his long and dangerous journey, having been up several nights without rest, it became apparent to all that Lincoln was tired, and would like to go to his room. After the party separated, Pinkerton went to the telegraph office and sent a message in code to his operators. The sounders clicked out—"Plums delivered nuts safely."

Lincoln came to regret his midnight ride into Washington. Later developments proved, however, that there was never a moment up to the time of his assassination that he was not in danger of death by violence.

CHAPTER 3

The North's Railroads
Meet the Emergency

INAUGURATION DAY, March 4, 1861, dawned cold and dreary, but toward noon the skies cleared, the sun came out, and the air warmed. After the inaugural parade, spectators gathered before the inauguration platform to witness the ceremonies, probably unaware that General Winfield Scott's sharpshooters, posted on the rooftops of the Senate and House buildings, watched their every move while army Secret Service operatives circulated among them as a precautionary measure against any overt attempt upon the life of the president.

Washington, in the words of General Scott, "was in such a state, that a dog-fight could cause the Capital's gutters to run with blood."

The crisis came very quickly. The attack on Fort Sumter occurred on April 15. President Lincoln's call for seventy-five thousand volunteers "to suppress combinations . . . too powerful to be suppressed by the ordinary course of judicial proceedings," and the War Department's order to concentrate all incoming troops in Washington (then a country village) without accommodations for a company of troops let alone an army of seventy-five thousand, suddenly drew attention to the North's railroads, particularly those lines centering on Baltimore.

Moreover, within the government there was no general staff, no strategic plan, no organized services of any kind. The United States Regular Army of thirteen thousand men and officers was to remain intact, while the burden of raising troops fell upon the shoulders of the governors of the northern states, such as John Andrew of Massachusetts and Andrew Curtin of Pennsylvania, to deliver their state's quotas of volunteer troops, who flocked to the colors with feverish bustle and patriotic fervor.

In the ensuing confusion, the nation was, in the words of Colonel W. T. Sherman, "attempting to make war without in the least knowing how."

The national crisis notwithstanding, the North wanted to put a quick end to the rebellion, providing that the military steps taken to quell it did not interfere with "business as usual." Inside and outside the government, however, there were those who welcomed the war as a means of getting rich, and hoped it would never end. The heyday of the war profiteer had arrived, and not a day went by on Wall Street without some new combination, a railroad promotion, or a new corner on the market.

"Every foul bird abroad and every dirty reptile up," said President Lincoln in despair. It became the reign of the shoddy, of thieving war contractors and influence peddlers. War contracts were let at 100 percent profit; diseased cattle, useless weapons and shoddy cloth were sold to the army with impunity and without government inspection.

Not the least of these opportunistic, political vultures was Simon Cameron, the most voracious politician of his time, who believed firmly in the Jacksonian adage that to the victor belong the spoils; who never forgot a friend, or an enemy; and who rewarded or punished them accordingly.

Cameron had come to Washington well versed in the business of questionable, though profitable, political practices, and was always quick to see the opportunities for making money. In 1832 he had opened the Bank of Middletown, Pennsylvania, set himself up as cashier, and made a fortune. As a politician, he wangled himself an appointment as commissioner to settle the claims of the Winnebago Indians, and further enriched himself by adjusting their claims by paying with notes drawn on his own bank. And since money is the major key to politics

Inauguration of President Abraham Lincoln.

Riflemen had been posted on the rooftops of the House and   Senate Buildings to watch for trouble.

FROM A PHOTOGRAPH BY MATHEW BRADY, AUTHOR'S COLLECTION.

and politicians, Cameron came into control of Pennsylvania's Republican party machine, a position from which he was never dislodged.

After making a fair showing as a Republican presidential candidate in 1860, it was only a step to the post of secretary of war in President Lincoln's cabinet, a post Cameron's political cronies had traded with Lincoln's campaign managers in exchange for Pennsylvania's vote for Lincoln. To Lincoln's ultimate disgust, the trade had been made without his knowledge or consent. With Cameron's appointment to the War Department, corruption became rampant.

Cameron was no stranger to railroad operations, having been a contractor for the construction of a number of railroads in Pennsylvania, which he later

combined in his own Northern Central; and as secretary of war, he dispensed War Department contracts for his personal enrichment with impunity. Before the Lincoln administration was in office a month, it became apparent to everyone that Secretary Cameron had every intention of awarding war contracts to his friends, particularly military transportation contracts favoring his own Northern Central Railroad.

The stage set for act one of the coming military railroad drama was Baltimore, a junction point for four leading eastern railroads: the Baltimore & Ohio, the Pennsylvania, the Philadelphia, Wilmington & Baltimore, and the Northern Central, the latter under the financial control and management of the Cameron family (Cameron's son James was its vice-president). Armed with his authority as secretary of war, Cameron was now in a position to dispense and control every rail transportation contract for the movement of troops and the enormous amount of war materiel and food needed to sustain the army in the field.

The most strategically important railroad to both sides was the Baltimore & Ohio, the largest, best equipped, and most efficiently operated rail line in the East, and the most solidly constructed. Since B & O trackage ran through Confederate territory at two points, with a line running into what is now West Virginia, it would soon become a bone of contention between the armies of North and South.

To Cameron, in peacetime the Baltimore & Ohio was a heavy competitor with his own Northern Central, particularly when the B & O established a terminal at Wheeling on the Ohio River, and could handle shippers' cargoes coming by riverboat from the west to Baltimore and mid-Maryland. With its western trackage in Virginia and eastern trackage in Maryland, its shops and main offices in Baltimore, the fate of the B & O hung on the question of whether or not Maryland would secede from the Union. Although most of Maryland was antisecessionist, there was much Southern sympathy in Baltimore. From the military point of view, the

B & O in federal hands would be a dangerous avenue of approach to the South. In Confederate hands, the line could be cut, isolating Washington, Baltimore, and Philadelphia from the west and the rest of the nation. The fate of the B & O rested on whether or not Maryland would join the Confederacy.

The Pennsylvania Railroad, with its terminal at Philadelphia a hundred miles east of Baltimore, was the junction point connecting Baltimore with New York, New Jersey, and New England. Harrisburg, Pennsylvania's capital city, lay a little over a hundred miles westward of Baltimore. The Philadelphia, Wilmington & Baltimore, and Cameron's Northern Central, linked Baltimore with the Pennsylvania at Harrisburg, providing Baltimore with a direct rail line to Pittsburgh and the Western Territories.

The Achilles heel of the North's marvelous military railroad facilities in the East was the B & O's thirty-mile, single-track spur line into Washington from Relay House, another B & O junction ten miles below Baltimore. Interdiction of this rail link could isolate the nation's capital from the rest of the nation at one stroke. (Cameron's Northern Central, a sixty-mile, single-track line from Harrisburg, also connected with the B & O spur at Relay House.)

Before the outbreak of the war, Cameron's North-

The Baltimore & Ohio Railroad's Junction at Baltimore, 1861.

The B & O represented an investment in excess of $30 million. Up-to-date rolling stock, locomotives, and modern machinery made it one of America's most costly railroads.
COURTESY BALTIMORE & OHIO RAILROAD.

Secretary of War Simon Cameron.

The all-powerful Cameron, his cabinet post a political pay-off, refused to curtail the activities of crooked war contractors. His Northern Central Railroad benefitted by his office's largess.

FROM A PHOTOGRAPH BY MATHEW BRADY, AUTHOR'S COLLECTION.

ern Central had formed a combine with the Pennsylvania and the Philadelphia, Wilmington & Baltimore railroads with the avowed intention of syphoning off all B & O business bound to and from Chesapeake Bay. It was an intense rivalry that left the executives of these lines on less than friendly terms.

When President Lincoln called for volunteers on April 15, the Northern Central, the Pennsylvania, and the Philadelphia, Wilmington & Baltimore received War Department orders to transport all troops arriving in Baltimore and Philadelphia from New York, New England, Pennsylvania, and the west, to Washington. The B & O management was neither consulted nor included in these transactions.

Secretary Cameron, his mind on his own personal interests, completely overlooked the fact that the B & O owned the only rail line into Washington, that federal troops arriving at Relay House would remain there unless John Garrett, president of the

B & O, participated in the War Department arrangements.

On April 15, coincident with Lincoln's call for troops, Samuel Felton, president of the Philadelphia, Wilmington & Baltimore Railroad; J. Edgar Thomson, president of the Pennsylvania; and Thomas Scott, the road's vice-president, knew all too well the problems Secretary Cameron's arrangement would cause—not to mention the fact that the bottleneck at Relay House, if Garrett's B & O did not participate, would mean no troop trains could move into Washington over the only rail line entering the capital city unless John Garrett and the B & O decided to cooperate.

Moreover, Cameron, Thomson, and Scott had been warned by so-called hostile parties that the B & O, "regardless of what its management might do," would not be permitted to keep its lines in operation during the crisis. How effective this secessionist threat was is evidenced by the stoppage of all through traffic over the B & O main line before mobilization of the first seventy-five thousand volunteers had been completed.

Two days later Thomson called on Garrett for a

John Worth Garrett.

As embattled president of the Baltimore & Ohio Railroad Garrett felt the heavy hands of Simon Cameron and "Stonewall" Jackson, both seeking to destroy his railroad—one by political pressure, the other out of military necessity.

COURTESY BALTIMORE & OHIO RAILROAD ARCHIVES.

consultation at Garret's office at Camden Station in Baltimore. At that meeting Garrett informed Thomson that his road was unprotected—that secessionist sympathizers were prepared to destroy his unguarded main line should he transport Union troops over it coming from the west.

Being loyal to the Union, Garrett agreed to move Union troops brought into Baltimore from Harrisburg and Philadelphia, using his own equipment. At the same time, however, he pointed out that Cameron had been quick to muster the Pennsylvania Militia into the Union Army to guard the tracks of his own Northern Central and Pennsylvania roads, denying the same protection to the B & O after learning of the secessionist threat against it.

Meanwhile, on April 18, the first contingent of Union volunteers arrived in Baltimore on the Northern Central's trains. Since there were no rail connections between the Northern Central and the B & O main line at Camden Station, the troops had to be marched across town on foot. En route they

The Camden Station of the B & O Railroad.

The main transfer point of volunteer troops bound for Washington, Camden Station was also main executive offices of the B & O.

COURTESY BALTIMORE & OHIO RAILROAD ARCHIVES.

Ordeal of the Sixth Massachusetts Regiment.

Attacked by an enraged mob of secessionists throwing rocks and wielding clubs while marching from the PW & B terminal to Camden Station these soldiers suffered fourteen killed or badly disabled.

COURTESY BALTIMORE & OHIO RAILROAD ARCHIVES.

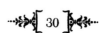

were set upon by secessionists who jeered and threw rocks at them. Fortunately, no one was seriously hurt.

Despite the present crisis and the shabby treatment accorded him by Secretary Cameron, Garrett was still willing to keep his agreement with Thomson and move federal troops to Washington. But a second warning by secessionists compelled Garrett to change his mind. On April 19, another secessionist attack occurred in Baltimore when the Sixth Massachusetts Regiment detrained from the cars of the Philadelphia, Wilmington & Baltimore Railroad and began their march across town to the B & O's Camden Station. They were set upon by a raging mob of secessionists, who stoned and clubbed many of them, while another Union regiment stood idly by at the President Street Station of the Northern Central awaiting orders to march across town.

Garrett immediately notified Samuel Felton of the P W & B that "in this state of things we [the B & O] cannot undertake to carry any more Northern troops over any part of our road." After a hurried conference between the inept Governor Thomas Hicks of Maryland and Baltimore officials, it was decided to notify Garrett that "the troops now here be sent back to the borders of Maryland." Felton then ordered that all trains en route to Baltimore be returned to Philadelphia, while trains arriving via the Northern Central be returned to Pennsylvania, apparently without giving thought to the national crisis.

And as if that weren't enough, the jittery Governor Hicks ordered the lines of the Northern Central and the Philadelphia, Wilmington & Baltimore cut outside the city limits! This idiotic order gave license to a wrecking crew of secessionists who caused almost irreparable damage to tracks, bridges, and telegraph lines between Baltimore and the Susquehanna River.

Furious at the damage done his own railroad, Cameron was even angrier when on April 19, he received a wire from Felton and Thomson, in Philadelphia, informing him of Hick's order that no more Union troops would be permitted to pass through Baltimore, adding that they were to wait for instructions. In a rage at this sudden turn of events Cameron wired back: "Governor Hicks has no right nor authority to stop troops coming to Washington. *Send them on prepared to fight their way through if necessary!*"

President Lincoln, anxious to hold Maryland in the Union since the state appeared to be loyal except for some secessionist elements in Baltimore,

reversed Cameron's order. After a hurried discussion at the War Department, the commanding general at Baltimore was instructed to withdraw all federal troops from the city.

In the middle of the confusion between Secretary Cameron and the railroads, large contingents of troops began to arrive at Pittsburgh, a day's train ride from Harrisburg. When Cameron's ill-considered order to have Union troops shoot their way into Washington had been overruled by President Lincoln, Thomas A. Scott and Samuel Felton, who had been in favor of Cameron's plan, devised an alternate plan to bring these troops to Washington.

Since the tracks of the Philadelphia, Wilmington & Baltimore were open to Perryville, at the mouth of the Susquehanna River, a fleet of tugs and ferryboats could carry the troops from Perryville to Annapolis, where they could entrain over the eighteen-mile Annapolis & Elk Ridge Railroad and connect with the B & O's Washington branch at Annapolis Junction.

"Secure the road between Annapolis and Washington," Scott wired Cameron from Philadelphia. "I will come and manage it for you if so directed." Cameron accepted Scott's offer, and he was immediately assigned to the job. Scott chose as his assistant young Andrew Carnegie, his superintendent of the Pittsburgh Division. (Carnegie had joined the Pennsylvania Railroad as Scott's personal secretary and telegrapher in 1853, for thirty-five dollars a month. "I couldn't imagine what I could do with so much money," was young Carnegie's comment upon receiving his first paycheck; but after twelve years with the road, at the age of thirty, he had succeeded Scott as superintendent of the Pittsburgh Division and proved himself an able railroad executive.)

The alternate Annapolis & Elk Ridge Railroad came under attack at once by secessionists. On April 20, General Ben Butler, commanding a Massachusetts regiment, had already left Philadelphia for Washington via the Annapolis route. He ferried his troops across Chesapeake Bay without incident, until it was discovered that secessionists had destroyed several miles of track west of Annapolis. Butler took matters into his own hands. Without waiting for official sanction from Washington, he took immediate military possession of the Annapolis road and put his men to work repairing the track. Such was the unofficial beginning of the United States Military Railroads.

Meanwhile, Cameron's questionable activities relative to the Baltimore & Ohio Railroad and its

Andrew Carnegie.
Superintendent of the Pennsylvania Railroad's Pittsburg Division, Carnegie, as assistant to Thomas Scott, conducted the first troop train into Washington, riding in the cab of the locomotive.

AUTHOR'S COLLECTION.

president John Garrett had not gone unnoticed. A storm of protest was heaped on the war secretary for his ruthless treatment of the road's president, whose loyalty to the Union cause was unquestioned. Unknown at the time, Garrett had acted as a self-appointed secret agent and had tipped off the War Department as to Confederate movements on many occasions. In view of Cameron's almost pathological desire to hurt Garrett and smother the B & O, it was Garrett's ability and loyalty that saved his railroad from government seizure.

Inevitably Cameron's manipulation of the railroads for personal profit during the national crisis caused the offensive breath of scandal to envelop the war secretary. Much to the embarrassment of the Lincoln administration, one of the questions raised was why the War Department refused to protect the B & O while it went out of its way to protect Cameron's Northern Central and the other lines. Even more embarrassing was the question of

why the Pennsylvania Railroad was able to publish notices that it no longer had the capacity to handle more government or civilian consignments to seaboard cities while the B & O, the largest rail line of all, remained virtually unused, and why all appeals to the secretary of war had gone unanswered. And there was the question of shipping rates, which had shot sky high, favoring the Northern Central and Pennsylvania.

Later, the Committee on Government Contracts, investigating complaints of mismanagement of military shipments "to serve the personal interests of Mr. Cameron and his friends," reported flagrant frauds.

Having rebuffed Garrett, Cameron now ordered General Ben Butler to occupy Relay House Junction and to stop all trains leaving Baltimore, thereby extending federal military authority over the B & O branch from Annapolis Junction to the outskirts of Baltimore. Then Butler moved into Baltimore and occupied the city. At the same time, Cameron appointed his friend, Thomas A. Scott, vice-president of the Pennsylvania Railroad, as assistant secretary of war for transportation and superintendent in charge of government railways and telegraphs, all of which placed the B & O's branch into Washington under federal control operated by officers of the Pennsylvania Railroad.

To keep the defiant Maryland secessionist minority under control, General Butler acted on President Lincoln's order that in suppressing insurrection against the laws of the United States he could control any resistance point between Philadelphia and Washington by "suspending the writ of habeas corpus."

On April 27, Butler arrested Ross Winans of the Maryland legislature upon his return to Baltimore from Frederick, and had him locked up under guard at his departmental headquarters at Annapolis, charged with secessionist activities. Winans was no small fish caught in Butler's dragnet. Born in New Jersey, the sixty-five-year-old Winans was a remarkable man. As an industrialist he had invented the friction wheel, a plow, axle bearings for railway cars; developed the eight-wheel, two-truck railway car system; and built the first successful steam locomotive for the B & O railroad. As chief engineer of the B & O, he operated the largest railway machine shops in the nation, and had already accumulated a personal fortune of $15 million.

But there was another side to Winans, in which the government was particularly interested: the secret weapon he had manufactured—the Winans

Annapolis & Elk Ridge Railroad, ca. 1865.

This Maryland short line carried the first contingent of Union volunteers to Washington in 1861, from Annapolis to Relay House Junction and then to Washington, D.C. Troops were ferried from Perryville to Annapolis, and carried by train to Washington, to avoid a confrontation with secessionists in Baltimore.

COURTESY BALTIMORE & OHIO RAILROAD ARCHIVES.

Major General Benjamin Franklin Butler and Staff.

On orders from President Lincoln, General Butler occupied the city of Baltimore and Relay House, suspended the writ of habeas corpus, and arrested all well-known secessionists.

Butler also seized both the B & O spur into Washington and the Annapolis & Elk Ridge Railroad to facilitate troop arrivals into Washington.

FROM A PHOTOGRAPH BY MATHEW BRADY, AUTHOR'S COLLECTION.

The Winans Steam Gun.

Ross Winans, a member of the Maryland House of Delegates and the B & O's chief of machinery, improved on a centrifugal steam gun invented by an Ohioan. The cannon, mounted on a steam-propelled carriage with a bulletproof cone, was reputed to fire 200 rounds a minute. The gun was captured by federal troops and Winans was arrested for secessionist activities.

COURTESY BALTIMORE & OHIO RAILROAD ARCHIVES.

The Seventh Regiment of New York Arriving at the B & O Station, Washington, D.C., 1861.

This station was the only railway terminal in the nation's capital during the Civil War.

COURTESY BALTIMORE & OHIO RAILROAD ARCHIVES.

William H. Seward.
Secretary of state in the Lincoln cabinet, Seward intrigued against the president and other members of the cabinet. He ordered the release of Ross Winans from federal custory.

From a photograph by Mathew Brady, Author's Collection.

Colonel Thomas Jonathan Jackson, CSA.
Jackson's strategy for capturing B & O locomotives and rolling stock to replenish Confederate railroads was a masterpiece of ad lib military deception. At Bull Run he became "Stonewall" Jackson. A military genius, he was shot by his own men accidentally at Chancellorsville a few months later.

Author's Collection.

steam gun, an incredible, rapid-firing gun mounted on a self-propelled carriage. It had a bulletproof cone-shaped shield to protect the gunners, and was reputed to be able to fire five hundred rounds a minute, calculated, it was said, to "mow down advancing infantry like a scythe." Winans had sent this weapon to Harper's Ferry for Confederate use; but it was seized by federal troops and found to be impractical in dealing out wholesale death. Following his arrest, Winans retained Reverdy Johnson as legal counsel, but it was Secretary of State William Seward who ordered his release from federal military custody.

By April 29, all rail communication had been restored between Washington and Annapolis Junction. Ironically, while trackage and rolling stock south of Annapolis Junction belonged to Garrett's B & O, no officer of that road was called upon to operate it for the War Department. Not many days later the Baltimore & Ohio removed its cars and locomotives from the Annapolis & Elk Ridge line. The only equipment in War Department hands was that on the rails south of Annapolis Junction.

Superintendent Scott's appeals to Samuel Felton and J. Edgar Thomson for equipment went all but unheeded. Although troops and supplies began a steady flow into Washington over the Annapolis road, at best it was no more than an expedient arrangement.

The first brigade of troops to arrive in Washington over the substitute route was transported by young Andrew Carnegie, in his new role as superintendent of railways. He rode in the cab of the first U.S. military train to enter the capital.

The war was fourteen days old. As the situation stood for the time being, Baltimore was under General Ben Butler's control, and Colonel T. J. Jackson and his Confederate Army occupied the B & O main line at Harper's Ferry.

By the end of 1861, the North's railroads would reach an amazing level of operation—financially depressed lines would almost overnight become prosperous carriers. By the end of the same period the Union Army boasted half a million men.

Harper's Ferry, Western Virginia, As It Looked in 1861.

The United States Arsenal site and buildings as seen from Loudon Heights. The post-Civil War Bollman Bridge, in the *left foreground, was washed out in the flood of 1936.*
Courtesy Baltimore & Ohio Railroad Archives.

CHAPTER 4

Raiders East- "Rupture of the Railroad at Cheat River Would Be Worth to Us an Army."

FOUR DAYS after the Confederate attack on Fort Sumter, on April 16, 1861, Captain John Imboden of the Staunton Artillery, CSA, met in a room in the Exchange Hotel in Richmond for a secret conference with two important southern railroad presidents: Edmund Fontaine of the Virginia Central and John S. Barbour of the Orange & Alexandria and Manassas Gap railroads.

Captain Imboden needed the indispensable cooperation of these men for a daring project he had in mind. Their consent was essential to its success since their railroads would be involved in an all-out foray against the United States Arsenal at Harper's Ferry.

The meeting lasted all night, involving arrangements for special trains, schedules, and other operational details for picking up his troops, supplies, and equipment at Charlottesville, Gordonsville, Culpeper, and other stations along the way. Governor Letcher's consent was needed for the undertaking, as a delicate political question was involved: Maryland might join the Confederacy and the governor didn't want to do anything to alienate the Maryland legislature.

Sometime around midnight they received the governor's consent, and at noon the following day Captain Imboden telegraphed his militia commanders to have their companies with their arms and equipment ready to entrain at their designated pickup points.

By sunset on April 17, Captain Imboden's railroad expedition rolled out of Richmond. Imboden himself was in charge of the leading train. Moving over the tracks of the Virginia Central and Orange & Alexandria railroads, they collected such regiments as the elegantly uniformed Albermarle Rifles, Monticello Guards, and Staunton Artillery. The war

had come as a fresh and romantic experience for many of these men who followed the "Stars and

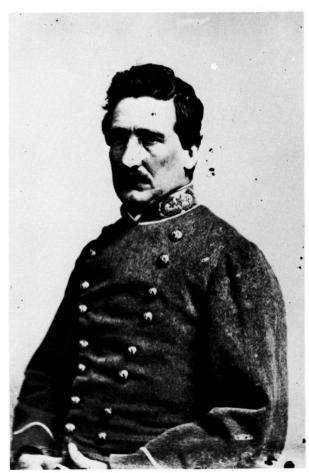

Captain John D. Imboden, CSA.

Imboden was the Confederate officer who conceived and executed the railroad expedition against the United States Arsenal at Harper's Ferry, Virginia, in 1861.

COURTESY VALENTINE MUSEUM, RICHMOND, VA.

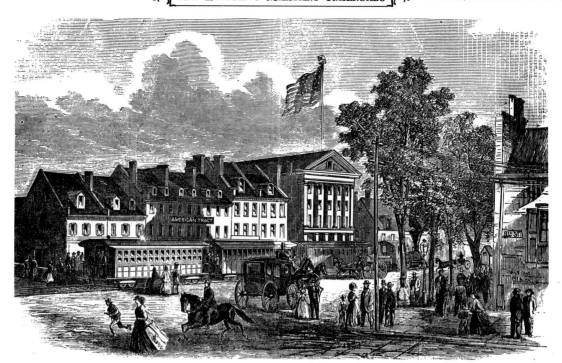

Richmond, Virginia, in 1861.

The tracks of the Richmond, Fredericksburg & Potomac Railroad on Broad Street, where Captain Imboden prepared his raid against the United States Arsenal at Harper's Ferry in June 1861.

Bars," and they weren't going to miss the fun while it lasted.

Shortly before Imboden's raiders reached Strasburg, Captain Imboden suddenly became aware that his train was slowing down, and when it rolled to a complete stop he made his way forward, climbed into the locomotive cab, and confronted the engineer, demanding to know the reason for the slowdown. In the course of the ensuing argument, the engineer wanted to know "why a Union man should haul rebel soldiers."

Furious at the delay, Imboden drew his revolver, cocked it, and aimed it directly at the engineer's head. That settled the matter—in a few moments Imboden's trains were underway once again. To guard against further delays Imboden rode in the cab for the rest of the way, his gun in his hand aimed at the engineer's head. The engineer gave no further trouble, and sometimes had his engine running at forty miles an hour.

When they reached Manassas Junction at dawn, Imboden's trains were hurriedly shunted over to the tracks of the Manassas Gap Railroad for the final run to Strasburg. From there it would be a march of a few miles to the railhead of the Winchester & Harper's Ferry Railroad for the final run.

The battle for the Baltimore & Ohio Railroad was building slowly, but an important question still begged an answer. Would Maryland join the Confederacy or remain in the Union? Until that question was answered—one way or another—the main line of the B & O would remain a sort of "no man's land"; neither side was willing to make any threatening military moves. One thing was certain—no matter which way Maryland decided, both contenders would alternate between building and destroying the railroad for temporary military advantage, each side using the line when needed, or destroying it to deprive the other of its use. To the Confederacy, the B & O was vital to its defense; to the Union, the line was a highway for southern invasion. J. M. Mason, Virginia's commissioner to Maryland, wrote:

> The preservation of this road . . . will be all important to the federal power—and of corelative importance to us to have it in our power, or if unable to hold it, to break it up at points where it will be impracticable to repair it in any convenient time. The numerous tunnels through the mountains, the numerous bridges across the river, and especially the expensive and complicated viaduct along the Cheat River in the Allegheny Mountains, furnish abundant places for irremedial damage, provided

we are in advance of the invaders. Nor would a large force be required, provided it was well distributed and under competent commanders.

The capture of the Harper's Ferry arsenal posed the second question. Could Confederate troops hold Harper's Ferry while the arsenal was put back in operation to manufacture urgently needed guns and ammunition, or would it be more advantageous to dismantle the machinery, much of it still intact from earlier federal attempts to destroy it, and move it south?

Situated in a beautiful gorge, a natural canyon surrounded by mountains, on a small peninsula flanked on both sides by the Potomac and Shenandoah rivers, Harper's Ferry was indefensible, a fact known to General Lee. A determined force with artillery could shell it out of existence from any of the surrounding heights. A large Union force advancing on it from Hagerstown and Cumberland could also make the position untenable.

Understanding the imponderables, as well as the risks involved, General Lee ordered Captain Imboden's militia companies reinforced, to hold Harper's Ferry as long as possible and to get the arsenal operating. The task of holding the town, the railroad, the arsenal, and the strategic mountainous region fell upon Colonel Thomas Jonathan Jackson, a graduate of West Point and a former professor of mathematics at the Virginia Military Institute—a military genius who sucked lemons for his dyspepsia.

The Manassas Gap Railroad, from Manassas Junction to Strasburg, Virginia, gave Union troops the means of cutting Jackson off from his reinforcements and supplies should his troops cross the Potomac River. To prevent this, Lee sent some additional militia companies to Manassas Junction to guard it against capture. This was the beginning of the "Manassas Line," the beginning of the Confederate military concentration that precipitated the first big battle of the war—Bull Run—in the coming July.

From the outset of the conflict the South had been in dire need of railroad equipment, rolling stock, and locomotives for its meager railroads. There were no locomotive shops and no locomotive builders of any consequence in the entire Confederacy. And the first Southern soldier aware of this deficiency was Colonel Jackson. Matters progressed rapidly between April and the first week in May, during which time Jackson, assigned to guard a fifty-mile sector of the B & O line, began to take particular cognizance of certain things, not the least

A Rare Engraving Showing Harper's Ferry Arsenal, 1861.

The United States Arsenal buildings and B & O viaduct can be seen along the edge of the Potomac River. The Latrobe *railroad bridge crosses the Potomac in the center of the picture.*

The Burning of the United States Arsenal at Harper's Ferry, Virginia, in 1861.

When Colonel Jackson took command of Harper's Ferry, he found that the previous fire damage had been superficial. *He later removed the gun-making machinery to Richmond, after dismantling.*

The B & O Potomac River Bridge at Harper's Ferry in 1861.

The covered span of B. H. Latrobe's massive wooden bridge, built in 1836, was destroyed by Colonel Jackson's raid in 1861.

COURTESY BALTIMORE & OHIO RAILROAD ARCHIVES.

Colonel Jackson Destroys the B & O Bridge at Harper's Ferry.

On June 15, 1861, on orders from General R. E. Lee, Jackson destroyed the important Harper's Ferry Bridge by blowing up the center span. Jackson and his troops then retired to Martinsburg, where they destroyed an enormous amount of railway equipment which he could not carry away.

COURTESY BALTIMORE & OHIO RAILROAD ARCHIVES.

of them being the heavy "coal drags" from Cumberland headed for Baltimore with coal for the United States Navy's eastern bases.

Jackson watched the long, heavy coal trains moving through his military zone around the clock to and from the coal mines. Here was the perfect opportunity, he reasoned, for collecting enough railway equipment to last the Confederacy a long time, should Maryland remain in the Union.

On May 6, once Maryland decided to cast her lot with the Union, Jackson received orders to destroy the B & O bridge at Harper's Ferry to prevent any possible advance of Union troops before they could seize control of the railroad. Now that political considerations were no longer in force, Jackson acted with his characteristic alacrity and audacity.

On Jackson's orders, Captain Imboden seized the bridge across the Potomac River at Point of Rocks, twelve miles below Harper's Ferry, and fortified the Virginia end of the bridge:

And as we expected a visit from General Butler's troops at Relay House on the B & O, it was my habit to keep awake all night to be ready for any emergencies, and to sleep in the daytime, making daily reports, night and morning, to Jackson. One

Sunday afternoon, a little over a week after we had occupied the post, I was aroused from my nap by one of my men, who said that there were two men in blue uniforms (we had not yet adopted gray) riding about the camp, and looking closely at everything; that be believed they were spies.

I went out to see who they were, and found Jackson and his staff officer [believed to be Henry Kyd Douglas]. As I approached them, he put his fingers to his lips and shook his head as a signal for silence. In a low tone, he said he preferred it should not be known he had come down there. He approved of all I had done, and soon galloped away. I afterward suspected that the visit was simply to familiarize himself with the line of the canal, and the railroad from Point of Rocks to Harper's Ferry preparatory to a bit of strategy, which he practiced a few days later.

The Baltimore & Ohio Railroad was double-tracked for a distance of about twenty-five or thirty miles from Point of Rocks to Martinsburg. The road's coal traffic from Cumberland to Baltimore was enormous, as the federal Government was stockpiling coal for the navy in any eventuality, and these coal trains passed Harper's Ferry at all hours of the day and night, as they do to this day. It was then that Jackson conceived a brilliant idea

B & O's "Artists'" Train in 1858.

In June of 1858, B & O sponsored a special train, carrying a large group of well-known artists and writers on a five-day trip to Wheeling, Western Virginia. Head-ended by a Mason *locomotive No. 232, the train crosses a Bollman iron suspension railroad bridge, an innovation in suspension bridges of the time.*

COURTESY BALTIMORE & OHIO RAILROAD ARCHIVES.

Point of Rocks, Western Virginia, in 1861.

This is the site where Colonel Jackson blockaded the B & O tracks and closed the line, entrapping 56 locomotives and 256 cars, between Point of Rocks and St. John's Run near Martinsburg.

COURTESY BALTIMORE & OHIO RAILROAD ARCHIVES.

A B & O "Pot-Hopper" Car, 1861.

Constructed of heavy wood with coal hoppers of cast iron, these cars were capable of forty thousand pounds capacity. Long trains of these cars carried coal to the Washington Nack Yard in 1861.

COURTESY BALTIMORE & OHIO RAILROAD ARCHIVES.

The Baltimore & Ohio Railroad and Chesapeake & Ohio

As shown in this rare photograph, coal from the western Maryland coal fields, brought to Cumberland by mule-drawn barges, was transferred to B & O "pot-hopper" coal cars for shipment to the Washington Navy Yard coal stockpiles. The C & O tow-

Canal Transfer at Cumberland, Maryland, in 1860.
...ath separates the B & O tracks from the Potomac River. The town of Cumberland, Maryland, can be seen in the background.

COURTESY BALTIMORE & OHIO RAILROAD ARCHIVES.

for raiding the B & O and obtaining the needed rolling stock for the South's railroads.

When he [Jackson] sent me to Point of Rocks, wrote Captain Imboden,

> he ordered Colonel Kenton Harper, with the Fifth Virginia Regiment, to Martinsburg. He then complained to President Garrett of the B & O, that the night trains, eastward bound, disturbed the repose of his camps, and requested a schedule that would pass eastbound trains by Harper's Ferry between 11 and 1 o'clock in the daytime.
>
> Garrett complied with Jackson's request, and thereafter for several days we heard the constant roar of passing trains for an hour before and after noon. But since the "empties" were sent up the road at night, Jackson again complained that the nuisance was greater than ever and, as the road had two tracks, he must insist that the westbound trains should pass during the same hours as those going east. Mr. Garrett promptly complied again, and we had then, for two hours every day, the liveliest railroad in America.
>
> One night, as soon as the schedule was working at its best, Jackson sent me an order to take a force across the river to the Maryland side the next day at 11 o'clock, and to let all westbound trains pass until 12 o'clock, to obstruct the road so that it would permit none to go east; so that it would take several days to repair it. He ordered the reverse done at Martinsburg. Thus he trapped all trains going east and west between these points.

To guard against recapture, Jackson ordered the destruction of all bridges in his sector, further consolidating his catch by blasting rocks onto the tracks at Point of Rocks. The trap was sprung, the surprise complete. The haul—fifty-six locomotives and three hundred fifty cars—constituted the largest capture of railroad equipment taken by either side in the entire war.

Jackson ran this equipment up to Winchester, over the Winchester & Harper's Ferry thirty-two mile railroad where they were removed by horsepower to the tracks of the Manassas Gap Railroad at Strasburg. Within four weeks Jackson also destroyed seventeen bridges, including the 837-foot Harper's Ferry Bridge. Then on June 2 he destroyed an important railroad bridge over the Opequon River, completing the destruction by running a train of fifty coal cars into the chasm of the Potomac River, where they burned with such intense heat the car wheels and axles melted. A newspaper reporter for the *National Intelligencer* who saw the destruction, wrote:

All along the railroad were scattered coal cars in long lines, with the coal still burning, having been set on fire by the "Noble and chivalric." They had kindled huge fires around them, burning all the woodwork and a great deal of the iron. They were all fine coal cars, holding twenty tons each. Here and there the road led above them, and, looking down we could see the inside—a mass of red hot coals. Some small bridges had been burnt with the cars on them, and giving way, the cars were left piled one on the other in the small streams below, all battered and bent. We counted the line of locomotives (forty-one or forty-two in all) red and blistered with the heat. The destruction is fearful to contemplate.

Whether Jackson had any remorse about the awful destruction he had visited upon those fine B & O locomotives and coal cars is open to conjecture, but in a letter to his wife Jackson had written that it had been "a sad work," done out of military necessity. "I had my orders," he wrote, "and my duty was to obey."

Returning to Martinsburg to continue his destruction of the B & O's extensive locomotive and car shops there, Jackson discovered that his fifty-six locomotives and three hundred fifty cars were still standing in the yards instead of being on their way to Richmond. These he promptly put to the torch. While the equipment burned, Jackson watched and apparently had some second thoughts; before it reached the standing locomotives he ordered the fire extinguished and sent for two of the South's top railway engineers, Hugh Longust and Thomas S. Sharp, and a select crew of thirty-five mechanics, laborers, and teamsters. Upon their arrival they were immediately put to work dismantling and salvaging the locomotives. Jackson then had them hauled overland by forty-horse teams to Strasburg, the nearest station and railhead of the Manassas Gap Railroad, for shipment to Richmond.

When Jackson's score was tallied by the B & O's harried officials, sixty-seven locomotives had either been burned or captured, stripped of their running gear, or dumped into the Potomac River.

On the evening of May 26, 1861, Major General George Brinton McClellan, an engineer and former railroad president, learned that Confederate Colonel George C. Porterfield, with a small force, was contemplating the destruction of the bridges along the B & O's main trunk line in the vicinity of Parkersburg and Wheeling, in western Virginia. Since this division of the B & O was the principal means of rail communication between Washington and the

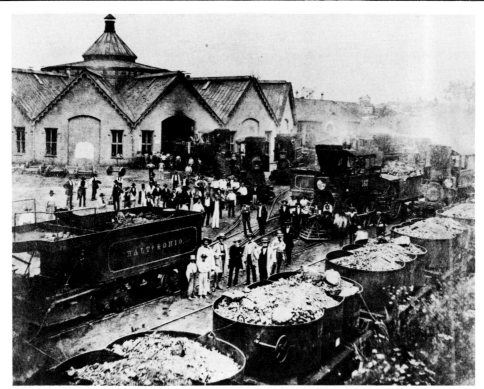

The Roundhouse at Martinsburg, Virginia, in 1861.

Winans's "camelbacks" and a line of three-pot gondola cars stand loaded in the foreground. Much railroad equipment and shop machinery were removed from these shops and sent to Richmond by Colonel Jackson. What he could not carry away, he put to the torch.

COURTESY BALTIMORE & OHIO RAILROAD ARCHIVES.

A Winans "Camelback" Locomotive at Martinsburg, 1861.

Intact, but looking the worse for wear, this "camelback" seems to have survived Jackson's raid. Youngsters in Union blue and kepis pose with the locomotive.

COURTESY BALTIMORE & OHIO RAILROAD ARCHIVES.

The Cumberland Valley Branch of the B & O, 1861.

Davis "Camel" No. 352, a 4–6–0, head-ends a ten-car mixed   *man "Winchester" type with four iron trusses.*
trains and poses for her picture on Passage Bridge, a Boll-

COURTESY BALTIMORE & OHIO RAILROAD ARCHIVES.

Federal Troops Arriving at Parkersburg, Western Virginia, 1861.

A part of General McClellan's twenty-thousand-man army   *western Virginia in the Union.*
of Ohio and Indiana regiments which came to help keep

COURTESY BALTIMORE & OHIO RAILROAD ARCHIVES.

west, the line became the main military objective of the first important, though little known, campaign of the war. It was also the first important military victory for the Union forces, because it secured western Virginia for the Union.

McClellan had for the campaign sixteen regiments of infantry, nine Indiana regiments, and two regiments recruited in western Virginia, plus two troops of cavalry and four batteries of six guns each. As each regiment numbered about seven hundred men, McClellan's entire force numbered about twenty thousand, from which a considerable number of troops were detached to guard the railroad.

Acting on information from his spies, McClellan wired Colonel B. F. Kelley, stationed at Wheeling, to take a column of troops along the main line of the railroad and post guards on all the bridges not yet destroyed, and to rebuild those already damaged. At the same time McClellan ordered Colonel Steedman to cross the Ohio River, occupy Parkersburg, and move his column by rail to Grafton, leaving adequate protection for Parkersburg and bridges along the route.

The energetic Colonel Kelley wasted no time in making his bridge repairs on the main line, and occupied Grafton at 2:30 P.M. on May 30, 1861. Delayed by time-consuming bridge repairs, Colonel Steedman arrived at Grafton to find that Colonel Kelley had already gone in pursuit of Porterfield, who had fallen back to Phillipi, thirty miles south of the rail line.

McClellan had planned his campaign well. With both trunk lines of the B & O railroad occupied by Union troops, McClellan now moved to destroy all Confederate forces in western Virginia, using both lines of the B & O to concentrate large forces of Indiana and Ohio troops in the vicinity of Grafton.

Meanwhile, seeing western Virginia slipping from his grasp, General Lee sent General Robert S. Garnett to supersede Colonel Porterfield and rush reinforcements over the Staunton Turnpike to Beverly, south of Phillipi, where Porterfield had taken a defensive position.

In the early days of the Civil War, western Virginia was still one of the most primitive, mountainous regions in North America, and this wilderness country posed some special military problems for General McClellan, not the least of them his complete dependence upon the Baltimore & Ohio Railroad. Wagon roads were practically nonexistent in many parts of this territory, and to move against Garnett in this immense forest region meant that he would have to move his troops forty miles to the south of his base at Grafton, thereby exposing his railroad base at Grafton to enemy attack and raiding parties. Extending his supply line overland through this wilderness would also invite active raiding parties.

McClellan left detachments at various points along the rail line between Grafton and the Ohio River as far as Rowlesburg, where the B & O's intricate Cheat River Viaduct, the immediate key objective in the struggle for western Virginia, was

A View of General McClellan's Base of Operations at Grafton, Western Virginia, in 1861.

A Bollman iron-span bridge, seen on the right spanning the Cheat River, was typical of B & O bridges during the war *and for some time afterward.*

COURTESY BALTIMORE & OHIO RAILROAD ARCHIVES.

Hotel and Station at Grafton, Western Virginia, in 1861.

Once regarded as an architectural masterpiece, Grafton Station was the scene of General McClellan's occupation and *the staging area for his western Virginia campaign.*

Courtesy Baltimore & Ohio Railroad Archives.

The Wilds of Western Virginia in 1861.

Western Virginia as it looked to Corporal "Nep" Roessler. A combat artist with the Union Army, Corporal Roessler sketched the wilderness region contested by Union and *Confederate forces, at the time the most primitive country in North America.*

From the sketchbook of Corporal "Nep" Roessler, Company G, 47th Ohio Volunteers; Author's Collection.

A Section of the B & O's Parkersburg Cutoff in 1861.

A B & O balloon-stacked American 4-4-0 poses for the camera on a wooden trestle on a lonely stretch of uneven track of the Parkersburg–Wheeling cutoff. The surrounding *country and forests testify to the primitive nature of the region.*

PHOTO FROM A HALF-STEREO PAIR, PHOTOGRAPHER UNKNOWN;
AUTHOR'S COLLECTION.

Sixteenth Ohio Volunteers Crossing Tray Run Viaduct in 1861.

Headed for Grafton, western Virginia, General McClellan's staging area and base, a troop train crosses Tray Run Via- *duct, near Rowlesburg, Chest River region.*

COURTESY BALTIMORE & OHIO RAILROAD ARCHIVES.

most vulnerable to destruction. Deeply concerned for the safety of the viaduct, and the protection of his supply line, McClellan detached Brigadier General Charles F. Hill and forty-eight companies, approximately 5,760 men, to guard them. In his orders to General Hill, McClellan, referring to himself in the third person, stressed the importance of the assignment:

> The commanding general has intrusted to you the most important duty next to his own in this territory viz: that of securing the base of his operations and line of retreat. At any cost—that of your last man— you will preserve the Cheat River line, Grafton, and the line thence to Wheeling. On this depends the entire success of the plan of operations.

Now that the lines were drawn, western Virginia became the first major military offensive of the war, and the Baltimore & Ohio Railroad the prime factor in the coming battle to drive the Confederacy out of the territory. Consequently, the military actions that followed between General McClellan and General Garnett were rough skirmishes and lively actions which burst across the region like a string of Chinese firecrackers. All the action took place within a radius of forty miles from Grafton, terminus of the B & O trunk line from Wheeling.

In large part McClellan had so far handled his campaign well, and his foresight in the military use of the B & O railroad as a tactical weapon and supply line gave him an advantage over his adversary, General Garnett. So long as the Union Army had a foothold in western Virginia and controlled the B & O to Grafton, west of Colonel Jackson's force at Harper's Ferry, there was nothing to prevent McClellan from reinforcing General Patterson at Chambersburg and mounting an attack against Jackson.

The loss of the Baltimore & Ohio Railroad early in the contest, in the wilds of the Cheat River

The B & O's "Artists'" Train Crossing Tray Run Viaduct, over the Cheat River Canyon in 1858.
This viaduct was the prime target of the Confederate forces in the western Virginia campaign in 1861.

COURTESY BALTIMORE & OHIO RAILROAD ARCHIVES.

region, posed a two-fold problem to General Lee at Richmond. There was the definite probability that the B & O line would become an invasion route. In addition, the Union forces coming from the northwest into the Shenandoah Valley could form a two-pronged drive against Richmond with Union forces already building up in Washington. This left Lee no choice but to destroy the B & O.

General Garnett had already realized the importance of the B & O's Cheat River Viaduct and had made it his sole objective. It destruction would deprive McClellan of the use of the railroad for months before repairs could be completed. Lee felt the same way about it, and wrote his field commander on July 1: "The rupture of the railroad Cheat River would be worth to us an army."

Moreover, should McClellan break out of western Virginia and cut the vital Virginia Central Railroad at Staunton, it would leave the strategic door open to Richmond and spell disaster for the Confederacy. But Garnett could find no way to penetrate McClellan's protective screen. Nevertheless, Garnett was instructed to prevent any drive McClellan might mount against Staunton and the Virginia Central.

As in most military encounters, however, fate had a hand in the solution of Lee's problem, in an order General Winfield Scott send to McClellan warning him not to overextend his line of communications, which restricted his operations for the moment to the Cheat River line. The remainder of this remote but important campaign developed into a pursuit between a railroad and an army: the pursued, General Robert Garnett's column; the pursuers, the Baltimore & Ohio Railroad and General McClellan's army.

On July 14, 1861, McClellan defeated General Robert Garnett's forces in a battle on Rich Mountain. Dislodged from his mountain stronghold, what had seemed to be an impregnable defensive position, to avoid certain capture Garnett began a precipitous retreat over the Staunton Turnpike, a move based on misleading information that McClellan had cut off his escape route at Beverly.

Fifty miles east of Beverly an all but impassable mountain range blocked his escape. The only way out of the trap was to go around a spur at the base of a mountain, through a narrow pass (while it was still open), and into the Shenandoah Valley where he could join other Confederate forces already there. To reach this pass he had to move over a road which lay fifteen miles south of the B & O's track east of Oakland, Maryland.

Divining Garnetts' escape route, McClellan sent an order to General Charles F. Hill to recall all his detachments now guarding the B & O railroad and bridges and bring them by special train to Oakland, and there to hurry them overland to intercept Garnett's column before it could pass around the mountain and head eastward. General Hill's telegraphic orders to his regimental commanders specified Oakland, Maryland, as the assembly point, roughly forty-seven miles from Grafton, almost the same distance Garnett's column had to travel on foot.

McClellan's quick, decisive action could have won him a brilliant success; but unfortunately neither the B & O railroad officials nor McClellan's officers were capable of taking advantage of the railroad facilities afforded them. What began as a brilliant strategic concept degenerated into a series of inextricable errors in which the Baltimore & Ohio Railroad could not adjust quickly enough to the military role it was expected to play at a moment's notice.

First, telegraphic communication broke down between McClellan and his field commander, delaying Hill's pursuit by twenty-four hours; his order of July 12 didn't reach Hill until 11 A.M. of the thirteenth. Second, no supply depot had been set up to provide wagon transportation for rations and supplies, nor were there artillery horses to haul the cannon. Consequently, Hill's regimental commanders could not take advantage of available rail transportation.

If McClellan's officers had problems getting the pursuit in motion, B & O officials at Baltimore and Grafton were in an even more confused state trying to get the troop trains organized. Since the line was single-tracked with turnouts, without train dispatchers to guide the runs the rail movement developed into a melee of trains running in opposite directions, inviting the danger of collision. Train crews threatened to quit their posts, army orders notwithstanding, until the mess was unravelled.

Twenty-four hours later, on July 14, General Hill got his pursuit started by dispatching two trains out of Grafton carrying six hundred troops and three cannon, and reached Oakland by ten o'clock that night. The next morning passed without the arrival of the rest of Hill's trains carrying additional troops and the horses for the cannon brought down the previous day. In the end, by the time General Hill was in position to cut off Garnett's escape the Confederate column had passed safely around the mountain spur. General Garnett was killed in a rearguard skirmish, but his officers had apparently

General Charles Hill, USA, in Pursuit of Garnett's Column, 1861.

After his defeat at Rich Mountain in western Virginia, General Garnett successfully saved his column from capture by moving through a mountain spur into the Shenandoah Valley. Hill's pursuit failed because of railroad mismanagement by both military and civilian personnel.

FROM THE SKETCHBOOK OF CORPORAL "NEP" ROESSLER, COMPANY G, 47TH OHIO VOLUNTEERS; AUTHOR'S COLLECTION.

been well briefed and skillfully carried off the retreat.

McClellan's plan to employ the B & O railroad as a tactical embellishment to his campaign had been a brilliant idea and would have worked had it not been for its faulty execution by his own officers and officials of the B & O. There had been more than enough locomotives and cars for the operation, but without train dispatchers to coordinate train movements over a single-track line the end result had been unnecessary delay and confusion. The first tactical use of the railroad in a military operation had been a failure for all intents and purposes, due mainly to the inexperience of both military and civilian personnel involved—but they were learning. Had the railroad movement been properly coordinated, Hill's entire contingent could have been carried to Oakland in two hours, and the game won.

Nevertheless, even with this first failure the tactical use of railroads in warfare had not been lost on General McClellan. In a letter to President Lincoln, he wrote: "It cannot be ignored. . . . the construction of railroads has introduced a new and very important element in war . . . for concentrating at particular positions, large masses of troops from remote sections . . . creating new strategic points and lines of operation."

Five weeks later McClellan's observation manifested itself on the battlefield of Manassas, when the railroad made the difference between victory and defeat for the Union Army.

The battle of Bull Run, or the First Battle of Manassas, began like the opening of the third act in an amateur comic opera. The Union Army's march to the battlefield in its naiveté was both hilarious and tragic. Neither Napoleon's colorful hordes nor King Arthur's knights could have challenged the originality and strikingly festive mood and appearance of these nondescript untrained, undisciplined citizen-soldiers. Patriotism and love of country was their motivating force. Many had never before fired an army musket, much less loaded one; and most had never heard a shot fired in anger.

The Seventy-ninth New York Highlanders marched in plaid fatigues, their officers in kilts. The Eleventh New York, as French Colonial Zouaves, marched in bright red pantaloons, white gaiters, blue shell jackets, and kepis. The Garibaldi Guards marched in the uniforms of the Italian carabinieri; the "Fighting 69th" marched "stripped to the pants" regiments from Michigan dressed as lumberjacks, wicked sheath knives and horse pistols stuffed in their wide belts. One New York regiment sported white duck trousers, blue blazers, and straw hats;

many carried trunks, valises, and housekeeping paraphernalia. One volunteer actually carried an ice cream freezer, "to make ices when the going got too hot."

There was no discipline. They broke ranks on the march, washed their feet in roadside brooks, looted houses along the way, and talked back to their officers, breaking every regulation. To Colonel William T. Sherman, a West Point Regular Army officer, "there was no greater curse than an invasion by a volunteer army."

Worse yet, there were no provost marshals to control the hordes of civilian spectators, congressmen, senators, and their wives in crinoline and carrying parasols and lunch hampers, who had "come to see the fight." Riding in horse and buggy, on foot and on horseback, they interfered with the movements of the troops and clogged the Warrenton Turnpike, the road to the battlefield. But the picnic atmosphere of this campaign was to be short-lived.

The battle began explosively, civilian gaiety swallowed up in the crises of dangerous effort. To Colonel Sherman, "men shot and mangled by shell and rifle fire, screaming with pain, were no less terrifying than horses running about with blood streaming from their nostrils or lying on the ground, still hitched to guns, gnawing their sides in death."

While the battle raged in the broiling July sun, the deciding factor was in the making at Piedmont, Virginia, a station on the Manassas Gap Railroad at the foot of the Blue Ridge Mountains, where trains awaited Colonel Jackson's brigade. The cavalry, artillery, and supply wagons had moved by road in the usual way, and the balance of General Joseph E. Johnston's infantry was expected to follow Jackson's brigade without delay to join General Beauregard's force already on the field. (On that Sunday morning, July 21, 1861, only three brigades of the Army of the Shenandoah, parts of Jackson's, Bee's, and Bartow's regiments, with the cavalry and artillery, had joined Beauregard then facing the Union Army under General Irwin McDowell, himself a novice at war.)

The Confederate Kirby Smith's brigade was still in the railway yards, and this delay might have easily caused a catastrophe to Beauregard. Fortunately, McDowell's troop movements were even tardier. Kirby Smith's brigade, coming by train, reached Manassas Junction while the battle was in progress and was immediately ordered to the field, instructed by Johnston to "turn" McDowell's right flank.

As the battle swirled in a tornado around the

Henry House and Henry Hill, victory, once within the Union Army's grasp, was lost when Jackson and his brigade of Virginians, hidden behind a stone wall, on command suddenly fired a disciplined blast of rifle fire into a charging column of Union troops. What began as a retirement became a stampede. Union soldiers streaming across the stone bridge over Bull Run overturned wagons and carriages in their haste and panic to escape. Valiant attempts by their officers to avert the panic were useless and the Union Army disintegrated.

Dazed with fright and mortification, catching the panic fever of the civilians, the Union troops streamed down the Warrenton Turnpike and choked side roads, not stopping until they crossed the Long Bridge, to drop exhausted on the sidewalks of the capital city.

The use of the Manassas Gap Railroad to concentrate troops at the right place at the right time gave the victory to the Army of the Shenandoah.

The First Battle of Manassas, or Bull Run, July 21, 1861.

In the first full-scale battle between Union and Confederate forces, victory went to the Confederate Army when reinforcements arrived by train at Manassas Junction. Alfred R. *Waud, an English combat artist, made this drawing on the spot. Waud accompanied Mathew Brady to the field.* AUTHOR'S COLLECTION.

Charge of the "Stonewall Brigade," July 21, 1861.
Jackson's troops leading the charge against the Union troops at Bull Run turned defeat into victory.

FROM AN ON-THE-SPOT DRAWING BY ALFRED R. WAUD,
AUTHOR'S COLLECTION.

CHAPTER 5

Balloon Stacks and Bayonets

INDESCRIBABLE CONFUSION reigned within the federal government the first year following the fall of Fort Sumter. But no department in the government suffered more from lack of intelligent supervision and direction than the War Department and its operation of the railroads, particularly those lines in and around Washington. Secretary Cameron's direction, motivated by personal financial interests, had hampered the railroads' military function.

The first step to correct this situation took place on January 31, 1862, when Congress authorized President Lincoln, as commander-in-chief of the army and navy, "to take possession of any and all railroads, and telegraph lines, in the United States, their rolling stock, their offices, shops, building, and all appendages and appurtenances, and to prescribe rules and regulations" concerning their operational and military priorities. Railroads, telegraph lines and their personnel were to be considered a part of the military establishment of the United States, subject to the rules imposed by the Articles of War.

At the same time, President Lincoln took another step in the right direction and rid himself of Simon Cameron by sending him out of the country as minister to Russia. Lincoln's replacement as secretary of war was Edwin McMasters Stanton, a former lawyer for the Illinois Central Railroad. A bundle of dogmatic energy, "opinionated to the point of insanity" some said, Stanton wielded his authority like a club. Ruthless in his efficiency, arrogant and brutal, Stanton held himself in no awe of high military rank, but he was precisely what Lincoln needed to bring order out of chaos in the War Department. Stanton "sneered and carped" behind Lincoln's back, but he got things done, and that was all Lincoln expected of him. Stanton dealt with war contractors as would a "hanging judge" dealing with

felons, and those coming under his jurisdiction never had any doubts about his authority.

On February 10, 1862, President Lincoln issued an order, countersigned by Stanton, appointing Daniel C. McCallum as military director and super-

Secretary of War **Edwin M. Stanton,** 1862.

Lincoln's replacement for Simon Cameron as secretary of war, Stanton, the ruthless, efficient, former counsel for the Illinois Central Railroad, wielded his authority like a club— but he got things done.

FROM A PHOTOGRAPH BY MATHEW BRADY, AUTHOR'S COLLECTION.

Daniel C. McCallum.

Lincoln's appointment as military director and superintendent of U.S. Military Railroads, McCallum, an experienced railroad man, was divisional superintendent of the Pennsylvania Railroad.

FROM A PHOTOGRAPH BY MATHEW BRADY, AUTHOR'S COLLECTION.

intendent of railroads in the United States, with sweeping authority "to take possession of, hold, and use all railroads, engines and cars . . . for the transport of troops, arms and ammunition and military supplies of the United States" to the exclusion of everything else when those roads were needed.

The most important railroad of immediate concern to both sides in the eastern theater of the war was the Orange & Alexandria, a standard-gauge line sixty-two miles long which terminated at Alexandria, Virginia, across the Potomac River from Washington. The Manassas Gap and the Richmond, Fredericksburg & Potomac railroads would also figure importantly in the coming campaign.

Strategically, the O & A was an avenue of invasion since it ran in an almost straight line through the Shenandoah Valley, parallel to the Blue Ridge Mountains as far as Lynchburg, where it connected with the Richmond & Danville and the Southside railroads approximately sixty miles from Washington, where it joined the Manassas Gap Railroad. At Gordonsville, Virginia, it joined the R F & P at Hanover Junction and terminated at Richmond, the new capital of the Confederacy, crossing the tracks of the Virginia Central running east.

A Section of the Orange & Alexandria Railroad, 1862.

An active section of the O & A main line, near Burke's Station and Union Mills. After War Department seizure, the O & A became one of the U.S. Military Railroads for the duration *of the war. Cars bear USMRR markings and soldiers guard the line.*

FROM A PHOTOGRAPH BY MATHEW BRADY, AUTHOR'S COLLECTION.

When the Confederate Army held Alexandria, the O & A terminal, it had been General Robert E. Lee's plan to construct a rail line connecting the Orange & Alexandria with the Loudon & Hampshire Railroad so that the rolling stock of the O & A, and its motive power, could be transferred south before the Union forces captured it.

Alert to the O & A's importance, the Union army seized the Orange & Alexandria terminal, and the city itself, before the Confederates could remove more than two locomotives, but what rolling stock they did not have time to remove had been put to the torch. All the Union Army could save were the large stocks of rails. The two locomotives the Confederates captured they renamed *General Beauregard* and *General Johnston* and sent them south under their own power to Richmond, where they were badly needed.

More disastrous to the Confederates, however, was the Union Army's capture of the Orange & Alexandria's large yards and shops, which the Union Army engineers quickly put into operation.

After consolidating their capture, United States Military Railroads' engineers extended their control of the line twenty-two miles into Virginia territory, westward to Manassas Junction, where they found that the retreating Confederates had destroyed the bridges east of Bull Run.

Meanwhile, the North's spring offensive against Richmond, designed to end the war quickly, got underway. General George B. McClellan, hero of the campaign in western Virginia, was placed in command of the Army of the Potomac. From July 1861 to March 1862, McClellan had trained his men and waited for favorable weather, spending months in the camps in and around Alexandria. The Lincoln administration, impatient at the delay, suggested a frontal assault against the Confederate Army at Manassas, at which McClellan had balked.

Finally, in response to a direct order from President Lincoln, issued in January, McClellan devised a plan for moving his army by water to Fortress Monroe, thence by way of the Yorktown peninsula to attack Richmond from the east. Lincoln reluctantly agreed with the plan, but he removed McClellan as general-in-chief.

General Irwin McDowell, in command of the Army of Virginia, Department of the Rappahannock, with forty thousand men, was based on the Potomac River at Acquia Creek, terminal of the Richmond, Fredericksburg & Potomac Railroad. Although ordered to cooperate with McClellan's

Office of the Military Director and Superintendent, U.S. Military Railroads.
250 G Street, Washington, D.C.

The Orange & Alexandria Roundhouse, Alexandria, Virginia, 1862.

The locomotive in the foreground was probably brought *bear USMRR markings.*
out for the photographer. Cars on the siding (upper right)

FROM A PHOTOGRAPH, PROBABLY BY MATHEW BRADY,
COURTESY BALTIMORE & OHIO RAILROAD ARCHIVES.

"Office Battery" of the U.S. Military Railroads, 1862.

U.S. Military Railroads Station at Alexandria, Virginia.

This station was also used as a hospital. The original drawings were made by William Marshall Merrick, a civil engineer working for the USMRR.

FROM THE SKETCHBOOK OF WILLIAM MARSHALL MERRICK, NEW YORK PUBLIC LIBRARY.

advance on Richmond, McDowell could not move at all because the Confederate Army, in its retreat to the Richmond defense line, had destroyed three miles of track and two bridges serving the Acquia Creek Depot. The Confederates had taken the rails with them, burned the crossties, and immobilized the line. Consequently, neither army could move in support of the other until this line had been restored.

The extraordinary man called upon to unravel this military railroad tangle was Herman Haupt, a brilliant civil engineer who at that moment was in Boston in the midst of a court battle with the governor of Massachusetts to recover his personal funds spent in constructing the Hoosac Tunnel for the Troy & Greenfield Railroad.

Haupt graduated at eighteen from the United States Military Academy at West Point, on July 1, 1835, and was appointed a brevet lieutenant in the Third U.S. Infantry, a commission he resigned two years later to become a civil engineer for the Norristown & Valley Railroad. A year later he was engaged in locating a railroad for the state of Pennsylvania. In 1840, he helped to construct a railroad between Gettysburg and the Potomac River, and aided in the construction of the York & Wrightsville Railroad. In 1847, Haupt was appointed principal engineer in charge of construction for the Pennsylvania Railroad; his organizational plans for the road were "adopted by the board without change."

Haupt arrived in Washington and reported to Secretary Stanton, who brought him up to date on the military railroad situation in Virginia: both McClellan's and McDowell's armies were immobilized until the Fredericksburg railroad was restored.

A precise, practical man, Haupt asked that his instructions be issued in writing and in due time received them, ordering him "to proceed to the headquarters of General Irwin McDowell on the Rappahannock, where he would receive further instructions respecting the engineering work he was to perform." Haupt accepted the assignment, again in writing, stating that he "had no military or political aspirations," but that he was "particularly averse to wearing a uniform" unless the uniform was a necessary requirement. As for pay, "I neither require any, nor care about it."

Haupt boarded a small steamer which had been placed at his disposal, and sailed down the Potomac to Belle Plain, where he found McDowell at his headquarters. After the amenities, Haupt, coming to the point, asked about the railroad situation. But McDowell interrupted, saying, "Why, Haupt, you don't seem to know me!" Haupt replied that he was not aware that they had ever met before. "Well," said McDowell, "that hurts my feelings. Don't you remember when I came to West Point as a plebe in 1834 that you took me into your tent during my first

Brigadier General Herman Haupt, USA, ADC.

A West Point graduate and railroad genius, Haupt, USMRR *in railroad bridge construction and military train operations.*
chief of construction and transportation, performed miracles FROM A PHOTOGRAPH BY MATHEW BRADY, AUTHOR'S COLLECTION.

Belle Plain, on the Potomac River, Virginia, 1862.

The scene of General (then Colonel) Haupt's arrival at Major General Irwin McDowell's headquarters at the Lacy House, where he reported for duty on April 27, 1862.
FROM A PHOTOGRAPH BY MATHEW BRADY, AUTHOR'S COLLECTION.

Acquia Creek Landing, Virginia, 1862.

Haupt's preliminary inspection found the "extensive wharfs and buildings burned out" by the retreating Confederate Army.
FROM A PHOTOGRAPH BY MATHEW BRADY, AUTHOR'S COLLECTION.

Office of the Provost Marshal, Acquia Creek, Virginia, 1862.

The Union Army's Military Police office, in the building in the background, and the group of "contrabands" (Negro refugees), make this terminal of the Fredericksburg Railroad (USMRR) *a busy place. Boxcars on siding bear the USMRR markings.*

FROM A PHOTOGRAPH BY T. J. O'SULLIVAN, AUTHOR'S COLLECTION.

encampment and extended to me your protection as an older cadet?"

On April 27, 1862, McDowell appointed Haupt as aide-de-camp on his staff, and two days later made a preliminary inspection tour of the wrecked rail line. He found that the "extensive wharf at Acquia Creek . . . covering more than an acre, and all the buildings" had been burned out. The Confederates had torn up the track for a distance of three miles and had carried away the rails. The crossties had been placed in piles and burned, and in several instances the bridge abutments had been destroyed. The roadbed had been traveled over by cavalry, and the rains had churned the clay surface into a quagmire.

Haupt had other problems, not the least of them the soldiers assigned to him as a work force. None of the men had any experience in laying track, and they had cut the crossties of varying lengths. Even the weather had refused to cooperate; drenching downpours made the working conditions unbearable, and the ties had to be laid in mud.

But Haupt was not the kind of a man who could be deterred by a little rain. Selecting some of his most intelligent officers as assistant engineers, with leveling instruments improvised from sticks Haupt and his crew worked around the clock, at night in pouring rain, laying and spiking rails by lantern light, completing the three miles of track in three days. "It was a hard-looking track when first laid," wrote Haupt, "and when the General rode out the first morning to inspect it, he expressed an opinion that an engine could never run over it. I requested him to suspend his judgment until the next morning, and look at the road then. He came as promised, and expressed surprise to find the track in good line and surfaced and ballasted with earth. . . ."

General McDowell had been a daily observer, "to watch the progress and encourage the men by his

Grading and Ballasting Track on the O & A (USMRR) Railroad, 1862.

A work train, behind the locomotive General Haupt, *stands on a siding. Haupt, in civilian clothes and wearing black hat, directs the track crew. Haupt was "averse to wearing a uniform."*

FROM A PHOTOGRAPH BY MATHEW BRADY, AUTHOR'S COLLECTION.

presence," and he commented that he had "never heard sweeter music than the click of the hammers" as the men pounded the rail spikes into place with the aid of lanterns.

By Saturday, May 3, a train carried the first load of lumber over the new rail from Acquia Creek to rebuild the Pohick Creek Bridge, a single span of about a hundred fifty feet and an elevation of thirty feet. About noon on that day, General McDowell, General Moorhead, and Secretaries of State and Treasury William H. Seward and Salmon P. Chase paid Colonel Haupt a visit and witnessed the "framing" of the bridge. To their surprise, fifteen hours later General McDowell rode across the structure on a locomotive.

The next big project was the reconstruction of the Potomac Creek Bridge, a span nearly four hundred feet long with an elevation of eighty feet above the water. Some logs had been laid for the crib foundations, but a week later Haupt was able to organize a sizeable work force by calling upon three companies of troops from the Sixth and Seventh Wisconsin and Nineteenth Indiana regiments under Lieutenants Harker, Pond, and Ford. Only 120 men reported for work from these companies; the rest had been "sickly" or "inefficient" or "unwilling to work on ropes and timbers eighty feet above the ground."

On May 14, Haupt telegraphed McDowell that because the men were "unwilling to climb about on the high trestles," he feared the work of bracing would be delayed. "With soldiers unaccustomed to such work," wrote Haupt, "with an insufficient supply of tools, with an occasional scarcity of food, and several days of wet weather, the work nevertheless advanced rapidly."

Moreover, Haupt reported that as soon as he had the "track timbers down and the track closed," he would test the structure by pulling an engine over it with ropes. "If it goes into the creek," wrote Haupt, "it will cease to trouble us for awhile. [The engine was the USMRR *Washington*.] If it reaches the other side, it will have a good road and may keep the track. We can readily get the cars over by planking between the track and pushing. The rains give us much trouble, but I will spare no effort to get an engine to the Rappahannock by Saturday, the 17th. The men are wet, dull, and no life or activity in them."

Even with these seemingly insurmountable difficulties Haupt completed the bridge in good time and with the road completed to Fredericksburg Haupt moved his headquarters to that city. There he witnessed a horrible accident. When the Confederates evacuated the city, they planted a number of mines with percussion fuses under the tracks around the depot to blow trains that tried to come into the station. Friendly "contrabands" had pointed out the locations of these explosives and the soldiers had removed a large number of them, placing them in a small brick building near the station that had once been used as a powder magazine. A careless sentry handled one of these mines, exploding it and setting off the entire number. The explosion shook the entire city, blowing the building to pieces—"not a brick left." The sentry disappeared; only a piece of his rifle was found some distance from the scene.

To make certain all the explosive had been removed, a locomotive was sent over the line pushing ahead of it a car heavily loaded with scrap iron to discharge any mines that had been left under the rails, but no more were found.

Later Haupt learned that President Lincoln and his cabinet had visited General McDowell at his headquarters and asked to see the Potomac Creek bridge. When the president returned to Washington he remarked to members of the War Committee that he had seen "a most remarkable structure that human eyes ever rested upon. That man Haupt has built a bridge across Potomac Creek, about 400-feet long and nearly 100-feet high, over which loaded trains are running every hour, and, upon my word, gentlemen, there is nothing in it but beanpoles and cornstalks."

Meanwhile, in the Shenandoah Valley "Stonewall" Jackson and his Army of the Valley, in a brilliant series of diversionary battles, defeated the forces of Banks, Shields, and Fremont at Kernstown, Cross Keys, Port Republic, Cedar Mountain, and Romney, and retired to join Lee who was facing McClellan before Richmond.

Since he was without McDowell's support, McClellan moved cautiously against Richmond, laid siege to Yorktown, which he captured without a fight, and fought a minor action at Big Bethel. With Jackson menacing Washington, President Lincoln detached a large body of troops from McClellan's

President Abraham Lincoln.
On February 10, 1862, President Lincoln issued the order appointing Daniel C. McCallum as director and superintendent of U.S. Military Railroads, with sweeping powers to operate any railroad in the United States for military purposes when necessary.
FROM A PHOTOGRAPH BY MATHEW BRADY, AUTHOR'S COLLECTION.

command for its defense, while McDowell was ordered to bring Jackson to battle and capture him at Front Royal, Jackson's reported position. Accordingly, McDowell, "leaving bag and baggage and knapsacks to be forwarded by river and rail," reluctantly began a series of forced marches through the Shenandoah Valley.

At the same time, Colonel Haupt with his construction corps left for the United States Military Railroad base at Alexandria, leaving instructions for Colonel Devereaux to reconstruct the Manassas Gap Railroad (which Devereaux soon "put in passable condition"). A few days later McDowell established his headquarters at Rectortown and his supply depot at Piedmont, four miles away.

When Haupt reached Piedmont, he ran head-on into a problem in bureaucracy. An army paymaster had taken over a boxcar which happened to be on the main line track and had set the car up as a pay office. The track had to be cleared, so Haupt told the paymaster he would have to give up the car, that a nearby house could serve just as well. Haupt

General Haupt's Famous "Bean

First of its kind, and built by Haupt in nine working days, the Potomac Creek Bridge when completed was tested by pulling the locomotive Washington across it with ropes.

and Cornstalk" Bridge, 1862.

Upon seeing the bridge, President Lincoln commented that the remarkable structure contained "nothing in it but beanpoles and cornstalks."

FROM A PHOTOGRAPH BY MATHEW BRADY, AUTHOR'S COLLECTION.

tried to explain to the paymaster, but the man was adamant and would not budge, saying that soldiers' pay was just as important as their rations. Haupt solved the problem by having a guard detail remove the desk, money chests, table, chairs, and papers. The paymaster followed meekly.

Earlier, Haupt had found the Manassas Gap Railroad inadequate to carry the enormous amounts of transportation that would be needed when McDowell moved against Jackson. Military interference with train movements was also a pressing problem. But most annoying was the refusal of subordinates in McDowell's Commissary and Quartermaster Departments to unload their cars promptly so they could be used again. Trains of cars waiting to be unloaded blocked the line and slowed other train movements. Haupt promptly reported this "railroad blockade" to McDowell, who immediately ordered his chief commissary officer to Piedmont to "superintend personally the unloading of these cars." The night was dark, the torrential rain made the work unpleasant, and the additional trains that Haupt had ordered from Alexandria had not arrived. After waiting all morning, Haupt sent an urgent message by courier to Colonel Devereaux, believing that officer had disobeyed his orders, "and was disposed to remove him."

On Monday, May 26, Haupt was making preparations to leave for Alexandria to reconstruct the Manassas Gap Railroad, which had been severely damaged, "and to throw troops and supplies into Front Royal" to head off Stonewall Jackson. Daniel Stone, whom Haupt was going to assign the task of repairing the Massaponix Bridge, handed him a letter from Secretary Stanton. The letter authorized Stone "to do anything he may deem expedient to open for use in the shortest possible time the Richmond & Acquia Creek Railroad," which left Haupt nothing to do "but play the part of a superintendent of transportation."

Haupt tendered his resignation at once, saying that "there was a serious defect in organization, which interferes with successful operations . . . that there cannot be *two* co-existent and equal heads in one Department." On the face of this it would not have been surprising had Stanton been playing a little game of duplicity, which he was sometimes prone to do when he thought it suited his purpose; but this one, it seems, backfired.

Apparently, Haupt's resignation under the circumstances had come to the attention of President Lincoln, who had great respect and admiration for Haupt, and on May 28, Haupt received General

Order No. 17, signed by Lincoln and countersigned by Stanton. The order read:

> All persons connected with the railroads, either in the Department of Construction or Transportation, will receive orders of Colonel Haupt, A.D.C., as if they were given directly by the Major General commanding the Department.
> Official
> By order of the President of the United States, Commander-in-Chief of the Army and Navy.
> Samuel Breck, A.A.G.

On June 3, Haupt received Colonel Devereaux's explanation as to why Haupt's order for the additional trains had not been carried out: "All my power save engines, *Rapidan, Fairfax, Delaware, Ferguson* and *Indiana*, were on the Gap Road. The *Fairfax* was (and is) too much out of order to run. Still, we press her as a switch engine, and are forced to use her on the main line, where she broke down on Saturday, delaying everything for hours. She switches and brings up cars from the Quartermaster and Commissary Departments. The *Rapidan* is the only engine we can trust to do the daily heavy work between Washington and Alexandria. . . . nevertheless she has been sent with heavy trains to Manassas to be forwarded to the Gap Road by your return power."

To fill the locomotive shortage Colonel McCallum seized three heavy "coal burners" from the Baltimore & Ohio Railroad to move General Ord's division to Front Royal, at the same time sending soft coal for these locomotives to Alexandria, which arrived there on Saturday night (these locomotives did not run out of coal until the following Monday). Colonel Devereaux was careful to point out to Haupt that more than three-quarters of the locomotives on the Manassas Gap Railroad were wood-burners. He added that Coal-Burner No. 70 limped in with her steam chest perforated by gunfire and that her cylinders were out of order, and "was of no use." All of which left only two locomotives operative for troop movements.

By Saturday, May 31, the Goose Creek Bridge and five others had been rebuilt; Haupt completed the work in a day and a half. While inspecting these bridges, Haupt received a message from McDowell, that the enemy had torn up a section of track on a high embankment west of the summit, and had thrown the rails and ties several hundred feet down the side of the mountain. They had also left a pile of wrecked cars at the east end of the break. Haupt sent word back to McDowell that he

One of Three "Coal-Burners" Seized from the B & O, 1862.

Winans's short-furnaced Camel No. 65, Phoenix, and two others of the same type, including No. 70, put out of com- *mission by gunfire, were seized from the Baltimore & Ohio Railroad to fill a USMRR shortage of locomotives.*

PHOTOGRAPHER UNKNOWN,
COURTESY BALTIMORE & OHIO MUSEUM ARCHIVES.

The Orange & Alexandria's (USMRR) Rappahannock Bridge, 1862.

Seen and drawn by William Marshall Merrick, civil engineer, USMRR.

FROM THE SKETCHBOOK OF WILLIAM MARSHALL MERRICK,
NEW YORK PUBLIC LIBRARY.

A U.S. Military Railroad Train Wrecked near Manassas, 1862.

*Always a sad sight, capsized military trains, if they were
not too badly damaged, were usually repaired and put back
in service.*

PHOTOGRAPH, PROBABLY BY DAVID WOODBURY OR JOHN GIBSON;
AUTHOR'S COLLECTION.

would be able to repair the damage, provided the rails and ties "were within reach, and no more bridges broken."

Haupt entrained that night and arrived at the site Sunday morning, June 1, at daylight. The reported damage was correct; Haupt found that the enemy had moved a dozen cars to the high embankment, had opened the track, and had pushed the cars over. Many of the cars had capsized, "making a bad wreck."

First, Haupt cleared the rails by pushing the remaining cars over the embankment since they were too badly damaged to save. He then divided his track gang into two working parties, starting one at each end of the break, working toward each other. Rails and ties which had been thrown over the mountainside were hauled back up to the trackbed by ropes. By 10 P.M. Haupt ran an engine over the new track and hurried to Front Royal, where he found "General McDowell riding through

the streets on horseback." A few hours later, General Augur's division was at Front Royal ready to pursue Jackson down through the Shenandoah Valley; but the move was too late to intercept the wily Jackson. For his failure to capture Jackson, General McDowell was relieved from his command and replaced by Major General John Pope.

The first two weeks of June 1862 saw the return of the Union Army from the Shenandoah Valley, demoralized and defeated. McDowell established his headquarters near Manassas, occupying the retaken line of the Orange & Alexandria Railroad. Meanwhile, the Manassas Gap Railroad was given sufficient military protection by General Geary's troops, posted along the line according to Haupt's instructions.

During this lull in active operations Haupt reorganized his construction corps with refugee Negroes, "contrabands" selected from the thousands who had poured into Washington, placing them

General Haupt's Track Crew at Work near Catlett's Station, 1862.

A bad break in the O & A line (USMRR) being put back into shape following a Confederate raid. If material was close at hand, the track was usually ready for use in a matter of hours.

FROM A PHOTOGRAPH, PROBABLY BY DAVID WOODBURY, AUTHOR'S COLLECTION.

General Robert E. Lee, CSA, 1862.

The commander of the Army of Northern Virginia, Lee removed McClellan's threat to Richmond by defeating the Army of the Potomac in the Seven Days' battles.

From a photograph by Mathew Brady, made in 1865; Author's Collection.

under civilian foremen and superintendents who trained them for the work.

On the morning of June 27, McClellan's Army of the Potomac was attacked in front of Richmond, at Beaver Dam Creek, by the entire Confederate Army, under Lee and Longstreet and reinforced by Stonewall Jackson. General "Jeb" Stuart's cavalry fell on McClellan's right flank and turned it at Old Church. McClellan then formed a new line of battle from Gaines House, along Mill Road to New Cold Harbor, and by three o'clock that afternoon his entire army had been driven back two miles.

The battle developed into a raging inferno of hissing steel and crashing explosives. McClellan's army fell back slowly along his entire front, beginning a retrograde movement that lasted seven days, each day fighting a bloody action—at Fair Oaks, Savages Station, Mechanicsville, and Harrison's

Landing, downriver from Richmond, after fighting a fearful holding action at Malvern Hill in which artillery, hub to hub, poured shells into the advancing Confederate line.

The Confederates' "fire never slackened nor abated," wrote George Alfred Townsend, able correspondent of the *Philadelphia Inquirer* in his eyewitness account of the Confederate advance:

> They loaded and moved forward, column by column, like so many immortals that could not be vanquished. The scene from the balloon, as Lowe informed me, "was awful beyond comparison—of puffing shells and shrieking shrapnel, with volleys that shattered the hills and filled the air with deadly whispers." Infantry, artillery and horse turned the Federal right from time to time, and to preserve the order of battle, the whole line fell back toward the Grapevine Bridge.
>
> It was with difficulty that I could make my way along the narrow corduroy, for hundreds of wounded were limping from the field to the safe side, and ammunition wagons were passing the

Major General James Ewell Brown Stuart, CSA.

A cavalry commander in the Army of Northern Virginia, the enterprising Stuart proved more than a match for McClellan in the Seven Days' battle.

Photograph probably by Vannerson or Cook of Richmond, Author's Collection.

The Battle of Fair Oaks (or Seven Pines), June 1862.

Fought only eight miles from Richmond, Fair Oaks was a bloody affair. The famous Twin Farmhouses are seen on the left of Alfred R. Waud's on-the-spot sketch. A manned howitzer redoubt stands at lower left.

The Battle of Fair Oaks.

Mathew Brady's photograph of the same scene, "where the battle raged hottest" in June 1862. General Daniel Sickles's brigade can be seen (blurred) in the upper right. More than four hundred Union soldiers were buried near Twin Farmhouses.

FROM A PHOTOGRAPH BY MATHEW BRADY, AUTHOR'S COLLECTION.

other way, driven by reckless drivers who should have been blown up momentarily. Before I could reach the north side of the creek, immense throngs of panic-stricken people came surging down the slippery bridge. A few carried muskets, but I saw several wantonly throw their pieces into the flood, and as the mass was unarmed I inferred that they had made similar dispositions.

Along side of the bridge many of the wounded were washing their wounds in the water; and the cries of the teamsters echoed weirdly through the trees that grew in the river. At nine o'clock we got underway—horsemen, batteries, ambulances, ammunition teams, infantry; and finally some great seige thirty-twos that had been hauled from Gaines House. One of these pieces broke down the tim-

bers again, and my impression was that it was cast into the current. When we emerged from the swamp timber, the hills before us were found brilliantly illuminated with burning camps.

Following his last-ditch stand at Malvern Hill, McClellan made no further attempt to check the Confederate juggernaut, bringing to a conclusion his grand enterprise of 1862. For his failure on the peninsula President Lincoln removed him from command of the Army of the Potomac.

Thus ended the spring campaign of 1862, in which the United States Military Railroads had played a major role, although not altogether successfully, despite the herculean efforts of Colonel Haupt.

The Field Hospital at Savage's Station, the Richmond, Fredericksburg & Potomac Railroad, June 1862.
Wounded from the June 27 battle are being treated by Union army surgeons.

FROM A PHOTOGRAPH BY MATHEW BRADY, AUTHOR'S COLLECTION.

McClellan's Army of the Potomac in Retreat across
"Grapevine" Bridge over the Chicahominy, 1862.

As witnessed by combat artist Alfred R. Waud, and correspondent George Alfred Townsend of the Philadelphia Inquirer.

The "Grapevine" Bridge.

As seen by Brady's camera in June 1862, army construction crews repair the rickety structure.

FROM A PHOTOGRAPH BY MATHEW BRADY, AUTHOR'S COLLECTION.

USMRR Gallery of Steam Power

Dᴜʀɪɴɢ ᴛʜᴇ course of the Civil War, the U.S. Military Railroads system built and purchased 312 locomotives and captured 106 more from the enemy; purchased 5,111 cars, constructed 55, and captured 409 more "within the zones of active operation."

The following gallery of photographs presents a sampling of the handsome, balloon-stacked war chariots which thundered over the rails of the USMRR and into the annals of railroad history of the United States.

The *General Haupt* of the U.S. Military Railroads in 1862.

Named in honor of the U.S. Military Railroads' great superintendent, Brigadier General Herman Haupt, this sleek war chariot saw long and distinguished service on the embattled lines of the Orange & Alexandria Railroad (USMRR) during the war. Designed and built by master locomotive builder William Mason, and delivered to the government on January 17, 1863, the General Haupt had sixteen- by twenty-two-inch cylinders and sixty-one-inch drivers. At the war's end in 1865 she was purchased by the Baltimore & Ohio Railroad in all her colorful war livery. She was retired in 1897.

Fʀᴏᴍ ᴀ ᴘʜᴏᴛᴏɢʀᴀᴘʜ ʙʏ Mᴀᴛʜᴇᴡ Bʀᴀᴅʏ, Aᴜᴛʜᴏʀ'ꜱ Cᴏʟʟᴇᴄᴛɪᴏɴ.

Locomotive *Fire Fly*, USMRR Engine No. 37.

Built by R. Norris & Son in 1862, Fire Fly had sixteen- by twenty-four-inch cylinders, fifty-two-inch drivers, and weighed 57,910 pounds. Fire Fly was one of twelve USMRR *locomotives purchased by the Baltimore & Ohio Railroad in 1865.*

NATIONAL ARCHIVES.

The U.S. Military Railroads' *W. H. Whitton*, 1862.

One of William Mason's sleek-looking American 4–4–0s, the Whitton had sixteen- by twenty-two-inch cylinders, sixty-one-inch drivers, and weighed 59,000 pounds. When the war *ended, the engine was purchased by the Baltimore & Ohio Railroad at Alexandria in 1865, and retired after long service in 1887.*

PHOTOGRAPHER UNKNOWN (PROBABLY CAPTAIN A. J. RUSSELL), NATIONAL ARCHIVES.

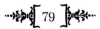

President Abraham Lincoln's Official Presidential Train.

The U.S. Military Railroads' only luxury passenger train, the ornately beautiful presidential coach was specially built by the Orange & Alexandria Railroad's shops at Alexandria.

President Lincoln never rode in it in his lifetime. The coach's first and last service was carrying Lincoln's remains to Springfield, Illinois.

U.S. MILITARY R. R.

Photographed (probably) by Mathew Brady,
Courtesy National Archives.

USMRR Locomotive No. 116 at City Point, Virginia, 1864.

Built by Rogers Locomotive and Machine Works in 1864, No. 116 weighed in at 60,000 pounds, had sixteen- by twenty-two-inch cylinders and fifty-two-inch drivers. The *young ladies decorating the tender were probably friends or relatives of the railroad men. No data are available as to her disposition.*

FROM A PHOTOGRAPH BY MATHEW BRADY, AUTHOR'S COLLECTION.

USMRR Locomotive No. 133 at City Point, Virginia.

Built by Danforth Cooke of Paterson, New Jersey, No. 133 stands before a log fort at City Point, General Grant's base of operations in the Petersburg Campaign of 1864. Received *by the USMRR on June 11, 1864, No. 133 had sixteen- by twenty-four-inch cylinders, sixty-one-inch drivers, and weighed in at 58,000 pounds.*

FROM A PHOTOGRAPH BY MATHEW BRADY, AUTHOR'S COLLECTION.

USMRR Locomotive No. 156 at City Point, Virginia, 1864.

Built by Baldwin and delivered to the U.S. Military Rail-roads on August 2, 1862, No. 156 saw service on the City Point Railroad in the last year of the war. Flag-decked, the engine poses for the photographer on a siding at City Point. It had fourteen- by twenty-four-inch cylinders and fifty-six-inch drivers. Its final disposition is unknown.

FROM A PHOTOGRAPH BY MATHEW BRADY, AUTHOR'S COLLECTION.

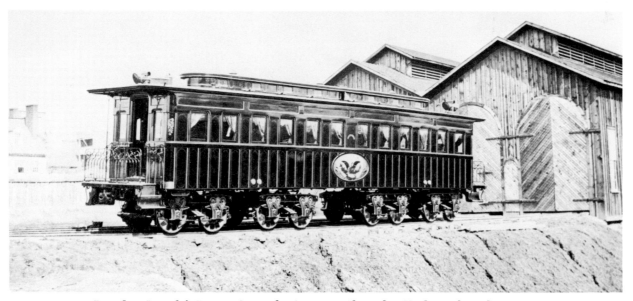

President Lincoln's Private Car in the Orange & Alexandria Yards at Alexandria, 1865.

The presidential car, built in the shops of the Orange & Alexandria and Manassas Gap railroads, was never used by Lincoln in his lifetime. Its only official journey was carrying his body to Springfield for interment.

FROM A PHOTOGRAPH BY CAPTAIN A. J. RUSSELL, *USMRR,* NATIONAL ARCHIVES.

Ironclad on Railroad Wheels, 1860s.

Bearing the familiar B & O insignia, these iron boxcars carried ammunition to the Union forces during the Civil War.

After 1862, cars carried the USMRR identification marking. The car body was supported on heavy arch-bar trucks.

COURTESY BALTIMORE & OHIO RAILROADS ARCHIVES.

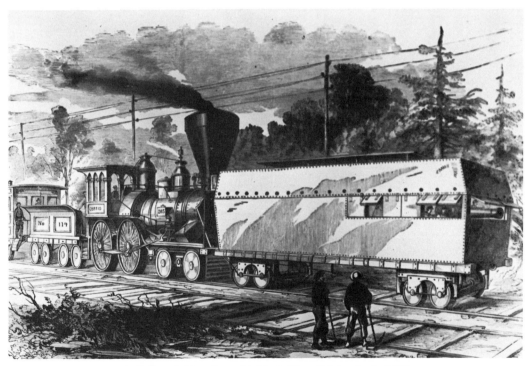

A Railroad Dreadnaught That Was Sidetracked, 1862.

In August, 1862, Peter H. Watson, assistant secretary of war, presented General Haupt with an armor-clad, bullet-proof car mounting a heavy canon. "The kindness was apparent," wrote Haupt, "but the present was an elephant. I could not use it and, being in the way, it was finally sidetracked on an old siding in Alexandria." But bullet-proof, iron-clad cabs on locomotives, to Haupt, "were indispensable."

FROM A CONTEMPORARY DRAWING, AUTHOR'S COLLECTION.

CHAPTER 6

The "General" Hangs Eight Men— and a General Loses a Battle

Shortly before the great battle of Shiloh Church on Sunday, April 6, 1862, Major General Don Carlos Buell and the Army of the Ohio had captured and occupied Nashville, Tennessee, one of the most important rail centers in the Confederacy. Buell had not been there long when he and his army were ordered to join General Ulysses S. Grant's forces operating in the vicinity of Fort Donelson on the Cumberland River.

Leaving a garrison at Nashville and another at Cumberland Gap to secure the area against any surprise moves the Confederates might make, Buell

Major General Don Carlos Buell, USA, 1862.

Commander of the Army of the Ohio, Buell captured Nashville, an important rail center, and then left to join forces with General Ulysses S. Grant on the Cumberland. Buell had hired James J. Andrews as a spy for his army, but had little confidence in his reliability in espionage.

From a photograph by Mathew Brady, Author's Collection.

Major General Ulysses S. Grant, USA, 1862.

Commander of the Union forces in the West, Grant was the only federal general who won victories and understood what the war was all about.

Photographer unknown, Author's Collection.

Nashville, Tennessee, in 1862.

At Nashville, an important railroad junction, Major General Ormsby McKnight Mitchell commanded the garrison under Buell's "discretionary orders," and planned the capture of Huntsville, Alabama, another important rail center.

FROM A PHOTOGRAPH BY COONLEY, AUTHOR'S COLLECTION.

also left a force of eight thousand men under Major General Ormsby McKnight Mitchell with "discretionary orders" to protect the region south of Nashville.

In Washington, Major General Henry Wager Halleck, chief-of-staff, a book soldier with no military experience and a self-styled master of military strategy, shuffled his papers and consulted his maps. The officer whom President Lincoln styled "a first-rate clerk," in total ignorance of the military situation in Tennessee, advised Mitchell to occupy Fayettesville, twenty-eight miles from Huntsville, Alabama, a Confederate stronghold, with particular orders to take over, if possible, the Memphis & Charleston Railroad there. If the military situation permitted, and the Confederates agreed to cooperate, Mitchell could try for Decatur, Georgia. If neither of these suggestions worked out, Mitchell was "to act according to circumstances"—in short, to "play it by ear."

Mitchell, the officer chosen to carry out this ambiguous assignment, was a former college professor, a "glory seeker" with no military experience whatever. With an all-consuming ambition to gain recognition as a military hero, Mitchell found himself in the not-very-promising position of guarding a railroad miles from the big actions. And so, with little chance that anything world-shaking would happen to further his soldierly fortunes, Mitchell decided to create his own opportunity to become a hero. His "discretionary orders" allowed him plenty of latitude for experimentation. And it was the combination of General Mitchell's ambition, and the ambition of an obscure quinine-salesman-turned-soldier, James J. Andrews, that brought about the greatest, most thrilling military operation of the entire war.

James J. Andrews, the real hero of this action, had become a soldier-spy for General Buell, who held some serious doubts concerning Andrews's pro-

Major General Ormsby McKnight Mitchell, USA, 1862.
College professor turned soldier, Mitchell, said to be a glory seeker, wanted public recognition as a military hero. General Buell later claimed that Mitchell did not order the Andrews Raid.

FROM A PHOTOGRAPH BY MATHEW BRADY, AUTHOR'S COLLECTION.

Major General Henry Wager Halleck, USA, 1862.
General-in-chief of the federal armies, Halleck regarded himself as a book soldier and master strategist. Lincoln referred to him as a "first-rate clerk."

FROM A PHOTOGRAPH BY MATHEW BRADY, AUTHOR'S COLLECTION.

pensity for espionage. Andrews had used his "cover" as a quinine salesman to spy for the Army of the Ohio; and while he might have had serious shortcomings in military espionage, Andrews was nevertheless a brave and daring man.

It was no secret that the military powers at Washington, and the Lincoln administration, wanted to relieve East Tennessee's "loyal population," a fact known to Mitchell. Moreover, since Andrews and Mitchell were both glory seekers, it was only natural that they collaborate in a project that could conceivably make them war heroes.

Both Mitchell and Andrews knew that Chattanooga, an important railroad terminus, was lightly garrisoned by Confederate troops. If they could bring about its capture, glory would be theirs. It was Andrews who had the audacious plan. He would take twenty trained, selected men in civilian clothes to infiltrate the enemy's lines at Marietta, Georgia, a station on the important Western & Atlantic Railroad. There, he and his men would steal a train, cut the telegraph lines, and run the stolen train northward to Chattanooga, burning the bridges behind them. Such was the first part of the

plan. At the same time, Mitchell with his army would attack the Memphis & Charleston Railroad at Huntsville, Alabama, and cut all communications, west and south. If successful, the operation would expose Chattanooga to capture and occupation without interference.

It was the kind of coordinated operation, though two hundred miles apart, that required precise timing, coordination, and solid communication facilities. With the imprecise Mitchell, and the extremely fragile telegraphic communications facilities available, such a daring venture was doomed to failure. Nevertheless, Mitchell and Andrews set April 11, 1862, as the target date for the joint operation, the theft of the train and the capture of the Memphis & Charleston Railroad at Huntsville, Alabama.

Andrews and his raiders exchanged their uniforms for civilian clothes and left on their separate missions, working their way south in small groups, taking separate trains at different stations along the way, all under the "cover story" of being Kentuckians on their way to Atlanta to join the Confederate Army. Right on target on April 11, Mitchell

James J. Andrews, 1862.

Leader and planner of the Georgia railroad raid, Andrews, "dressed in a Prince Albert coat, white shirt, stiff collar and knotted tie," carrying an expensive pair of saddle bags over his arm, in disguise as a rich planter, almost got away with raid, but bad judgment and lateness brought about his downfall and capture. He was hanged as a spy.

PHOTOGRAPHER UNKNOWN,
COURTESY ATLANTA HISTORICAL SOCIETY.

attacked Huntsville at 6 A.M., routed the garrison, and captured a number of freight cars and fifteen locomotives. Mitchell then threw his force across the main line of the Memphis & Charleston Railroad, his part of the scheme completed without incident or retaliation.

Had Mitchell let matters stand as planned with Andrews, the chances are that the operation would have been successful. But Mitchell committed the incredible blunder of completely forgetting all about Andrews and his men. Sending a detachment eastward along the tracks, Mitchell destroyed several bridges, captured five more locomotives, and attempted to destroy the important railroad bridge at Bridgeport and others at Decatur, Georgia. But the Confederates beat him to the punch by wrecking the east span of the bridge themselves and then withdrawing. Mitchell never gave a thought to the fact that by wrecking his own communication and rail lines he had placed Andrews and his raiders in great danger.

But Andrews had also made a mistake—he started a day late, on April 12, 1862. On that day at precisely 6 A.M., conductor W. A. Fuller "highballed" his engineer, Jeff Cain, at the throttle of the loco-

The Atlanta Railroad Station in 1862.

Known as the "old car shed," built in 1854, both shed and station were destroyed by General Sherman in 1864, prior to the March to the Sea.

COURTESY ATLANTA HISTORICAL SOCIETY.

motive *General*, head-ending the northbound passenger train. Rain had started when the train pulled out of the station with three empty boxcars coupled ahead of the coaches and "dead-headed" to Chattanooga.

While the *General* and its train headed for Marietta, Andrews and his men purchased tickets, boarded another train without causing any undue attention, and rode to Big Shanty, the station marked for the theft of the train.

Aboard their train, Andrews noticed that many trains were running or standing on sidings every ten miles or so, adding a warning note to his plans. The Western & Atlantic Railroad was typical of the single-track rail lines of the time, with turnouts and sidings to permit trains to run in each direction, scheduled to pass each other at given times and places.

As the *General* and her train pulled into Big Shanty, Andrews and his men seated throughout the cars heard conductor Fuller announce, "Twenty minutes for breakfast!" While the passengers and

train crew rushed for the restaurant, Andrews and his men dropped off on the opposite side of the train unnoticed. Andrews himself moved toward the boxcars while his engineer slipped forward and into the *General's* cab.

With his men safely aboard the boxcars, Andrews quietly uncoupled the passenger coaches and climbed into the cab, and the *General* slowly pulled out of the station. Oddly enough, a camp of four thousand Confederate soldiers on the opposite side of the track took no notice of the departing train, but conductor Fuller, at breakfast, was startled by the sound of his locomotive pulling out of the station. Followed quickly by his engineer, Fuller started on foot in pursuit of the *General*, but Andrews quickly outdistanced them. Up to this time Fuller had no way of knowing that the men who stole his train were federal soldiers out of uniform. He thought they were Confederate deserters who would abandon the train as soon as they made their escape.

Having obtained copies of the train schedules,

The Locomotive *General* at Big Shanty, Georgia, 1862.

At the start of the "Great Locomotive Chase," the General, head-ending a mixed passenger and freight train, waits while her crew eat breakfast in the Lacey Hotel dining room. Andrews and his party of twenty, including two soldier- *engineers, William Knight and Wilson Brown, and their fireman, Alf Wilson, boarded the train and engine cab, in full view of a sentry at Camp McDonald, to begin the eighty-seven-mile race that made railroad history.*

From an original watercolor by Wilbur G. Kurtz, Courtesy Atlanta Historical Society.

William F. Fuller

The conductor of the train stolen by Andrews and his raiders, Fuller began his chase after the General *on foot. He finally commandeered the locomotive* Texas, *and captured the* General *only after latter engine ran out of fuel.*

Andrews was familiar with the track he was to cover. He also knew where they would meet the trains coming from the other direction—two regularly scheduled, and the third an unscheduled freight. Thus far Andrews had planned carefully and had made no mistakes except that of starting a day late. Nevertheless, by pulling out of Big Shanty he had gained twenty minutes, and for the moment he would have no collisions with on-coming, unscheduled trains.

Reaching Etowah Station, Andrews saw an old locomotive, the *Yonah*, standing on a siding with steam up. Seeing that she was old and slow, he did not stop to disable her—another fatal mistake.

At Kingston, thirty miles from Big Shanty, Andrews found the train from Rome, Georgia, waiting to transfer passengers from Fuller's train which Andrews had stolen. But when the *General* was recognized, hauling only three boxcars instead of passenger coaches, explanations were demanded of Andrews. Keeping his wits about him, Andrews coolly explained that he was running a "special" carrying three cars of gunpowder for General Beauregard at Corinth. When Andrews asked about

Camp McDonald, Recruiting and Training Center, 1862.

At Big Shanty, Henry Whitely, Company F, Fifty-sixth Georgia Regiment, saw Andrews and his raiders take over the General *and three boxcars, suspecting nothing. The camp was across the tracks from the Hotel Lacey.*

The Locomotive *Yonah* at Etowah Station, Georgia, April 12, 1862.

The Yonah *stands before the turntable. In the background, Andrews and his raiders in the* General's *train didn't give a thought to the steamed-up* Yonah *and the danger she posed,* *so they didn't stop to disable her. This was a fatal over-sight.*

FROM AN ORIGINAL WATERCOLOR PAINTING BY WILBUR G. KURTZ, COURTESY RALPH RIGHTON.

Unexpected Train Meeting at Kingston Station, Georgia, April 12, 1862.

At Kingston, Andrews and his raiders meet the train from Rome, waiting to transfer passengers from Andrews's train. When the General *was seen hauling three boxcars, explan-* *ations were demanded. Andrews told his inquisitors that his train was a "special," hauling ammunition for Beauregard.*

FROM AN ORIGINAL WATERCOLOR BY WILBUR G. KURTZ, COURTESY RALPH RIGHTON AND THE ATLANTA HISTORICAL SOCIETY.

the local freight, he was informed that it was expected at any moment. Andrews then backed his train onto a siding and waited. Moments later the expected freight arrived, its locomotive carrying a red flag indicating that another train followed behind.

Andrews kept his head, bellowing at the freight conductor, "What does it mean that the road is blocked in this manner, when I have orders to get this powder to Beauregard?" The trainman's answer came as a shock to Andrews, who suddenly realized his own mistake by starting a day late on his mission. Mitchell had attacked and cut the Memphis & Charleston Railroad and the trains that had escaped were now heading in his direction!

Andrews immediately changed his attitude and became apologetic. His imposing appearance bore validity when he asked if the conductor of the local train would please back his train to a safe distance from the "powder cars." The perplexed conductor complied, and Andrews put on a good act, moving among his questioners while he kept an eye on the telegraphic office, pretending exasperation that there was no train order for him to clear the track ahead of him.

After an interminable wait the second train arrived. But suspicion was still apparent among his questioners, who little guessed that Andrews's main reason for pretending to wait for a message was to be sure no messages of inquiry about him were sent.

Another train now arrived, also carrying a red flag, and Andrews could do nothing but "sweat it out." An hour and a half passed while Andrews's men waited in breathless silence in the boxcars, expecting at any moment to find themselves trapped.

Finally the last of the local freights passed into the sidings and Andrews's "powder train" again headed for Chattanooga. At Kingston, four miles beyond, Andrews had stopped long enough to cut the telegraph lines and pry up some rails when he was startled to hear a train whistle coming up behind him! He and his men made a run for the train and started for Adairsville where, according to schedule, he expected to find the southbound express on a siding waiting for him to pass. Instead, Andrews found the siding occupied by a mixed train, which meant that the express was obviously running late and was somewhere between Adairsville and Chattanooga.

Andrews then decided to chance it and make the run of nine miles for Calhoun and get there before the southbound express did. The *General* was a fast locomotive and could possibly make it, so Andrews "opened her up"—to a speed of a mile a minute over a not very stable roadbed. Again Andrews's luck was with him. He reached Calhoun to find the express train already there, and using his story of "carrying powder to Beauregard," he was allowed to pass.

As far as Andrews knew the express was the last of the southbound trains and the track was open to Chattanooga and safety. Off they went again, ripping up track and cutting telegraph lines. Destroying track was a problem since they didn't have the tools for such work, and all they could do now was to burn the Oostenaula Bridge behind them. After that, the rest of the way probably could be made in safety.

While they were ripping up the rails, a locomotive whistle was heard behind them again and they were compelled to abandon the work. On came Fuller at full throttle. Andrews could only reason that his pursuers could make quick repairs, and unless Fuller's locomotive could be derailed by one of his breaks, burning the Oostenaula Bridge would be impossible. To make matters worse it began to rain, soaking the timbers.

Fuller, a remarkable, tenacious man, had kept up the chase at full throttle. He and his engineer, Jeff Cain, had first started after Andrews in a handcar taken from a track crew. When they came to Andrews's break in the track the handcar derailed and went into a ditch, but it took only a few minutes to get it back on the rails.

At Etowah, Fuller found the *Yonah*. Commandeering the old engine, Fuller pressed her for all she was worth, reaching Kingston only five minutes after Andrews had left! What Andrews never realized was that the three freight trains he had backed on a siding were below the "Y" which connected the Rome line with the main line, further slowing up Fuller.

Dropping the *Yonah* for the engine belonging to the Rome train waiting on a siding, Fuller uncoupled the engine, the *Texas*, the same type of 4-4-0 locomotive as the *General*, and again took up the chase, his engine running in reverse. Fuller's locomotive was almost derailed when it reached the broken rails at Adairsville, but Cain saw the break in the line and reversed his engine. Near Calhoun the *Texas* struck the third break at full speed, but miraculously ran over it without derailing! Fuller was now only minutes behind his quarry.

Andrews now uncoupled one of the boxcars and

Conductor Fuller and the *Texas* in Hot Pursuit, April 12, 1862.

The Texas, having dropped its freight cars, continues the pursuit. Fuller and his engineer Jeff Cain keep the Texas *running in reverse at full throttle. The General and its train can be seen in the distance.*

FROM AN ORIGINAL WATERCOLOR BY WILBUR G. KURTZ, COURTESY RALPH RIGHTON AND THE ATLANTA HISTORICAL SOCIETY.

The *Texas* Approaches the Tunnel at Tunnel Hill, April 12, 1862.

The General and Andrews's raiders have already cleared the tunnel near Dalton with the Texas in close pursuit. Fuller *has dropped his man Henderson at Dalton, to get a message through.*

FROM AN ORIGINAL WATERCOLOR BY WILBUR G. KURTZ, COURTESY RALPH RIGHTON AND THE ATLANTA HISTORICAL SOCIETY.

let it roll backward, hoping for a collision. But Fuller slowed his engine down until the rolling boxcar met his rear coupler. He then pushed the car ahead of him. As Fuller began to draw closer, Andrews uncoupled another car. Fuller handled it the same way, but the *Texas* slowed down. The two racing locomotives now reached the Oostenaula Bridge, but Andrews could not stop to burn it. Meanwhile, the *General's* fuel and water began to run low, and at Resaca, Fuller paused in his pursuit to push the two boxcars into a siding, which again gave Andrews time to cut telegraph lines.

It now became apparent to Andrews that unless he reached the bridges at Chicamauga and destroyed them, his mission would end in total failure and capture. The *General* was pushed to the limit, at times running at ninety miles an hour. Once again a slim chance presented itself: Andrews men pushed out the rear end of the last boxcar, and the "stringers" Andrews had intended as fuel to burn the bridges were dropped onto the track in the hopes of derailing the speeding *Texas*. But this, too, failed. Andrews then dropped a rail onto the

track on a blind curve. The *Texas* struck it head-on with a terrific shock, but the locomotive did not derail.

Now matters became desperate for Andrews and his men. Running into Dalton, Andrews again cut the telegraph lines. Fuel and water were fast being used up and burning the Chicamauga bridges was a forlorn hope. The *Texas* was visible behind them, her pilot and tender swarming with soldiers. Some distance beyond Dalton, Andrews and his men built a barrier across the track to gain time to reach the covered bridge while they piled wood in the middle of their last car and set fire to it with brands from the engine, running on her last head of steam.

Despite the rain, the fire miraculously caught and the burning car was hauled onto the bridge and uncoupled on the center span. The bridge roof caught fire, but the *Texas* caught up, entered the burning bridge, and slowly pushed the burning car out into the open and onto a siding.

The end of the chase was only minutes away. Seeing the hopelessness of his situation, Andrews ordered his men to jump and make a run for the

The End of the Great Locomotive Chase, 1862.

Two miles north of Ringgold, Georgia, eighty-seven miles from Big Shanty, the General's *race ended, the gallant locomotive having run out of fuel. The* Texas, *running in reverse for forty-eight miles of the pursuit, is seen in the background of the picture, coming up fast. Although Andrews's men take to the woods, Confederates captured all twenty of the raiders before the week was out.*

FROM AN ORIGINAL WATERCOLOR BY WILBUR G. KURTZ, COURTESY ATLANTA HISTORICAL SOCIETY.

The Fate of a War Hero, September 1864.

Standing on a siding of the Georgia Central Railroad, the General, *her cab shot away, her boiler, steam chest, and balloon stack shot-riddled, minus her headlight, awaits an* unknown fate. Later rescued, the General *became a war* hero.

PHOTOGRAPH PROBABLY BY GEORGE N. BARBARD OF THE U.S. ARMY'S TOPOGRAPHICAL ENGINEERS, MADE IN SEPTEMBER 1864.

Locomotive *General* of the Western & Atlanta Railroad.

Stripped of her original guard frames, the General, full of years and honors a century later, spends her days at the *Louisville Depot of the Nashville, Chattanooga & St. Louis Railway. In 1961, the General was reconditioned to run*

under her own power in the road's shops, to take part in the pageant commemorating the centenary of the Great Locomotive Chase of 1862, when she relived her adventure of a century before.

COURTESY NASHVILLE, CHATTANOOGA & ST. LOUIS RAILWAY.

woods. But he had delayed too long: the woods were full of Confederate soldiers, and one by one Andrews and his men were picked up.

The chase had been remarkable, pursuer and pursued speeding a distance of fifty and a half miles in sixty-five minutes, the *Texas* making twelve stops and running in reverse all the way. Only after running out of fuel was the *General* caught, two miles north of Ringgold, Georgia. (Both the *General* and the *Texas* were built in Paterson, New Jersey, and both engines lived as fitting monuments for one of the greatest sagas of railroading in America.)

Sadly, the daring Andrews and eight of his men received their death sentences by courts-martial, and they were hanged in Atlanta, Georgia, on June 7, 1862.

The spring and summer of 1862 began badly for the Union forces in the eastern theater of the war. On June 26, while McClellan was fighting for his life in the swamps of the Chicahominy eight miles from Richmond, Major General John Pope replaced General Irwin McDowell as commander of the Department of the Rappahannock because of McDowell's failure to capture Jackson in the Shenandoah Valley.

It was Colonel Haupt's misfortune to find himself suddenly subordinate to an officer of John Pope's character and personality. Where Pope was an incompetent, pompous braggart, Haupt was knowledgeable and resourceful, a genius in his field who went right to the point of the matter in hand. Had Haupt's superior officers followed his suggestions, the battles they conducted could have had happier endings. Haupt's awareness of what was going on around him and his alertness of mind overshadowed these characteristics in his superior officers, which sometimes made for awkward situations.

Upon assuming command of the Department of the Rappahannock, with characteristic bullheadedness Pope, turned over the operation and maintenance of the military railroads to the Quartermaster Department and, wrote Haupt, "did not recognize me in any way, and gave me no instructions." Pope indicated that "a separate and independent department for the construction and operations of railroads was unnecessary . . . that railroads were used for the transportation of army supplies" so they belonged under the control and management of his Quartermaster Department.

General McDowell tried to explain to Pope how helpful Haupt and the railroads had been, that Pope was making a bad mistake in making the alteration. Haupt called on Peter H. Watson, assistant secretary of war, to explain the state of affairs. Haupt informed him that he was returning to Massachusetts, saying that if he was needed again Watson could send for him and requesting Watson to keep him "posted occasionally as to movements."

Shortly thereafter, Haupt received an urgent telegram from Watson: "Come back immediately—cannot get along without you; not a wheel moving on any of the roads." The battle of Cedar Mountain had been fought and lost, and the state of the military situation was, to say the least, deplorable.

Incompetency in the military was still on the rise in the War Department. On July 23, during Haupt's brief absence, Major General Henry Wager Halleck had been appointed general-in-chief of all United States armies in the field. In the interim, Pope had created unbelievable confusion in the ranks of the military railroads.

Haupt returned as requested. After an interview with Assistant Secretary Watson, he boarded an engine and rode to the point nearest Pope's headquarters, a farmhouse near Cedar Mountain, where he found Pope, McDowell, and members of the staff. "I was cordially welcomed back," wrote Haupt, "especially by McDowell, and General Pope was quite civil. . . ."

After being apprised of the situation, Pope instructed his chief of staff Colonel George D. Ruggles to accept any orders Haupt wanted issued in the commanding general's name. General Order No. 23, dated August 18, 1862, reads: "all railroads, especially the Orange & Alexandria Railroad within the limits of the Army of Virginia, are placed under the exclusive charge of Colonel Herman Haupt." The order also specified that "no other officer, whatever his rank, shall give any orders to any employee of the road, whether conductor, engineer, or other agent . . . respecting the running of the trains, construction or repair of the roads, transportation of supplies or troops" except on the explicit authority of Colonel Haupt. This order was followed the next day by an order from Secretary Stanton extending Haupt's authority to embrace "all the railroads which are or may hereafter be included within the lines of operation of the Army of Virginia."

Meanwhile, Lee assumed personal command of the Army of Northern Virginia and moved it to Pope's front, finding it encamped on flat ground facing the Rapidan River with the Rappahannock at its back, dependent upon the supply line of the Orange & Alexandria Railroad which crossed the

The Battle of Cedar Mountain, 1862.

One of the key battles of Jackson's Valley Campaign to clear the Shenandoah Valley of federal occupation, Stonewall Jackson defeated General Nathaniel Prentiss Banks. The battle was a diversionary tactic to reduce McClellan's force facing Lee before Richmond.

FROM A DRAWING BY LT. FREDERICK F. CAVADA, 14TH PENNSYLVANIA VOLUNTEERS.

Rappahannock Bridge, Richmond, Fredericksburg & Potomac Railroad (USMRR), 1862.

Constructed under the supervision of Daniel Stone, of General Haupt's Construction Corps, the R F & P bridge was 600 feet long and 43 feet above high water. This bridge was later damaged by vandalism of Union troops on a mistaken order.

PHOTOGRAPH BY CAPTAIN A. J. RUSSELL, USMRR, NATIONAL ARCHIVES.

bridge at Rappahannock Station—a supply line which could be cut by simply destroying the bridge.

At the time Haupt returned Pope was completely unaware that Lee and the powerful Army of Northern Virginia were on his front, only a day's march away. However, on August 18, Pope mounted his horse "and rode off to review one of his Corps, but returned in haste in about an hour with the information that the enemy was in full force in front and advancing rapidly." Pope then ordered Haupt to do all in his power to remove the supplies at Culpeper, where a large amount had been collected. Pope then ordered a general retreat across the Rappahannock, which was accomplished in the nick of time as it had been Lee's intention to entrap Pope's army between the Rapidan and Rappahannock. Lee's cavalry under Jeb Stuart was supposed to have burned the Rappahannock Bridge and cut the Orange & Alexandria Railroad in Pope's rear; but Lee's cavalry was two days late, and Pope by that time was safely across the river, in line of battle on the north bank. Lee now resorted to a flanking movement.

Having carried out his instructions at Culpeper to reload the supplies and send them "to a safe distance in the rear," Haupt reorganized railroad transportation, "which had been thrown into confusion from the usual causes, military interference, neglect to unload and return cars. . . ."

On the afternoon of August 22, Haupt returned to the front "to ascertain the requirements of the army in the way of transportation." Lee, Jackson, and Longstreet had launched a frontal attack which had been temporarily unsuccessful. Looking for information, Haupt found Pope "some distance from the railroad, sitting under a tree on a hill overlooking the valley and country below." In the course of their conversation, Haupt mentioned to Pope that "he had seen the enemy's wagons moving along the river," something Pope should have seen for himself. Believing this to be a flank movement, Haupt asked Pope how far he had sent his scouts up river. Pope's answer was "Not very far." Haupt then asked, "Is that far enough? What is to prevent the enemy from even going as far as Thoroughfare Gap and getting behind you?" Pope replied, "There is no danger."

Manassas Junction, Orange & Alexandria Railroad, USMRR.

Stonewall Jackson, with three brigades, on an all-night march through Thoroughfare Gap, attacked Pope's Supply base at

Manassas Junction. What they couldn't carry away, they destroyed.

FROM A PHOTOGRAPH BY CAPTAIN A. J. RUSSELL, NATIONAL ARCHIVES.

Feeling very "uneasy" about Pope's faltering reply, Haupt returned to his train and started back for Alexandria to check on matters there. When Haupt reached Manassas Junction, the telegraph operator handed him a message from Pope. "The enemy in largely superior force has turned my right flank," it read, and requested Haupt to "retire the rolling stock to a safe distance."

Lee's forces were moving quickly, and the train following Haupt's had been "fired into and captured." At the same time, Jeb Stuart's cavalry had made a shambles of Pope's headquarters. Since Pope had previously ordered a large amount of rolling stock to the front, which was now between himself and the enemy, had Haupt been a half hour later he too would have been captured.

Haupt and his engine reached Burkes Station where he met General Phil Kearney in the act of moving a part of his troops by train. Haupt beckoned Kearney into the station so as not to be over-heard, explained the situation, and showed him Pope's telegram. Kearney then asked Haupt for a pilot engine and two flatcars to send an advance guard ahead of his troop trains. Haupt immediately furnished the equipment and Kearney went on his way. (That was the last Haupt saw of General Kearney. He was killed in an action at Chantilly.)

The odd part of all this was that McClellan, having been relieved by Pope at Lincoln's orders, had been sojourning at Alexandria, less than twenty miles away, within cannon sound, with ninety-one thousand veteran troops, survivors of the seven days' battles, sitting around idly.

While Lee, Jackson, Longstreet, and the entire Confederate Army were pounding Pope to pieces, what was happening on Pope's front was reflected behind the lines and on the railroad. Haupt informed Pope that the conductor of train no. 6 from Catlett's Station had reported that his train had been fired into by Confederate troops at

USMRR Locomotive *Fred Leach* Out of the Running, 1862.

The Fred Leach *is probably the locomotive Colonel Haupt refers to in his telegram to General Halleck, at Washington, dated August 27, 1862: "I sent an engine and cars of a construction train . . . to Fairfax to bring off the wounded if possible. The engine was fired upon by cavalry or guerril-* las two miles west of Burkes, and compelled to return without wounded." Later, most USMRR locomotive cabs were armored to protect engineers and firemen from snipers' bullets.

FROM A PHOTOGRAPH, PROBABLY BY CAPTAIN A. J. RUSSELL, USMRR, NATIONAL ARCHIVES.

Catlett's, and that his engineer had opened the throttle and run through the rebels at full speed, the trainmen throwing themselves on the floors of the cars to avoid the bullets. Haupt further told Pope that he would hold trains at Alexandria and await further instructions, and went on to explain that "we have 2100 troops here [Alexandria] in cars. The fire was from both sides of the track, but most heavy from the east side of the track." Correctly, Haupt supposed it to be a cavalry dash.

On that same day, August 22, Haupt reported another problem. He might have to "turn the sick and wounded out of the cars and into the street." He would be unable to send troops forward if he had to run his trains into Washington with wounded, to stand for hours unloaded while troop trains were needed. "My first care is to send forward troops," he wrote Pope. "I hope to send forage forward tomorrow."

By midnight of August 23, Haupt anxiously awaited the arrival of four trains, long overdue, when a conductor carrying a lantern came in to report that the four trains he had been waiting for had been stopped only four miles out of town on orders of General Sturgis, who would not allow them to be moved. Haupt immediately wired General Halleck and then started for Sturgis's headquarters in company with Colonel J. D. Devereaux, a superintendent of the USMRR.

They found Sturgis at his headquarters, seated in an armchair and surrounded by his staff, evidently "under the weather." Seeing Haupt, Sturgis exclaimed, "Well! I am glad you have come, for I have just sent a guard to your office to put you under arrest for disobedience of my orders in failing to transport my command!"

Haupt replied calmly that he was acting under the orders of General Halleck, and that as far as his "personal comfort" was concerned, his "arrest would be a welcome relief." Could the general spare a

U.S. Military Railroads' Yards at Alexandria, Virginia, 1862.

The main base of railroad operations in the eastern campaigns in Virginia, these yards, formerly the Orange & Alexandria Railroad terminal near Washington (USMRR) *was strategically important since the line ran into Virginia. The line was the bone of contention to both armies.*

FROM A PHOTOGRAPH BY MATHEW BRADY, AUTHOR'S COLLECTION.

blanket "and a corner on the floor"; since he had not had any sleep for days, he would welcome a few hours rest. Haupt went on to make Sturgis understand that he was assuming "a very grave responsibility," that the trains were loaded with wounded and the surgeons were waiting for them at the depot. And if that were not enough, the locomotives were running out of wood and water, and serious delays would be caused in forwarding troops to General Pope.

At the mention of Pope's name, Sturgis exclaimed, "I don't care for John Pope one pinch of owl dung!" When it began to dawn on Sturgis that he was out of line, he called one of his staff over and whispered in his ear. Haupt could not hear what Sturgis told the officer, but he learned some time after that Sturgis had taken it upon himself to order the locomotive engineers to uncouple their trains, run back to Alexandria, refuel, and then return! Since the railroad was single-tracked, the order was ridiculous and could not possibly be executed.

Then an orderly came in and delivered a dispatch to Haupt from General Halleck which read: "No military officer has any authority to interfere with your control of the railroads. Show this to General Sturgis, and if he attempts to interfere, I will arrest him!"

Haupt tried to make Sturgis understand that the message had indeed come from General Halleck, but he "seemed to think that the dispatch had come from General Pope." Sturgis "exploded," exclaiming several times, "I don't care for John Pope one pinch of owl dung!" At last, Colonel Devereaux took the paper from Haupt, handed it to Sturgis, and finally convinced him that the message really had come from Halleck.

When it finally dawned on Sturgis, he asked, "Who did you say? Yes, I respect his authority. What does he say?"

"He says that if you interfere with the railroads," said Devereaux, "he will put you under arrest." "He does, does he?" muttered Sturgis. "Well, then, take your damn railroad!"

With incidents like this it was a wonder that the Army of the Potomac and the Army of Virginia functioned at all. Sturgis's interference with train movements kept ten thousand men out of a battle which had been raging for two days. Assistant Secretary Watson wanted Haupt to prefer charges and have Sturgis court-martialed; but as Sturgis was not, in Haupt's words, "in normal conditon" at the time, and was afterward willing to carry out instructions, acknowledging that the delays were his fault, Haupt dropped the matter.

Colonel Haupt had a point: "it was simply absurd to wait for days to secure rail transportation, when a single day's march would have carried the troops to the battlefield," especially when the railroad was single-tracked, and had only limited cars and engines.

During the Second Battle of Manassas, Lee, Jackson, and Longstreet outsmarted, outmaneuvered, and outfought Pope and the Army of Virginia. Defeated, on August 26, Pope retreated, which for a second time in a year brought about a panic that spread to Washington. Haupt managed to keep the trains running as far south as Warrenton Junction, using every car that had wheels, all loaded to capacity with food, ammunition, and troops. Haupt had advised Halleck that he could move twenty thousand troops per day, if conditions permitted; that if Pope were to maintain the Rappahannock line, controlling the rail line was his only means of doing so; and that there were twenty thousand troops of McClellan's army coming in to Alexandria.

The indescribable confusion, chaotic beyond belief, is best described at firsthand by Colonel Haupt's telegraphic messages between himself, the army officers, and the War Department:

•

August 25, 1862, 5:05 A.M.

Major General Pope:

We will get off Hooker's command during the day and night. Sturgis has been the cause, directly and indirectly, of more than 24 hours delay in transportation of troops and supplies.

A Baltimore & Ohio engine, sent forward, blocked the track six hours by getting out of order on the road. When cleared, an engine got off the track; this caused more delay. I have now ordered that no more cars shall be loaded on track south of Alexandria. The loading of troops will be done on Washington track, so as to keep main track clear. We have just dispatched six trains for Hooker. General Heintzelman and staff are in car just moving off. Cox will go forward in the morning.

Long bridge broke with Baltimore engine yesterday; it is now repaired.

H. W. Haupt

•

August 25, 1862, 9:45 A.M.

Major General Pope:

I have not only sent forward every car loaded

with forage and commissary stores that has been delivered to us, but I have gone personally late at night to the Commissary and Quartermaster to urge them to load cars, even beyond their requisitions, that there should be no deficiency.

H. W. Haupt

•

War Department
August 25, 1862, 10:40 A.M.
Colonel Haupt:

When you cannot get orders from General Pope, land the troops where you deem most convenient, but as near to General Pope's army as you can.

H.W. Halleck
General-in-Chief

•

August 26, 1862, 8:50 A.M.
Major General Halleck:

I am just informed that the four trains following the engine *Secretary* are captured, and that the rebels are approaching Manassas with artillery. These may be exaggerations, but the operator and agent are leaving, and prompt action is required. It is unfortunate that a portion of our forces did not march. I await instructions.

H. W. Haupt

•

August 26th, 1862 [time not stated]
Major General Halleck:

The following telegram has just been received from Manassas: The engine *Secretary* was being followed by four other trains which are in great danger, as there is no communication. The wire is cut between Manassas and Warrenton. We have transportation for 1,200 men; this number might be sent to Manassas to protect the road while we repair it. I suppose the bridge at Bristoe will be destroyed.

H. Haupt

•

August 26, 1862 [time not stated]
General Halleck:

Operator at Manassas says: "I am off now sure." I directed the agent to run the two engines at Manassas forward, wait until the last moment, and then escape on the engine if a real necessity existed. Operator has just commenced message to Headquarters of General Pope when wire was cut. It is clear now that the railroad can be relied upon only for supplies. No more troops can be forwarded; by marching they will protect communication; in cars

they are helpless. Our capacity by this raid will be much reduced.

H. Haupt

•

August 26, 1862, 11 A.M.
D. C. McCallum:

So far Bull Run is safe. Four trains empty cars lost at Bristoe. Rebels have possession of Manassas. Some of our artillery taken and used against us. Damage at Manassas not known. Sent out 3,000 men last night, also a large wrecking and construction force to Union Mills, where track is blocked by a collision in rear.

H. Haupt

•

Incredibly enough, while the Army of Virginia was fighting for its life on the plains of Manassas, it appears that on orders from General Halleck, Haupt went in search of the officers Halleck had ordered Haupt to find, but "could find none!" "The attractions of Washington City," wrote Haupt, kept most of the general officers in that city! (The battle was only twenty miles away!)

On August 25, Jackson with his "foot cavalry" coming through Thoroughfare Gap at "route step" struck at Bristoe Station. Near nightfall they heard several train whistles of Haupt's empty trains making a dash for Alexandria to pick up more troops and supplies.

Jackson's men tried to stop the second train as it came on by throwing obstructions on the track, and watched as the onrushing train pushed the obstructions aside. Then they poured a volley of rifle fire into it.

Jackson's men then found a derailing switch and opened it, this time ready to pour rifle fire into the engine's cab. Moments later the third train rushed on, the engineer unaware that the derailing switch had been opened. The engine struck the derailer, ran off the track, the cars trailing after it, and went over an embankment with an enormous crash. Then another of Haupt's trains, this time with twenty cars, followed the first over the embankment, crashing on top of the first.

Haupt's third train came along moments later, but the engineer saw the wreckage on the track ahead in time, reversed his engine, and backed it down the track out of danger. Wasting no time, Jackson's next target was Pope's massive supply depot at Manassas Junction. After leaving "Peg-leg" Ewell and three brigades at Bristoe Station, Jackson marched his wornout troops through the night, hit-

The Second Battle of Bull Run, August 30, 1862.

Pope, with victory almost in his hands though cut off from his reinforcements, had attacked Jackson's force the day before. But Lee marshalled the entire Confederate Army and turned victory into another defeat for the Union Army.

FROM AN ORIGINAL DRAWING BY ALFRED R. WAUD, LIBRARY OF CONGRESS.

Military Railroading the Hard Way on the Gap Road, 1862.

USMRR work party, with block and tackle, attempt to reclaim a locomotive derailed and thrown over an embarkment of the Manassas Gap Railroad by Stonewall Jackson's men, who threw a derailing switch, opened the throttle, and let the engine do the rest. This sort of thing was a frequent occurrence.

FROM A PHOTOGRAPH BY CAPTAIN A. J. RUSSELL, USMRR, COURTESY NATIONAL ARCHIVES.

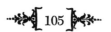

Where Stonewall Jackson's "Tornado" Struck—Manassas Junction, August 1862.

Two views of the appalling destruction of General Pope's supply depot at Manassas Junction. Jackson, with two regiments of infantry and a large detachment of Jeb Stuart's cavalry, ran off the guard and captured "two miles" of warehouses and loaded freight cars in one of the greatest captures of the war. What Jackson's men could not carry away, they destroyed. Ghostly chimneys stand as silent sentinels guarding the devastation.

From a photograph by Mathew Brady, Author's Collection.

ting Manassas Depot at dawn the following morning with two regiments of infantry and part of Stuart's cavalry.

What Jackson and his men found in Pope's enormous supply depot staggered them. The lavishness with which the North supplied its armies gave rise to the Confederate axiom "The enemy has everything! You need everything!" Not believing their own eyes, Jackson's men, as hungry as wolves, addressed themselves to looting of Pope's warehouses with systematic thoroughness. They found them piled to the rooftrees with a variety of goods and supplies more befitting a hotel than an army in the field: meat in enormous quantities and barrels of whiskey, flour, coffee, and sugar of the best grade. Other warehouses produced clothing, from uniforms and shoes to overcoats.

And there were the costlier luxuries which, to Jackson's ragged soldiers, had been as far out of reach as the moon: canned lobster, cake, candy, wines, and fine cigars by the case. For the cavalry, there were the horse accoutrements, McClellan saddles, saddlebags, and coverings.

Equally important, the railroad yards were filled with rolling stock, loaded freight cars, some with forage for Pope's horses. Realizing that all these incredible stores could not be carried away, much as he would have liked to have done, Jackson hurried along the looting process, left Manassas Junction a burning wreck, and retired his weary soldiers to a point near Groveton, in a position to unite with Lee or Longstreet or both.

Pope had lost his battle, and the casualties had been heavy indeed. The problem of caring for so many wounded and removing them back to the hospitals in Washington to receive medical attention called for clear, unemotional heads. Unfortunately, while Pope's army was in retreat to Washington in near panic, Secretary Stanton, in a moment of compassion, committed the colossal blunder of inviting the citizens of Baltimore and Washington to volunteer as nurses, to assist the surgeons in caring for the wounded on the battlefield. To Haupt, Stanton's invitation was "an impulsive and kindhearted, but ill-advised act."

On August 30, D. C. McCallum, director of United States Military Railroads, wired Haupt, his hands already full of railroad problems, to furnish trains to Washington to carry the volunteers to the battlefield. Haupt tried to have Assistant Secretary Watson prevail on Stanton to rescind the order, "even though it might be a mistake."

Over his own strenuous objections, Haupt sent a train to Washington, and when it returned to Alexandria "it was packed full, inside and on top. Some of the women had even forced themselves into the cars, which were ordinary freight cars without seats." That night Superintendent Devereaux, after inspecting the train, begged Haupt to have it sidetracked: "half the men were drunk, and nearly everyone (men and women) had bottles of whiskey."

On that same night, at 11:15 P.M., Haupt telegraphed Watson that a large number of the nurses who came on "last night" were "drunk and very disorderly." Angry, Haupt sent written orders to the officers in command to arrest everyone who was drunk and return him (or her) by the next train.

Thus ended the Second Battle of Manassas, which paved the way for Lee's invasion of Maryland, to go into history as the battle of the railroads.

CHAPTER 7

"Tough Times on the Railroad"

O N SEPTEMBER 1, following Pope's defeat at the Second Battle of Manassas, the Army of Virginia and the Army of the Potomac were merged into a large striking force. McClellan was given a second chance to redeem himself, and he began a reorganization of the army under the protection of the forts and defenses in and around Washington.

All active operations of the United States Military Railroads were temporarily suspended; but Haupt, now a general ever active, kept his men busily engaged in car and locomotive repairs while he himself experimented with new and faster methods to rebuild railroad bridges and, conversely, to destroy them.

Haupt had many original ideas along these lines, especially prefabricated bridges that could be quickly installed over a break. Destroying locomotives was given some special attention. Haupt's report on *How to Destroy Locomotives and Bridges* was a guidebook on railroad wrecking for the War Department's future use. "Rendering locomotive engines useless to an enemy, is often a desideratum," wrote Haupt, "and to render locomotives unfit for service . . . the most expeditious mode is to fire a cannon ball through the boiler." Since railroad cars, both passenger and freight, were built of wood they were easy to destroy: "Cars are readily destroyed by burning," wrote Haupt, "and no instructions are necessary."

The destruction of bridges was another matter entirely, and Haupt gave this subject the attention it deserved. As usual, he was specific. "On the destruction of bridges," he wrote, "which may be desirable in retreat," in time period "not exceeding five minutes, requires apparatus so simple that it can be carried in the pocket or a saddle bag." The apparatus Haupt referred to was a "torpedo," which

consisted of a metal tube, seven-eights of an inch in thickness and eight inches in length, "with a head and nut—the head to be two inches in diameter, and about an inch thick. A washer of the same size as the head must be placed under the nut at the other end, with a fuse hole." A tin cannister for holding the black powder was an inch and three-quarters in diameter, open at both ends. When the powder was inserted in the tin cannister, the ends were closed and bolted together, forming the case.

At the bridge site to be destroyed, a hole the same size as the cylinder was bored with an augur into the wooden timber, usually a main support. "The torpedo, head downward, is hammered into the hole in the bridge timber," wrote Haupt. "The explosion, if a main support, brings down the whole structure. Ordinary cigar-lighters, which burn without flame and cannot be blown out, are best suited for lighting the fuse."

The early days of September of 1862 were portentous of the events to come. By September 7, McClellan and the Army of the Potomac left Washington in search of Lee's Army of Northern Virginia, its whereabouts unknown for the moment. The nation watched with anxiety Lee's advance into Maryland and McClellan's race to get between Lee and the cities of Baltimore, Washington, and Philadelphia, building toward the battle at Antietam.

Antietam battlefield lies in a little peninsula bounded by the Antietam Creek and the Potomac River, only ten miles from Harper's Ferry and a short distance from the town of Sharpsburg, Maryland. Lee's selection of this battle site was not determined by personal choice, but by the military exigencies of the moment, for on the morning of September 16, everything about this lovely country-

Long Bridge over the Potomac River, ca. 1862–1863.

Looking from the Washington end of the bridge toward Virginia, Long Bridge provided the rail link between the *capital city, Fort Runyon, and Alexandria Station of the Orange & Alexandria Railroad (USMRR).*

PHOTOGRAPHED BY CAPTAIN A. J. RUSSELL, USMRR,
AUTHOR'S COLLECTION.

First Train over Bull Run Bridge, August 30, 1862.

Colonel Haupt began reconstruction of Bull Run Bridge on or about August 27, and completed the work on August 30. Haupt then asked for two hundred men to protect it from *raids, since he considered the bridge "our most exposed point."*

FROM A PHOTOGRAPH BY CAPTAIN A. J. RUSSELL, USMRR,
NATIONAL ARCHIVES.

Washington Station, Maryland Avenue, U.S. Military Railroads, 1863.

William Marshall Merrick's drawing of the USMRR station, within sight of the Capitol dome, differs slightly from Mathew Brady's photograph of the same scene. Merrick has taken liberties with the drawing by completing the dome on the Capitol, which was not completed until after the war.

Fort Corcoran, One of the Forts Protecting Washington, 1862.

McClellan's reorganization of the Army of the Potomac *circling Washington, D.C.*
began under the protection of the forts like this one en-

USMRR Locomotives and Rolling Stock Stored at the Maryland Avenue Depot in View of the Capitol.

To keep them out of reach of rebel cavalry raids, these *tracks of the Alexandria & Washington Railroad, a seven-*
locomotives and cars were stored here for safety's sake dur- *mile military rail link with the O & A at Alexandria.*
ing the early years of the war. Equipment was run over the

Locomotive and Repair Shops of the Orange &
Alexandria Railroad (USMRR) at Alexandria, Virginia, in 1862.

Spare car wheels and reclaimed spare parts strewn about are all a part of the yard scenery. Bales of hay, forage for artillery and cavalry horses, piled in the background, await transportation.

FROM A PHOTOGRAPH BY CAPTAIN A. J. RUSSELL,
COURTESY NATIONAL ARCHIVES.

A USMRR Sawmill in the Yards at Alexandria, 1863.

The sawmill, mounted on railroad wheels, was used to cut bridge timbers, crossties, and fuel for the wood-burning locomotives. The sawmill could be moved to any point in the yards or on the main line.

FROM AN ORIGINAL DRAWING BY WILLIAM MARSHALL MERRICK,
SKETCHBOOK III, COURTESY THE NEW YORK PUBLIC LIBRARY.

The Orange & Alexandria Car Sheds, Repair Shops, and Buildings at Alexandria, Virginia

During the war this was the U.S. Military Railroad's base of operations. Lines of flatcars loaded with lumber for bridge building and repairs stand on sidings. Millions of board feet of lumber were used, much of it going to waste. Drainage ditches, track ballasting, and stub switches are much in evidence.

FROM A PHOTOGRAPH BY CAPTAIN A. J. RUSSELL,
COURTESY NATIONAL ARCHIVES.

Superintendents and Foremen of the U.S. Military Railroads, 1865.

Photographed at Alexandria, Virginia, probably in 1864, these unsung heroes of the USMRR construction crews are all but forgotten. For the most part unarmed and defenseless civilians, they performed untold feats of courage and daring, building bridges under fire, laying track, and gener- *ally keeping the USMRR's supply and troop trains running under heartbreaking conditions. Many engineers and trainmen lost their lives, victims to cavalry and guerrilla raids. No individual identification of the men in this picture exists.*

FROM A PHOTOGRAPH, PROBABLY BY MATHEW BRADY, COURTESY NATIONAL ARCHIVES.

Alexandria Station of the U.S. Military Railroads.

The log stockade enclosed the entire USMRR station and railroad yards to guard against cavalry raids. The high *bastions at each corner of the stockade were pierced for artillery, mounted on platforms within.*

FROM AN ORIGINAL DRAWING BY WILLIAM MARSHALL MERRICK, USMRR, SKETCHBOOK III, COURTESY THE NEW YORK PUBLIC LIBRARY.

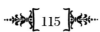

Testing the Strength of a "Shad-Belly" Bridge, 1862.

Reinforced by crossed board trusses, the "shad-belly" bridge was tested by loading it with iron rails loaded on a flatcar, *until it broke at two tons per foot.*

From a photograph by Captain A. J. Russell, USMRR,
Author's Collection.

General Herman Haupt's "Shad-Belly" Bridge.

Built of board trusses, the "shad-belly" bridge is here being tested for deflections at the government yards at Alexandria, *Virginia.*

From a photograph by Captain A. J. Russell, USMRR,
Author's Collection.

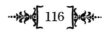

Haupt Arch and Truss Bridge over the Rappahannock River, 1862.

A railroad engineering genius, Haupt constructed prefabri- cated military bridges used extensively during the war. A *small log block house on the embankment on the right pro- tects the structure from cavalry raids.*

FROM A PHOTOGRAPH PROBABLY BY CAPTAIN A. J. RUSSELL, USMRR,
COURTESY NATIONAL ARCHIVES.

"Rendering Locomotives Useless to an Enemy . . ."
"The most expeditious mode is to fire a cannon ball through the boiler!"

FROM A PHOTOGRAPH BY MATHEW BRADY, AUTHOR'S COLLECTION.

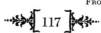

"Torpedo" Used in Bridge Destruction, 1862.

Invented by General Haupt as a quick means of destroying railway bridges, the torpedo, shown being assembled, was made of two cylinders, one inside the other, containing black powder. Closed at each end and fused, the "torpedo" was fired by a cigar lighter. A hole was augured in a main bridge support and the cylinder inserted. The explosion brought the bridge down.

FROM A PHOTOGRAPH BY CAPTAIN A. J. RUSSELL, USMRR,
AUTHOR'S COLLECTION.

Destroying Track.

General Herman Haupt demonstrating his method of twisting iron "T" rails out of shape permanently. A USMRR locomotive stands in the background.

FROM A PHOTOGRAPH BY CAPTAIN A. J. RUSSELL, USMRR,
AUTHOR'S COLLECTION.

side became of vital importance to Lee. His own army was dangerously separated and Lee found himself with only eighteen thousand men, the combined forces of his own and Longstreet's, Jackson's, and Daniel Harvey Hill's divisions, facing McClellan's host of more than ninety thousand.

By midafternoon on September 16, McClellan feinted at Lee's left and ran head-on into John Bell Hood's Texas regiments, whose arrival on the field increased Lee's forces to twenty-five thousand by the following dawn.

Before sunrise of the seventeenth, the federal general Joseph Hooker began the "bloodiest single day's action of the war" by attacking Jackson on the Confederate left, destroying Lawton's, Hayes's, and Trimble's brigades, and opening a wide gap in Lee's line. Then a flood of blue-jacketed soldiers—Hooker's men—climbed over a post-and-rail fence

and rolled down the Hagerstown Pike toward the Dunker Church. Hood's men desperately fought them off, exhausting their ammunition but holding on until they were driven off by Mansfield's federal brigades.

At that critical moment, Lee ordered up Anderson's and Walker's brigades, then four miles away. But the Hagerstown Pike, swept by a murderous enfilading fire, proved a terrible obstacle. Sumner's corps attacked again, only to be thrown back by McLaws's reinforcements.

By midmorning McClellan opened his second battle against the Confederate center. Then began the terrible struggle in the "Bloody Lane" where again enfilading fire left thousands dead in the sunken road and the fence corners.

At 1. P.M. Burnside's men attacked across the stone bridge across the Antietam. Once across they could have turned Lee's right flank but for three thousand men of A. P. Hill's division, who, after a forced march from Harper's Ferry, a distance of

Tearing Up Rails.

Destroying tracks by the "corkscrew twist" method, here demonstrated by a USMRR work crew. Rails were rendered useless and could not be twisted back into shape.

From a photograph by Captain A. J. Russell, USMRR,
Author's Collection.

fifteen miles, rushed onto the field, swept Burnside's men down the slopes and back across the bridge, and saved the day for Lee. The battle was over by sunset. McClellan, though he had twenty thousand troops in reserve, had no further interest in continuing the contest. Had McClellan continued the battle that day, it is possible that Lee would have been defeated and the war shortened.

While McClellan and Lee fought at Antietam, at Alexandria Haupt received a telegram from General Heintzleman of McClellan's army asking Haupt to "make an examination of the tracks and bridges of the Orange & Alexandria Railroad as far as Bull Run, stating that a considerable force of the enemy was reported to be at Centreville, and that the Pennsylvania Second Cavalry had been ordered to go as far as Bull Run "to cover Haupt's reconnaissance."

Not waiting for the cavalry escort, Haupt made his own personal examination, found the road "in good condition," and then left for Hagerstown to

report his findings on Friday, September 19, two days after the battle. Upon his arrival, Haupt found Governor Curtin of Pennsylvania and Generals John F. Reynolds, John A. Wright, and Edward McPherson, officers of the Pennsylvania Militia.

Early that night, rumor had it that "a sizable force of the enemy" was about to attack Hagerstown. A council was held to consider the withdrawal of the Pennsylvania Militia beyond the state line, since the troops had been called out to defend their own state—Curtin, for "political reasons," did not wish to risk an attack on their own territory! The question was put to a vote in Haupt's presence.

"The vote was a tie," wrote Haupt, "but Governor Curtin was very uneasy, and it was decided to retire the Pennsylvania Militia by 1 P.M., but the alarm was false." The truth was that Lee's army, exhausted with fighting, was already moving across the Potomac into Virginia without a thought of attacking anybody.

The next day Haupt rode over the Antietam bat-

Major General Joseph "Fightin' Joe" Hooker, USA.

Hooker directed the opening action against Stonewall Jackson at Antietam and did well; but at the Second Battle of Manassas, when all the general officers were needed, General Haupt writes: "The attractions of Washington kept most of the General Officers in that city." Hooker was one of them, and did not get into action until August 29, 1862.

FROM A PHOTOGRAPH BY MATHEW BRADY, AUTHOR'S COLLECTION.

The Battle of Antietam, Maryland, September 17, 1862.

Lee's invasion of Maryland ended in this battle, called the "bloodiest, single day's action of the Civil War," what could be called the North's first victory. For his failure to consolidate it by pursuing Lee, McClellan was removed from command by President Lincoln.

FROM AN ORIGINAL OIL PAINTING BY CAPTAIN JAMES HOPE, USA COMBAT ARTIST, AUTHOR'S COLLECTION.

tlefield, where he found soldier details engaged in burying the dead of both armies. After a short interview with McClellan at headquarters, Haupt left for Frederick, by way of Boonsboro, and thence by rail to Baltimore & Washington. At Monocacy, to his surprise Haupt found two hundred boxcars loaded with army supplies standing on sidings, where they had been for a week. At Haupt's insistence, General Wool assigned an officer to oversee their unloading. On that same day, W. P. Smith, superintendent of the Baltimore & Ohio Railroad, requested Haupt to send a force of carpenters to repair the damage to that road, which was done at once.

Being an observant man, Haupt noted that after Lee crossed the Potomac, McClellan did nothing to stop him, allowing Lee to extricate his army and reoccupy the line of the Rappahannock. Haupt also found that Lee's men had reconstructed a bridge on the Orange & Alexandria Railroad (USMRR), had repaired the line, and were running trains as far as Bristoe, five miles south of Manassas, carrying off all the disabled U.S. Military Railroad engines, rails, car wheels and axles that had been abandoned after Pope's defeat.

On the strength of this news Haupt sent a force to Bristoe on the chance of recapturing a train the rebels had commandeered. Haupt's men hid themselves in the woods, ready to block the train on its return trip. Everything went well until one of Haupt's men was spotted by the Confederate engineer. Quickly reversing his engine, the engineer backed his train toward the Rappahannock and safety.

On November 1, McClellan wired President Lincoln that his army "had crossed the Potomac," at the same time complaining that the main reason for his sixteen-day delay in his pursuit of Lee was due to his "sore-tongued and fatigued" horses. Lincoln promptly replied, posing the question, "Will you pardon me for asking what the horses of your army have done since the battle of Antietam that fatigues anything?" Stung into action, McClellan began moving his army southward.

About this time General Rufus Ingalls came to Haupt's headquarters at Rectortown. Haupt had serious doubts about the location, knowing McClellan's sloth-like movements, and he also knew that McClellan's army had not reached the line of the Manassas Gap Railroad. Nevertheless, Haupt

U.S. Military Railroad Car Barges on the Potomac River, 1862–63.

Loaded USMRR boxcars being towed on barges down the Potomac River to the Aquia Creek terminal of the Fred-

ericksburg Road. Two barges lashed together and straddled with railroad tracks comprise the car floats.

From a photograph, probably by Captain A. J. Russell, Courtesy National Archives.

told Ingalls that he would risk going with him personally to find McClellan, and ordered an engine and two flatcars for a guard unit which they picked up at Fairfax Station.

The first part of this junket was uneventful, until they reached Manassas and started on the "Gap Road," over which not a wheel had rolled since the spring campaign. The rails, overgrown with weeds and grass, caused the locomotive's drivers to slip badly. After several miles of this, the sand in the sand dome ran out.

The soldiers aboard the flatcars got off and walked ahead of the locomotive, placing pebbles on the tracks which when crushed by the drivers "helped the adhesion." And if this were not enough, after running several miles in this fashion the engine's water gave out. Finding a couple of water buckets aboard the tender, the soldiers dipped the buckets in whatever streams and puddles could be found along the track, but the engine still lost traction power. Haupt then uncoupled the two flatcars, taking on board the tender as many of the soldiers as he could and leaving the rest to walk along the tracks.

Haupt and Ingalls reached Rectortown by midnight, but found no sign of McClellan or the Army. And since it was no longer safe to linger Haupt and Ingalls returned the same way they had come. Sometime later that night they found a lone cavalryman from Maxcy Gregg's command roaming about, supposedly on picket, and the rumor was that Colonel John S. Moseby and his guerrillas were in the area of the railroad.

"How it happened that we weren't captured has always been a matter of surprise to me," Haupt wrote later. "For the puffing of the steam and the slipping of the wheels made a noise that could be heard for more than a mile, giving notice to the enemy in the vicinity."

Later that night, passing Fairfax, Haupt was informed by the conductor of a train they met that it had been fired on near the last bridge they had crossed. When he returned to Fairfax, Haupt sent a guard to the bridge location. The bridge was intact, so he sent some soldiers out to scour the woods in the vicinity, but all they found were numerous horse tracks, which proved conclusively that the firing had come from mounted troops, probably Moseby's.

The days that followed Antietam were troublesome for Haupt and the United States Military Railroads. In his attempts to restore the Manassas Gap and Orange & Alexandria railroads (USMRR) he found that most of his problems were caused by

irresponsible federal troops—more damage was done the railroads "by our own soldiers than by the enemy."

"Camps had been established near the roads, and near the stations," wrote Haupt in a report to the War Department, "and the soldiers would tear up sidings and switch stands, burn the wood provided for engines, wash clothes and their persons with soap in the streams and springs which supplied the water stations . . . and many of the engines were stopped on the road by foaming boilers caused by soapy water."

And there were the vexatious and consistent problems Haupt faced when careless, and sometimes stupid, generals left their military supply boxcars standing on siding for days before having them unloaded—even after these generals had been advised numerous times of the problems they caused the railroads. But most discouraging of all to Haupt was the vandalism. A telegram Haupt received from J. J. Moore, his engineer of tracks and telegraphs, outlined these acts of unnecessary

Major General William P. Heintzelman, USA, 1862.
Heintzelman ignored Haupt's request for troops to guard the Orange & Alexandria Railroad from the enemy, as well as the "vandalism on the part of our own troops."
FROM A PHOTOGRAPH BY MATHEW BRADY, AUTHOR'S COLLECTION.

General Haupt's Boxcar Dilemma of 1862.

Scores of boxcars, many empty, await disposition at Manassas. Haupt's complaint against army officers for not unloading boxcars promptly was not unfounded. Haupt went *in search of the cars, found them, ordered them back many times for use elsewhere.*

FROM A PHOTOGRAPH BY CAPTAIN A. J. RUSSELL, USMRR, COURTESY NATIONAL ARCHIVES.

vandalism "which occurred daily" along the line of the Orange & Alexandria Railroad.

Haupt wrote to General Heintzleman immediately. "Not a guard was to be seen on the road between Fairfax Station and Union Mills," he wrote, "although we have five bridges in that interval. Our railroad men do not shirk any duty, however hazardous, if I direct them to proceed. They have occupied the most exposed positions; some of them have been killed and some captured, *but we cannot afford to risk them unnecessarily.* I have therefore presumed to inquire as to the arrangements for guarding the roads, and the numbers and positions and instructions of the troops detailed for this duty, in order that I might be able to give directions and assurances to our men based on personal knowledge of the facts."

Having put Heintzleman on the spot, Haupt reiterated that his "frequent calls . . . were becoming annoying," and although he had not heard from Heintzleman, Haupt pointed out that "from past experience" with Heintzleman he had "but little confidence that the lines will be guarded properly," no matter the urgency.

To McClellan's query concerning the condition of the railroads in Virginia, and whether or not they could be counted on to move six hundred tons of supplies daily, Haupt sent this angry reply on October 26, 1862, at 2 P.M.:

The destruction of the Aquia Creek and Fredericksburg Railroad was an unfortunate piece of vandalism on the part of our own troops. I reported to General Halleck that the destruction of this road was also unnecessary, and highly censurable. The Potomac Creek Bridge was nearly 80-feet high and 400-feet long. Nearly all the available timber within reach was used in its construction. This bridge was blown down and burned. The reconstruction of the Rappahannock Bridge at this season will be difficult, and the structure, if rebuilt, precarious. Timber at this time is very scarce. . . . Would it not be best to rely on boat and pontoon bridges at Fredericksburg? The wharf at Acquia Creek was a very complete affair, covering nearly an acre and a half, with double tracks and commodious buildings. It cannot be reconstructed as it was in four months. The material cannot be procured in any reasonable time.

Haupt also pointed out that because of the lack of guards his losses in rolling stock to the enemy were "402 cars captured or destroyed, and we have now less than 300, only a part of which are avail-

Kettle Run Bridge, Near Bristoe Station, 1862.

Repaired hastily by Haupt's construction corps, an engine and twelve cars of ammunition wait to cross. Smoke rises from the engine's stack behind the cut in the embankment. Conductor C. M. Strein reported to Haupt: "the bridges over Broad Run, between Bristoe and Manassas and over Bull Run were burned . . . engines and cars at Bristoe were burned and destroyed."

FROM A PHOTOGRAPH BY CAPTAIN A. J. RUSSELL, USMRR, COURTESY NATIONAL ARCHIVES.

General Herman Haupt's Rebuilt "Bean and Cornstalk" Bridge at Potomac Creek, 1862.

Destroyed unnecessarily by Union troops after all Haupt's labor, an investigation of the matter was dropped when it *was learned Burnside had ordered the destruction "on the advices of others."*

FROM A PHOTOGRAPH BY CAPTAIN A. J. RUSSELL, USMRR, COURTESY NATIONAL ARCHIVES.

U.S. Military Railroads Construction Corps, at Burnside's Wharf at Aquia, 1862.

The terminal of the Richmond, Fredericksburg & Potomac Railroad, this wharf was the base of the Army of the Poto- *mac's supplies in the Fredericksburg campaign in December.*

FROM A PHOTOGRAPH BY CAPTAIN A. J. RUSSELL, USMRR, COURTESY NATIONAL ARCHIVES.

Major General Ambrose Everett Burnside, USA, 1862.

Appointed to the command of the Army of the Potomac, replacing McClellan in 1862, Burnside lost his head at Fredericksburg, and by his mistakes caused a senseless *slaughter in the December battle. Haupt had advised Burnside not to depend on the Orange & Alexandria Railroad for his supplies, since the road had been badly damaged.*

FROM A PHOTOGRAPH BY MATHEW BRADY, AUTHOR'S COLLECTION.

U.S. Military Railroads Construction Corps Headquarters.

Construction Corps headquarters at Bealton, Virginia, as it looked on November 14, 1863, following the Gettysburg campaign. The round, cone-shaped tents were called Sibleys *—the rest of the camp comprises simple army wall tents. USMRR Construction Corps personnel were on twenty-four-hour call.*

FROM AN ORIGINAL DRAWING BY WILLIAM MARSHALL MERRICK, USMRR, COURTESY THE NEW YORK PUBLIC LIBRARY.

able." When Haupt's alarming reports concerning the "unnecessary vandalism by our own troops" reached General Halleck, he wanted an investigation begun at once, until it was discovered that the destruction had been ordered by General Burnside, "on the advices of others," and the investigation was dropped.

On November 6, Haupt telegraphed Watson at the War Department to inform him that the road "beyond Piedmont, over the Goose Creek bridges," had been examined and found to be unharmed. "We will have tough times on the railroad," continued Haupt in his report, and reminded Watson of the trouble encountered supplying McDowell the year before. "That was in June," wrote Haupt, "when grass could be obtained. Now, 60,000 animals must be fed exclusively by rail. . . ."

On November 5, 1862, Haupt had been advised confidentially that McClellan was to be relieved of his command, that both President Lincoln and Secretary Stanton had "been out of patience" with McClellan for his failure to pursue Lee after Antietam. Haupt "esteemed McClellan highly," but as a commander "he was too slow and his caution excessive." Two days later, as Haupt joined him for supper, McClellan was apparently unaware of his removal for he was still issuing orders to Haupt at Rectortown, requesting that the line to Warrenton "be put in running order as soon as possible in order that the movement of troops need not be delayed."

While momentous events had been taking place on the rolling farmlands of Pennsylvania and Maryland that year of 1862, concurrent military activity in the west was beginning to assume major proportions. The first two months of 1862 witnessed the emergence of a young general named Ulysses S. Grant, who quietly went about his business of winning the war in his sector.

Here both sides were prepared for intensive operations. In January, Grant had attacked Fort Henry on the Tennessee and reduced it, and the following month attacked and captured Fort Donelson, and thereby destroyed the Confederate first line of defense on the Cumberland. Nashville, Fort Pillow, Island No. 10, New Madrid, Corinth, and Chattanooga were also earmarked for attack and capture.

In February, Grant ordered the *Carondelet*, one of the U.S. Navy's river flotilla of ironclad gunboats, commanded by Rear Admiral Henry N. Walke, "to ascend the Tennessee River and thoroughly destroy the bridge of the Memphis & Ohio Railroad," very skillfully cutting General Albert Sidney Johnston's communications with Bowling Green and Columbus.

Then, on February 14, after an eleven-mile march, Grant, in a concerted land and gunboat assault, attacked Fort Donelson on the Cumberland River, which capitulated after two days of fighting. Meanwhile, General Don Carlos Buell, commanding the Department of the Ohio, began moving on Bowling Green, the center of the Confederate

Main Station and Yards at Nashville, Tennessee, 1864.

The Nashville & Chattanooga Railway station at Nashville epitomized the enormous war-damaged condition of the *South's railroads in the last months of the war. Rolling stock and rails suffered the most damage.*

FROM A PHOTOGRAPH BY GEORGE N. BARNARD,
AUTHOR'S COLLECTION.

defense line, approaching southward along the Louisville & Nashville Railroad.

Seasonal torrential rains had raised the waters of the Cumberland River and enabled Grant's ironclad gunboats to navigate as far south as Alabama, thereby endangering the Memphis & Charleston Railroad which ran along the river bank and was therefore vulnerable to attack from gunboats.

Nashville, Tennessee, Grant's next prime target, was one of the Confederacy's important railroad centers and the largest military supply and munitions depots in the west. Enormous warehouses supplied both Lee's army in Virginia and Johnston's army in Tennessee. Nashville was also an important ordnance manufacturing center.

Grant's destruction of the Mobile & Ohio's railroad bridge over the Tennessee River now made it impossible for Johnston and General Leonidas Polk to join forces, which in turn compelled Johnston to withdraw his force from his fortified position at Bowling Green and to abandon his plan to fight Buell at Big Barren, putting the Cumberland between his own and Buell's forces.

With the first rumors of Johnston's withdrawal from Bowling Green to Murfreesboro Nashville's citizens began to panic, believing they were being abandoned to the federal armies. Panic is contageous and virulent, and when Nashville's citizens discovered the rumor to be true they became terror-stricken. The three railroads out of Nashville—the Nashville & Chattanooga, which ran through Murfreesboro and east to Chattanooga; the unfinished Central of Alabama, which had no terminal but which ran to Columbia; and the Louisville & Nashville, to Murfreesboro and Stevenson—suddenly became avenues to safety.

The panic-stricken citizens descended on the railroad stations and mobbed them. When freezing, torrential rains, and the arrival in the city of the wounded survivors of Fort Donelson and Johnston's retreating columns from Bowling Green were added, all the incentives for a full-scale riot were present. Civilians overran the railroad stations in force, packed every car that had wheels and an engine to haul it, and paid astronomical fees for any kind of transportation available. General Johnston's failure to seize military control of the railroads for the removal of wounded and the enormous stockpiles of military stores caused great losses in meat, foodstuffs, and ammunition. But it was not long before the trains carrying civilians out of town were recalled to carry the sick and wounded south, and the removal of stores was accomplished as quickly as the disorganized and brokendown transportation would permit.

Military train movements from Murfreesboro to Corinth, another important rail center, over the Memphis & Charleston Railroad "was simply impossible," wrote General Jeremy F. Gilmer, "without sacrificing the supplies and munitions on which the subsistence and armament of the command depended. The entire transportation capacity of the railroads was taxed to the utmost and even the immense quantities of meat and other commissary stores were left at Nashville, Murfreesboro, and Shelbyville, Fayettesville and Huntsville. Again the movement was made over the leading roads to Shelbyville, Fayetteville and Huntsville, expeditiously as possible, considering the numbers of troops to be transported . . . with the imperfect organization of the [Confederate] railroads as it then existed."

Nevertheless, Johnston concentrated at Corinth, with troops moving over the Mobile & Ohio Railroad from Columbus, Johnson, and Humboldt. The Mississippi Central carried five thousand troops from New Orleans. General Braxton Bragg brought ten thousand more over the Mobile & Ohio from Mobile, Alabama, and Pensacola, Florida.

While this heavy troop concentration was taking place at Corinth, General Halleck, who apparently regarded himself as some kind of military genius, reinstated the astute and competent General W. T. Sherman and ordered him to take his division to Eastport, Mississippi, by river steamer. Once landed, Sherman was to march his division across a narrow strip of marshy swampland and cut the Memphis & Charleston Railroad. Not once did Halleck realize that General Johnston did not depend on this railroad for supplies, and no one understood the meaning of the move, least of all Halleck, its innovator.

The weather fought on the side of the Confederate army. Drenching rains and swampy ground bogged his men down and Sherman was compelled to abandon this senseless operation and return to his transports. Sherman then moved back downstream, disembarked his division at Pittsburgh Landing (Shiloh), and pitched camp on the high ground above the river.

On February 19, the Confederates blew up the two bridges across the Cumberland to keep them out of federal hands, the most important being the new Louisville & Nashville Railroad bridge. Rising waters caused by the heavy rainfall accounted for the destruction of two bridges belonging to the Nashville & Chattanooga Railroad and to all intents and purposes the evacuation of Nashville came to a standstill.

Meanwhile, the trains which had carried Nashville's refugees out of the city had picked up Johnston's wounded and taken them to Chattanooga. Riding in unheated boxcars, the wounded men suffered greatly, and exposure to cold and wetness aggravated their pain and caused many to succumb. But Nashville had seen the last of the Confederate Army. The next soldiers Nashville's citizen would see in their streets would be wearing blue uniforms.

It had been General Johnston's plan to join forces with P. T. G. Beauregard's forces, then at Jackson, Mississippi, to protect Memphis, Tennessee, and the river, with the object of engaging and defeating Grant before he could join forces with Buell's army.

Corinth, Mississippi, at the time, was the junction of two important railroads—the Mobile & Ohio, running north to south; and the Memphis & Charleston Railroad, running east and south, deep into Confederate territory. It was therefore only natural that Johnston concentrate his forces at Corinth; and if the combined federal forces should be defeated, the entire rail transportation facilities of the Confederacy north of Vicksburg and west of Chattanooga would be saved. If the tables were turned and Johnson should be defeated, the railroads would be lost to the enemy.

More than a month had passed since the fall of Nashville without sign of any movement on the part of the federal forces, but the lull was soon to be over. Having rid himself of Halleck's interference, Grant assumed command of the entire army on March 17. Following Sherman's advice, Grant concentrated his forces on the bluff above Pittsburgh Landing, ordering the rest of his scattered forces to join him there.

An extremely competent soldier, Grant regarded Corinth as "the great strategic position at the West, between the Tennessee and Mississippi rivers, and between Nashville and Vicksburg" (Jefferson Davis called it "the Gibralter of the Confederacy"). Grant also knew that with Corinth under his control he would be in complete command of the Confederate Army's rail transportation, and toward that end he planned to attack Corinth as soon as Buell's forces could join him.

One of the ablest of the Confederacy's commanders, General Albert Sidney Johnston was not about to wait until he faced Grant and Buell together. If he could defeat Grant before Buell could join forces with him, he could in turn defeat Buell. Therefore, Johnston with his army of forty thousand men set out for Pittsburgh Landing, only twenty-three miles away, and in three days deployed in the vicinity of Shiloh Church.

At six o'clock on the morning of April 6, 1862, General Johnston advanced in line of battle and surprised, attacked, and dispersed Grant's advance units, overrunning their camps and forcing Prentiss's division back on the second federal line. In no time at all the Confederates enveloped the entire divi-

sion. After several hours of bloody fighting, Grant's army was pushed back to within six hundred yards of the Landing, on an overhanging bluff near the river's edge. Only after desperate work by Grant and his officers were the federal lines finally restored. Because of confusion in the Confederate ranks, and poor communications between units, the Confederates lost their initial advantage of surprise.

By nightfall the battle settled down to sporadic firing of the pickets. During the night, Buell's force of twenty-five thousand men arrived, crossing the river on pontoon bridges by torchlight. Grant opened his counterattack at five o'clock the next morning, supported by his gunboats in the river, but the heavy-caliber naval rifles of the gunboats failed to make any impression on the Confederate line. Finally, after sustained attacks lasting five hours, the battle ended. The Confederate Army withdrew and Grant's forces occupied their old camps. Both armies, weakened by losses and fatigue, did not renew the contest.

Chattanooga, Tennessee, 1863–1864.

An important strategic railway center, and a prime objective of both contending armies, Chattanooga changed hands twice and underwent a siege. Grant defeated Bragg in the battle for Chattanooga and recaptured the city. Bragg retreated to Dalton, Georgia.

FROM A PHOTOGRAPH, PROBABLY BY GEORGE N. BARNARD, AUTHOR'S COLLECTION.

CHAPTER 8

Raiders West—
"We Could Have Gone to Vicksburg!"

In the west General Henry W. Halleck, who had thus far been wrong in his military assessments and judgments, decided after Shiloh "to take command in the field." Apparently, Halleck, commander of the Department of Mississippi, jealous of his younger subordinate Grant's recent successes, had decided to grab some of the public limelight for himself (Grant was promoted to major general and relegated to minor operations). With one hundred twenty thousand men he began a movement against Corinth, Mississippi. To say that Halleck was overly cautious would be a gross understatement, for he literally dug his way to his objective; every mile of his advance the men stopped to dig useless trenches and fortifications.

Moreover, Halleck had ordered General Don Carlos Buell, the officer who had arrived in time to save the day at Shiloh (Pittsburg Landing), to move on Chattanooga along the line of the Memphis & Charleston Railroad, which he was to restore as he went along. This Buell knew to be a waste of time, since that particular railroad was an unnecessary element in his campaign. The long line was generally vulnerable to cavalry and guerrilla raids and for all practical purposes was indefensible. Buell carried out Halleck's orders, but the time taken to repair the rail line caused the army long delays since the earlier destruction had not been limited to torn-up trackage; General Mitchell had thoroughly destroyed most of the bridges, which had to be rebuilt if the line was to be used at all.

Meanwhile, an important change had taken place at Tupelo, Mississippi. The Confederate high command had decided to replace General P. T. G. Beauregard with Lieutenant General Braxton Bragg, a short-tempered, "high-born" officer with ability. It did not take Bragg long to divine Buell's intentions against Chattanooga. Bragg acted accordingly, ordering General Bedford Forrest, one of the South's more astute cavalry officers, to delay Buell's advance as long as possible. Forrest acted at once.

By June 12, Buell's men had repaired the Memphis & Charleston Railroad to within thirty miles of Chattanooga, working slowly for more than a month in the stifling summer heat to repair a railroad they would never use. (That same month, General Halleck was recalled to Washington to become general-in-chief of all the Union armies.) Buell, who had known all along that the operation he was engaged in on Halleck's orders was a lost cause, now assumed the personal responsibility for changing them. Buell sent detachments to repair the Nashville & Chattanooga Railroad so he could use that line to supply his army when it reached Stevenson, Alabama, and reopen his old line of supply between Louisville and Nashville, completing his repairs as far as Bridgeport.

When all this had been accomplished, the axe fell. On July 13, in a hit-and-run tactical raid, Forrest captured a small garrison at Murfreesboro, wrecked a section of Buell's recently restored railroad, and retired to McMinnville. "The consequences of this disaster were serious," wrote Buell. "The use of the railroad from Nashville, which had been completed the very day before, and which I was depending on to throw supplies into Stevenson, for a forward movement, was set back two weeks; the force of Forrest threatened Nashville itself and the whole line of railroad through Tennessee."

On July 21, Forrest again rode out of McMinnville, reached the outskirts of Nashville, and set Buell's timetable back another eight days by cutting another section of the railroad. On that

Military Bridge over the Tennessee River at Chattanooga.

Built entirely of wood, the nine arch trusses, or cantilevers, and the approach ramps are well constructed, although the bridge deck seems to sag in places.

FROM A PHOTOGRAPH, PROBABLY BY GEORGE N. BARNARD, AUTHOR'S COLLECTION.

same day Braxton Bragg moved his army out of Tupelo, Mississippi, and advanced on Chattanooga, leaving General Earl Van Dorn to defend Vicksburg and General Sterling Price to keep a weather eye on Grant.

Bragg's route to Chattanooga was roundabout to say the least. First, he moved his infantry to Mobile, Alabama, by way of the Mobile & Ohio Railroad, at the same time moving his cavalry and artillery horses overland. At Mobile, he ferried his infantry across Mobile Bay and up the Tensas River, reached the railhead of the newly constructed Alabama & Florida Railroad, moved his men by rail to Montgomery, Alabama, and via the Montgomery & West Point Railroad on to Atlanta. Then they went to Chattanooga over the tracks of the Atlantic & West Point Railroad. While Bragg was engaged in his involved troop movement, Forrest kept Buell pinned down at Huntsville, Alabama, which allowed Bragg to move unmolested.

The Union Army's railroad situation in middle and western Tennessee was good. With both areas, and a portion of Mississippi and Alabama, in federal hands, the outlook was bright and somewhat promising. Federal lines now ran from Stevenson, Alabama, to Kentucky, a distance of about twelve hundred miles, three hundred of them running parallel to the tracks of the Memphis & Charleston Railroad. Once the Confederacy controlled about 10 percent of the total railroad mileage, including twelve railroad junctions and a rail supply line which had carried ammunition, food, forage for animals, and subsistence for two hundred thousand soldiers. Now the Confederacy held not a single railroad north of Mississippi and Alabama, and no lines running southwest of Virginia. The Confederate military railroad situation in Tennessee and Mississippi looked gloomy indeed.

"The operations in Western Tennessee and Kentucky, and in north Mississippi," reported Colonel Daniel McCallum, general manager of the U.S. Military Railroads in 1866,

were distinct and separate from those at Nashville, and although under the control of the general superintendent of the latter point, they required and received very little attention as compared with those leading to the front.

The Nashville & Chattanooga Railroad, 151

The Nashville & Chattanooga Railroad Bridge over the Tennessee River, at Chattanooga.

The track gauge was five feet, laid on crossties three inches thick. Support timbers, running lengthwise under the rails, measured six by six inches. Timber uprights of the same size rest on the original stone piers. Despite their "jerry-built" appearance, open-deck truss bridges of this type were capable of supporting fairly heavy trains—two tons to the inch.

FROM A PHOTOGRAPH, PROBABLY BY GEORGE N. BARNARD, AUTHOR'S COLLECTION.

miles, was the great main line over which passed all the supplies for the armies of the Cumberland, the Ohio and the Tennessee, through the campaigns which terminated with the occupation of Atlanta. Over this single line of railroad the provisions, clothing, camp equippage for the men, forage for the animals, arms, ammunition, and ordnance stores, reinforcements, and all the varied and miscellaneous supplies required for a great army engaged in an active campaign, were sent to the front; and by it were returned the sick, wounded, disabled and discharged soldiers, refugees and free men, captured prisoners, and materials deemed advisable to send to the rear. Portions of the road had been in use for military purposes since April of 1862. . . .

Thus the Confederacy had little if any use of the Memphis & Ohio, the Tennessee & Ohio, the Memphis & Charleston, the Central Alabama, the Mississippi Central, the Louisville & Nashville, and the Nashville & Chattanooga railroads. Much of this railway mileage had been recaptured from time to time during the year, but the Union armies recovered it and controlled the lines, although in

many places these lines had been severely damaged. The remarkable thing in all this was that the federal government, through the U.S. Military Railroads, restored these lines, even long after the war ended.

General Halleck occupied Corinth, Mississippi, on the day of its evacuation. Following his appointment as general-in-chief, Halleck turned the Department of West Tennessee over to General Grant, along with all the territory held by the Union armies in northern Mississippi. In August, on Halleck's orders Grant sent E. A. Paine's and Jeff C. Davis's divisions, one of which was garrisoned at Nashville, across the Tennessee River to bolster Buell who was moving northward through middle Tennessee to engage Bragg. Then on June 11, General William Starke Rosecrans succeeded to the command of the Army of Mississippi, relieving General John Pope, in Grant's military District of West Tennessee.

General Earl Van Dorn, commanding all the Confederate troops in Mississippi except Sterling Price's independent command, now devised a plan

"Section 9" of the Atlantic & West Point Railroad.

One of the Southern railroads that carried General Bragg's troops, this lengthy timber trestle is typical of railroad trestles of the period. The 4–4–0 balloon-stacked locomotive entering the scene, is not identified by name or number.

FROM A PHOTOGRAPH, PROBABLY BY GEORGE N. BARNARD, AUTHOR'S COLLECTION.

to drive the Union forces out of northern Mississippi and western Tennessee, in a concerted movement with Bragg in Kentucky (Bragg had always believed that the Kentuckians had been coerced into remaining in the Union). This Confederate troop concentration spelled trouble for the Union forces in West Tennessee, where some forty to fifty thousand federal soldiers had been loosely scattered by Halleck over the district occupying the vicinity of the Memphis & Charleston Railway, from Iuka to Memphis, a stretch of about one hundred fifteen miles. On interior lines, this loose troop concentration covered the Ohio and Mississippi rivers from Paducah to Columbus, Ohio, Jackson, Bethel and other places on the Mississippi Central and Mobile & Ohio railways. As General Rosecrans wrote,

The Memphis & Charleston Railway runs not far from the dividing lines between the States, with a southerly bend from Memphis eastward toward Corinth, whence it extends eastwardly through Iuka, crosses Bear River and follows the Tuscumbia Valley on the south side of the east and west reach of the Tennessee River to Decatur. Thence the road crosses to the north side of this river and

unites with the Nashville & Chattanooga road at Stevenson en route for Chattanooga. The Mobile & Ohio Railway, from Columbus on the Mississippi, runs considerably east of south, passing through Jackson, Tennessee, Bethel, Corinth, Tupelo and Baldwyn, Mississippi, and thence to Mobile, Alabama. The Mississippi Central, leaving the Mobile & Ohio at Jackson, Tennessee, and Holly Springs, Grenada, runs to Jackson, Mississippi. All this region . . . and the adjoining counties . . . although here and there dotted with clearings and farms, settlements and little villages, is heavily wooded. Its surface consists of low, rolling oak ridges of diluvial clays with intervening crooked drainages traversing narrow, bushy, and sometimes swampy bottoms.

Corinth's strategic importance to both sides was based on three factors. First, the Mobile & Ohio Railroad crossed the Memphis & Charleston, only ninety-three miles from Memphis. Second, this controlled all train movements in both directions. Third, Corinth was close to Hamburg and Pittsburgh Landing on the Tennessee River, where supply steamers could ascend the river at its lowest water stages, a military transportation plus.

Major General William Starke Rosecrans, USA, 1864.

Commander of the Army of Mississippi, Rosecrans's impetuosity got him into trouble. At Corinth, he objected to Grant's order not to march on Vicksburg, not being "well enough prepared." At Chattanooga, Rosecrans fell into the same trap he set for Bragg and was himself besieged.

FROM A PHOTOGRAPH BY MATHEW BRADY, AUTHOR'S COLLECTION.

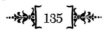

The Mobile & Ohio Railway Station and Tishomingo Hotel at Corinth, Mississippi, October, 1862.

The Mobile & Ohio Railway was one of the strategic railways, with the junction at Corinth, defended by General *Earl Van Dorn's forces. Van Dorn was defeated by Rosecrans, and the lines became supply lines for the Union Army*

Corinth is situated on low flat ground along the Mobile & Ohio Railway, flanked occasionally by low, rolling ridges covered with oaks and heavy undergrowth. "The streams are sluggish and not easily fordable," wrote General Rosecrans,

> on account of their miry beds and steep, muddy clay banks. Water in dry seasons is never abundant, and in many places is only reached by bore-wells of one hundred to three hundred feet in depth, whence it is hoisted by rope and pulley carrying water buckets of galvanized iron pipes from four to six inches in diameter, and four to five feet long, with valves at the lower end. These matters are of controlling importance in moving and handling troops in that region. Men and animals need hard ground to move on, and must have drinking water.

Such was the nature of the battlefield to come.

The battle for the railroads at Corinth, Mississippi, on October 3 and 4, 1862, was a desperate, bloody affair between the Army of the Mississippi under General W. S. Rosecrans and the Confederate forces under the command of Major General Earl Van Dorn. Fiercely contested on both sides, Corinth equalled in intensity the larger battles fought that year.

Van Dorn "had been in hopes that one day's operations would end the contest and decide who should be the victors on this bloody field; but ten miles' march over a parched country on dusty roads without water, getting into line of battle in forests and undergrowth" ended that hope.

The heat of the day was fierce and the air still. The Confederates opened the battle at 4:30 A.M. with a six-gun battery salvo and advanced to the attack. But when they reached the Union lines, the crossfire of the Union batteries broke up the Confederate advance. During the fighting a part of the Confederate line reached the edge of town, which, wrote Van Dorn, "had developed into a hand-to-hand contest being enacted in the very yard where General Rosecrans had his headquarters, and in the streets of the town."

At first Rosecrans's heavy artillery had been silenced. But when all seemed lost for the Union forces, fresh Union reserves from Iuka, Burnsville, and Rienzi arrived on the scene and ripped into the Confederate ranks. The encounter was furious and the Confederate line gave way. The fighting almost became a personal matter among the contestants, all realizing the importance of the railroads they defended.

Sometime afterward, General Price said of the three-day battle: "The history of this war contains no bloodier page, perhaps, than that which will record this fiercely-contested battle. . . . the gallant conduct of the officers and men under my command . . . who stood to arms through this struggle . . . have acquired . . . a halo of glory as imperishable as it is brilliant."

The Confederates lost Corinth and the railroads; and Van Dorn, removed from his command for his failure, bowed "to the opinion of the people whom I serve." When the battle ended, Rosecrans, elated by his victory, telegraphed General Grant: "We have defeated, routed and demoralized the army which holds the Lower Mississippi Valley. We have two railroads leading down toward the Gulf through the most productive parts of the State, into which we can pursue them with safety. . . . We have whipped them, and should now push them to the wall and capture all the rolling stock of their railroads. . . ."

But Grant felt that after its ordeal at Corinth Rosecrans's army "needed more preparation" to take on Bragg; and to Halleck, at Washington, he wired: "on reflection, I deem it idle to pursue further without more preparation, and have for a third time ordered his [Rosecrans] return."

It was cool October weather now, and the roads "were in prime condition, along the Mississippi Central to Grenada, and especially below that place," Rosecrans wrote, unhappy with the outcome of his bout with Grant, "was a corn country—a rich farming country—and the corn was ripe. *If Grant had not stopped us, we could have gone to Vicksburg!*"

In the East, with the winter of 1862–1863 approaching, on November 6, Lee and his army moved into camp at Culpeper, Virginia, while McClellan and the Army of the Potomac encamped at Warrenton. The Orange & Alexandria Railroad below Manassas Junction once again became the important line of supply for the Union forces.

Dissatisfied with McClellan's performance after Antietam, President Lincoln removed him for good. "I said I would remove McClellan if he didn't pursue Lee, and I must do so," said the president, and handed the command of the army over to General Ambrose E. Burnside. Upon receiving the appointment Burnside told Lincoln that he felt he was not qualified to handle such a large command —and he set out to prove that he was not.

Once again, enter General Herman Haupt. When Burnside took over command on November 9, Haupt carefully and painstakingly informed him

A Group of Union soldiers at Corinth, October 1862.

Taken a few days after the battle, these Union soldiers, comprising both infantry and cavalry, pose for the camera. *Railway line and warehouses can be seen in the background.*

PHOTOGRAPH PROBABLY BY GEORGE N. BARNARD, COURTESY NATIONAL ARCHIVES.

Winter Quarters of the Fifty-second Illinois Volunteers, Corinth, October 1862.

In the custom of the times, the contesting armies settled down in winter quarters built by the soldiers themselves. *Most military operations ended with the coming of winter, since bad weather made the roads impassable.*

FROM A PHOTOGRAPH, PROBABLY BY GEORGE N. BARNARD, COURTESY NATIONAL ARCHIVES.

The Foreground of Battery Robinette, Corinth, Mississippi, 1862.

Taken by an unknown photographer, the picture was made immediately after the fiercely contested action before the *bodies of the men and horses killed in the action were recovered.*

BY AN UNKNOWN PHOTOGRAPHER, POSSIBLY ARMSTEAD,
COURTESY NATIONAL ARCHIVES.

that under the present conditions the Orange & Alexandria Railroad would be inadequate to supply his large army, and that if he operated along the line of the O & A, he could expect transportation and supply problems. The newly restored line did not have enough sidings to accommodate long trains; as yet there were no water or wood stations; the road's capacity was less than half that needed to supply the Army of the Potomac.

And there was an even more serious aspect to the use of the line. The line would undoubtedly be raided in the coming campaign, and there was special danger to the bridges. In fact, Haupt pointed out, the entire line would have to be heavily guarded and patrolled constantly. Finally, Haupt insisted that there be no more interference from army quartermaster and commissary officers in train operation, that cars be unloaded promptly and returned, that Burnside allocate enough men and officers to see that they were unloaded properly.

These rules and conditions had to be strictly enforced for, "without this," said Haupt, "the supply of your army is impossible. No man living can accomplish it!"

Haupt's warning to Burnside and the War Department must have had the proper effect for the advance line of the Orange & Alexandria Railroad was abandoned and Burnside marched his army to Stafford Heights, across the Rappahannock River, in plain sight of Fredericksburg.

Meanwhile, Haupt had made the Richmond, Fredericksburg & Potomac Railroad serviceable. He repaired the Aquia Creek docks at the road's terminal, and again bridged Potomac Creek with a prefabricated truss structure. Cars and locomotives were shipped to Aquia by barge down the Potomac, and by the time Burnside had his army encamped at Falmouth the line was ready.

By all odds, the battle of Fredericksburg on December 13, 1862, was the greatest military blun-

The Army of the Potomac Crossing the Rappahannock to Engage Lee at Fredericksburg, December 13, 1862.
Under fire from Berdan's Sharpshooters hidden in the shell-damaged houses, Burnside's men succeeded in consolidating *a beachhead on the riverbank.*

DRAWN BY AN UNKNOWN ARTIST, PROBABLY EDWIN FORBES,
AUTHOR'S COLLECTION.

der of the war. Lee had positioned his army on Marye's Heights above the town, behind a stone wall running parallel to the road. The Union forces had to march over a long plain in gradual ascent before they could come within shooting distance of Lee's men stationed behind the wall.

In addition, before Burnside's men even reached the plain they had to cross the Rappahannock on pontoon boats and march through the town, with Lee's sharpshooters behind every window and door ready to pick them off. Undoubtedly, every officer on Burnside's staff realized that a frontal attack against such a strong position was wrong, but Burnside, out to prove himself, thought otherwise.

Burnside opened his battle with an artillery barrage, which reduced the town but which did not seem to dislodge Berdan's Sharpshooters, who picked off Burnside's men trying to launch the pontoon boats. Once his men got the boats across, Burnside marched his men through town, formed on the plain, and ordered charge after charge against Lee's solidly entrenched line. Burnside continued to order the senseless advances until his officers, sickened by the awful slaughter, balked at carrying out his orders. But not until nearly nineteen

thousand men were either dead, wounded, or missing, did Burnside give in.

The battle had raged all afternoon, and the field was littered with the wrecks of men and horses, "the dead rolled out for shelter for the living, dead artillery horses breast-works for little groups of blue-coated men." The stirring but terrifying sight of thousands of blue-uniformed soldiers, with flags waving and cannon roaring; the men advancing up the hill in the winter sunlight firing as they went, caused Lee to comment to his officers: "It is well that war is so terrible, otherwise we should grow too fond of it."

With darkness came the end of the battle, but Stonewall Jackson opened a cannonade, the muzzle flashes scorching the cold night sky. Later that night, as if to illuminate the carnage, the Northern Lights flickered over the wounded and dead. Thus ended the campaigns of 1862. The war would go into its third year.

With the coming of spring, on April 1, General John Imboden, who had won his spurs as a captain in 1861 with his raid on Harper's Ferry, decided to have another try at wrecking the Baltimore & Ohio Railroad in a raid designed to break up the steady

The Army of the Potomac Crossing the Pontoon Bridge over the Rappahannock River, December 13, 1862.

Once across the river, the Army of the Potomac marched through the burning town of Fredericksburg to attack Lee's army behind Marye's Heights, an almost impregnable posi- *tion. Burnside's blunder in ordering frontal assaults caused enormous casualties.*

FROM A DRAWING BY ALFRED WAUD, MADE ON THE SPOT;
AUTHOR'S COLLECTION.

flow of supplies to the Army of the Potomac. Imboden succeeded somewhat, but the line began functioning again shortly thereafter.

In May, Hooker, having replaced Burnside for his failure at Fredericksburg, began his command at Chancellorsville, Virginia, in a battle that again spelled disastrous defeat for the Army of the Potomac and its new commander, and gave immortality to Stonewall Jackson for his flanking movement, crossing the "T" of O. O. Howard's Eleventh Corps and rolling up the entire Union line and routing it. It was an incredible victory for Lee, but it was not without a heavy price. The night before the battle, while Jackson was reconnoitering his lines, he was accidently shot by his own men and died as a result of his wounds.

In the summer of 1863, Lee made his second cast toward ending war in northern territory. With the reluctant consent of Jefferson Davis, Lee began his advance into Pennsylvania, his objective—Harrisburg, on the Susquehanna River. Beginning at Culpeper, across the O & A's tracks which Lee had ordered left unharmed, he crossed into Maryland, wrecked the B & O Railroad at one point, crossed

the Potomac, and advanced to Hagerstown, destroying the Cumberland Valley Railroad and the Northern Central Railroad at York, Pennsylvania. After destroying the Pennsylvania Railroad's main line, Longstreet isolated Washington.

At the same time that Hooker was removed, General Herman Haupt, chief of construction for the U.S. Military Railroads, was given complete authority over the operations of the railroads in Maryland and Pennsylvania. Haupt had guessed Lee's intention to destroy the Pennsylvania, B & O, and other lines, and further realized what it would mean to the federal government if Lee were permitted to cut all rail and telegraphic communication between Washington and the rest of the nation.

Lee's army, moving from victory to victory, marched hundreds of miles across hostile country only to pile up on the crest of a ridge now called the "High Water Mark," at Gettysburg. At Round Top, Little Round Top, Big Round Top, the Peach Orchard, the Wheatfield, Devil's Den, and Bloody Angle, Lee's veterans were to learn what it meant to waver under fire.

Anxiety haunted every Union officer, not the least

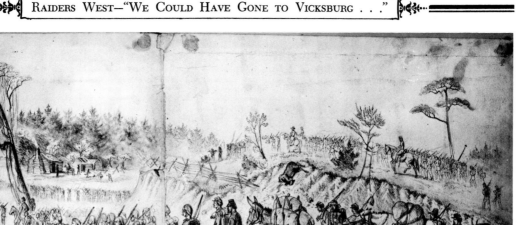

Hooker's Advance on Chancellorsville, Virginia, April 30, 1863.
The Army of the Potomac on the march to Chancellorsville, passing along the north bank of the Rappahannock River.

AN ORIGINAL DRAWING BY EDWIN FORBES MADE ON THE SPOT;
COURTESY LIBRARY OF CONGRESS.

of them General Haupt, who arrived at Harrisburg on the evening of June 30 to see Thomas Scott and make plans for the defense of the railroads in the area, especially the Baltimore & Ohio. Haupt learned from Scott that General R. S. Ewell had already moved through Carlisle, and that Jubal Early and his force were moving west toward Chambersburg. Scott had also told Haupt that he had organized his own "scouts" to keep informed of Lee's movements.

Haupt divined that Lee had already learned of Hooker's removal and was now concentrating his army to do battle. What Hooker did not know was that Jeb Stuart and the Confederate cavalry were off somewhere chasing wagon trains so that Lee was moving blind, with no cavalry advance and no way of knowing the enemy's intentions.

With Meade moving on a collision course, unless he changed his line of march, in Haupt's opinion, a battle was inevitable. Accordingly, Haupt wired Washington what he had learned from Scott, then hurriedly boarded an engine and set out for Baltimore. As a former resident of Gettysburg, Haupt knew all its roads, bypaths, and the surrounding country. He also knew that from Baltimore the Northern Central ran to Hanover Junction, Pennsylvania, and west via the York & Cumberland; and that Early had already burned out the bridges on

both roads, The B & O, he found, was still open to Frederick, where it would be necessary to supply the army by wagon road.

The tiny Western Maryland Railroad, a short twenty-nine-mile line, had its nearest terminal at Westminster, about twenty miles from the battle zone, but the line was inadequate, with no sidings to take long trains, no turntables, telegraphic line, or water stations. The line, Haupt found, could only handle four trains a day—and to supply the army, Haupt needed thirty trains a day.

When Haupt arrived at Westminster on July 1 the battle had already started and the terminal was the center of wild confusion and speculation. Hundreds of wagons from Meade's trains had gathered there and pandemonium reigned—quartermasters and teamsters shouting and yelling, officers demanding supplies, almost bordering on riot. To get away from the noise and confusion and think matters over, Haupt climbed into one of the wagons to decide on his course.

Haupt's fertile mind conceived a plan—he left his temporary sanctuary and hunted down the nearest telegraph station and commenced sending urgent wires. On July 2, while the battle still raged, from USMRR headquarters at Alexandria came four hundred members of the Railroad Construction Corps under Adna Anderson, Haupt's trusted superintendent, with tools, equipment, lanterns, and water buckets, followed by another train loaded with kindling wood for locomotives and the train crews. Impressed B & O rolling stock began to arrive in the Baltimore yards, and without wasting time Anderson sent his crews to open the Northern Central at Hanover Junction and work westward to the York & Cumberland, toward Gettysburg. The rest of the crews were sent to keep the Western Maryland in repair at all costs.

While the trains were being made up in the yards and loaded with provisions at Baltimore, Haupt then telegraphed the Quartermaster Department that he was ready to move the trains and that it now rested with them to see to it that the trains were promptly unloaded and returned. Since there were no passing sidings or crossovers the trains would be run in groups of five trains each, spaced at intervals of eight hours, giving each departing train enough time to unload and return before the next group of trains started.

By July 3, as the battle's outcome was being decided for history, Haupt was moving fifteen hundred tons of supplies over the Western Maryland Railroad daily, while the returning trains were bringing out the thousands of wounded to the Baltimore hospitals. Lack of turntables was no hindrance, since the engines ran backwards from Westminster in close order.

As soon as the track was clear, five other trains started in the other direction. When the engines needed water, Haupt's crews used their buckets at nearby trackside streams and filled the engines' tanks. By these devices, Haupt had increased the

Hanover Junction, Hanover, Pennsylvania.

Photographed by Mathew Brady sometime in November of 1863, after the Gettysburg Address; the clothing of the soldiers and civilians indicate winter. General Haupt brought out the Gettysburg wounded in July through this junction for transfer to Baltimore hospitals.

FROM A PHOTOGRAPH BY MATHEW BRADY, AUTHOR'S COLLECTION.

Another View of Hanover Junction, Pennsylvania, in 1863.

Probably made at the same time by Mathew Brady, this picture shows more of the junction and its track arrange- *ment. It has been said that the tall man standing on the platform with the umbrella is President Lincoln.*

FROM A PHOTOGRAPH BY MATHEW BRADY, AUTHOR'S COLLECTION.

Western Maryland's operating capacity beyond the wildest dreams of its owners.

By four o'clock on the afternoon of July 4, Haupt wired Halleck that the Northern Central was operative as far as Hanover Junction and that the Gettysburg Railroad was open to Littleton, where, incidently, Haupt had found General Daniel Sickles (Sickles lost a leg at Gettysburg in the action of the second day and Haupt send him on to Washington in a special train).

The incredible Haupt had now opened a second line, running in supplies and removing the wounded via Hanover Junction, and by 11:00 P.M. sent another telegram to Halleck at Washington from Oxford, seven miles east of Gettysburg, announcing that two hours' more work would complete the rail line to the battlefield.

Meade, the federal commander at Gettysburg, elated that he had bested Lee, sent a telegram to

President Lincoln saying: "We have swept the enemy from our soil!" But Meade's telegram did not have the effect on the president it was meant to have; Lincoln's reaction to it was one of unbounded exasperation. "When will our generals ever get it through their heads that the whole country is our soil!" he exclaimed.

General George Gordon Meade's failure to pursue Lee and follow up his advantage astonished Washington. Lee's army had been badly mauled, and when, after ten days had passed, there was no pursuit to finish off the Army of Northern Virginia, Haupt hurried to Washington to beg Stanton to issue a peremptory order to Meade to move after Lee at once. For some unknown reason, no such order was given.

While the Army of the Potomac rested, Haupt restored the Northern Central to operating condition over its entire length, also completing repairs

Major General George Gordon Meade, USA.

The sixth commander of the Army of the Potomac in a little over a year and a half, Meade fought at Gettysburg and, like his predecessors, failed to follow up his gains. He, too, was replaced—by Ulysses S. Grant.

FROM A PHOTOGRAPH BY MATHEW BRADY, AUTHOR'S COLLECTION.

Gettysburg—The Third Day, July 3, 1863.

The turning point in the war of the Southern Confederacy is depicted here in Paul Philippoteaux's painting Picket's Charge. *Pettigrew's, Trimble's, and Garnett's brigades dash themselves to pieces against the federal line.*

FROM THE PAINTING BY PAUL PHILIPPOTEAUX,
COURTESY GETTYSBURG BATTLEFIELD PARK.

General Robert E. Lee on His Horse, Traveller.

Disappointed at the outcome of his second northern invasion to end the war in the Confederacy's favor, Lee said, "It was all my fault."

FROM A PHOTOGRAPH BY GEORGE COOK OF RICHMOND,
COURTESY VALENTINE MUSEUM, RICHMOND, VA.

The Orange & Alexandria Railroad (USMRR) Fairfax Station, 1863.

Since the O & A was the target of cavalry and guerrilla raids, General Haupt was compelled to warn General Burn- *side that he could not depend on this rail line for his supplies, unless certain conditions and rules were imposed.*

FROM A PHOTOGRAPH BY CAPTAIN A. J. RUSSELL, USMRR,
COURTESY NATIONAL ARCHIVES.

to the Cumberland Valley Railroad as far as Chambersburg.

Finally, on July 14, Stanton ordered Haupt to drop his work in Pennsylvania and return to Alexandria. After their gigantic confrontation on the farmlands of Pennsylvania the contending armies moved back into Virginia, and again it fell upon Haupt to supply Meade's army by way of the Orange & Alexandria road, now more exposed than ever to guerrilla and cavalry raids.

While the battle of Gettysburg was being fought, cavalry raiders and freelance guerrillas had again worked over the Orange & Alexandria and Manassas Gap roads, the lines which Haupt now needed to supply the Army of the Potomac on its return south. From Alexandria to Warrenton the entire line was plagued with the night raiders of Colonel John S. Moseby's partisans, whose specialty was railroad wrecking and bushwacking.

At this time, Moseby and his men were still unidentified, and the soldiers guarding the tracks, usually outnumbered, were terrified by their forays. These raids became so bad that Haupt, unable to get any adequate patrols to guard his railroads, was

granted the authority to raise his own guard units to defend the lines. Haupt would have preferred large cavalry patrols on an around-the-clock basis, but the War Department was reluctant to furnish them. Nevertheless, by August 1, 1863, the Manassas Gap Railroad was open to Front Royal, and the trains of the Orange & Alexandria were in operation as far as Rappanhannock Station.

Once across the Rapidan River, a greatly disappointed Lee made no apologies for his failure at Gettysburg. "It was all my fault," he said. And the war went on from there.

Haupt's service to the Union Army in the systematic evacuation of the wounded from the stricken field of Gettysburg was a remarkable feat of clear thinking, resourcefulness, and energy. By rapidly converting supply trains to hospital cars for the return trips to Westminster, Haupt was able to evacuate over fifteen thousand wounded and disabled soldiers to the hospitals at York and Harrisburg, Pennsylvania, and to the larger hospitals at Baltimore, Philadelphia, and New York.

Lee had not been that fortunate with his wounded, not having a General Haupt on his staff.

Lee's wounded were evacuated in horse-drawn army wagons and carts over bumpy roads with little or no medical attention. For this reason, if for no other, Meade could offer no excuse for not pursuing Lee and ending the matter. And so Lee was permitted to retire to Orange Court House, south of the Rapidan River, to rest and refurbish his exhausted army unmolested.

In the west, concurrent with the Gettysburg campaign, Grant was planning his campaign against Vicksburg, the Confederacy's "Gibralter of the West." After completing his communications line via the Yazoo River, Grant attacked Vicksburg vigorously in May and June 1863 and tried to carry the Confederate entrenchments by assault. When the attempt failed, Grant settled down to a siege of forty days, having driven General John C. Pemberton back on his main defense line in a three-day running fight. Cut off from communication on all sides, Pemberton prepared for a long siege and hoped for a miracle.

With no food supplies forthcoming the people of Vicksburg fared as badly, if not worse, than Pemberton's army. They dug caves in the clay hillsides and lived on mule meat, rats, and dogs. The daily bombardments from the Union land batteries and gunboats killed many of those civilians foolish enough to venture forth during the regular shellings. Outside Vicksburg Grant tightened his grip on the doomed city, planning the final attack to be staged on July 6. But Lieutenant General John C. Pemberton, his army starved out, asked for surrender terms on July 3, at the same time that Lee, at Gettysburg, was making his last desperate cast with "Pickett's Charge." Vicksburg fell on July 4, after holding out for forty-seven days.

In the Vicksburg campaign the railroads played a minor role (except for Colonel B. H. Grierson's cavalry raid against the Mobile & Ohio Railroad, which wrecked the line in three places—at Columbus, Kentucky, and Okolona and Tupelo, Mississippi; the raiders cut the Vicksburg line west of Meridian and then rode from one end of Mississippi to the other in sixteen days, completely cutting the Vicksburg lines with Louisiana, except for the rail line to Jackson).

The Confederacy was now split in two; Port Hudson, above Baton Rouge, fell to General Nathaniel Prentiss Banks on July 8, and the whole length of the Mississippi River was open.

A View of the Orange & Alexandria Roundhouse and Terminal at Alexandria, Virginia, 1863.

After Gettysburg, Haupt was ordered to Alexandria by Stanton to handle the reconstruction of the line, which had suffered heavy damage during Lee's retreat.

FROM A PHOTOGRAPH BY CAPTAIN A. J. RUSSELL, USMRR, COURTESY NATIONAL ARCHIVES.

Grant's Siege and Battle for Vicksburg, 1863.

Vicksburg, starved out after a siege of forty-seven days, surrendered on July 4, 1863. General John C. Pemberton's capitulation to Grant opened the Mississippi River to Port Hudson and the Gulf.

BY AN UNKNOWN ARTIST, AUTHOR'S COLLECTION.

CHAPTER 9

Sherman: "The Quicker You Build the Railroad..."

OF ALL the far-flung, colorful campaigns of the Civil War, Chattanooga provided the moment in which the railroad and the railroad man really proved themselves. At Chattanooga, the railroad became the significant element in a major campaign action. Both sides originated the idea at the same time, but for different reasons—one for transporting reinforcements for an offensive, the other for transporting troops to repair a blunder and break a siege.

It all came about in September of 1863, in the third year of the war. Grant's forces were near Vicksburg, Bragg's army was facing Rosecrans's Army of the Cumberland at Murfreesboro, while General Joseph E. Johnston's army was still in Mississippi, supposedly in position to reinforce Pemberton at Vicksburg and break the siege.

"I do not believe in luck in war any more than luck in business," Grant once said to John Russell Young, the correspondent who accompanied Grant on his world tour after the war. "Luck is a small matter, and may affect a battle or movement, but not a campaign or a career. . . . there is nothing ideal in war."

Vicksburg had not been a matter of luck with Grant, but a cold, calculated, and carefully planned campaign with its share of hard slugging. If General Rosecrans and the Army of the Cumberland depended on luck at Chattanooga, they got it—and all of it bad.

In many respects Chattanooga was a campaign unlike previous campaigns of equal magnitude and intensity during the conflict. The nature of the terrain fought over was as divergent as the personalities of the officers who directed the contending armies, General William Starke Rosecrans and General Braxton Bragg. Rosecrans was intelligent,

brave, impetuous, disorganized, with flashes of talent; Bragg was irascible, quick-tempered, re-

Lieutenant General Joseph Eggleston Johnston, 1864.

A native Virginian and a West Point graduate, General Johnston was removed as commander of the Army of the Tennessee by Jefferson Davis "for his failure to arrest the advance of the enemy." Although Johnston was never defeated during the war, it was the opinion of many who knew him that Johnston's temperament was not suited to aggressive military action, but his evasive tactics against Sherman were flawless.

FROM A PHOTOGRAPH BY GEORGE COOK,
COURTESY THE VALENTINE MUSEUM, RICHMOND, VA.

Lieutenant General Braxton Bragg, CSA, 1864.

Tall, bearded, and ungainly, Bragg, a West Point graduate and former plantation owner, won a decisive victory over Rosecrans at Chickamauga, but Grant roundly defeated him at Chattanooga. Bragg retreated to Dalton, Georgia, where Davis removed him from command and replaced him by General Joseph E. Johnston.

FROM A PHOTOGRAPH BY GEORGE COOK,
COURTESY THE VALENTINE MUSEUM, RICHMOND, VA.

markably intelligent and protective of his prerogatives, and a brave man.

After Vicksburg capitulated, Grant had urged General Halleck and the government to authorize a movement against Mobile, Alabama, to draw Bragg away from Rosecrans at Murfreesboro. Grant's plan had been heartily approved and he telegraphed Rosecrans to move against Bragg, but Rosecrans delayed, even though Bragg's large and well-equipped army was almost equal to Rosecrans's.

Months passed and still Rosecrans refused to budge. In Washington, Halleck and the administration became tired of waiting and sent Charles A. Dana, assistant secretary of war, to look into the matter of the recalcitrant general. Dana's report on Rosecrans was anything but glowing. "I have never seen a public man possessing talent with less administrative power, less clearness and steadiness

in difficulty, and a greater incapacity than General Rosecrans."

But when Rosecrans finally did move, he did it skillfully, maneuvering Bragg south of the Tennessee River, beyond Chattanooga. "The news that Vicksburg could not hold out over two or three weeks having reached us," wrote Rosecrans,

we began our movements to dislodge Bragg from his entrenched camp on the 24th of June, 1863. It rained for seventeen consecutive days. The roads were so bad that it required four days for Crittenden's troops to march four miles. Yet, on the 4th of July, we had possession of both the enemy's entrenched camps, and by the 7th, Bragg's was in full retreat over the Cumberland Mountains into the Sequatchie Valley, whence he proceeded to Chattanooga, leaving us in full possession of middle Tennessee, and the damaged Nashville & Chattanooga Railway with my headquarters at Winchester, fifty miles from our starting point.

After crossing the Tennessee River, Bragg burned the railroad trestle at Bridgeport, Alabama, but this had not stopped Rosecrans since he had pontoon boats and the pontoniers prepared for such a contingency. An observer noted, speaking of these soldiers, "they unload the pontoons from the wagons, run them into the water, put the scantling from boat to boat, lay down the plank, and thus make a good bridge on which men and horses, and wagons, can cross. They can bridge any stream between this and the Tennessee in an hour, and put a bridge over that in probably three hours."

"If he had stopped and entrenched [at Chattanooga] and made himself strong," wrote General Grant, "all would have been right, and the mistake of not moving earlier partially compensated." But Rosecrans did not stop there. He crossed the Tennessee River, marched due east between two mountain spurs, and wisely placed himself in a position in which he could either move his army down the Chattanooga Valley and push Bragg into the Tennessee River or threaten Bragg's main supply line, the Western & Atlantic Railroad. The next move was now Bragg's, and when he discovered what Rosecrans had done it was too late for him to do anything but evacuate Chattanooga and fall back on Dalton to cover his railroad. In the course of this retreat, Bragg suddenly turned at Chicamauga Creek and attacked Rosecrans with all he had.

The bloody battle at Chicamauga lasted three days. Bragg's sudden offensive in the heavily forested region caught Rosecrans with his units widely scattered. Rosecrans managed to get his units together, but the desperate fighting along a line six miles long through thick woods forced Rosecrans's army to fall back on Chattanooga. Defeated, with heavy losses, they took a position on a narrow plain between Missionary Ridge and the Tennessee River, near where the tracks of the Nashville & Chattanooga Railroad and a wagon road ran around the base of Lookout Mountain "with little room to spare."

Bragg now occupied the heights of Lookout Mountain and Missionary Ridge, in a strong position which extended in a line from the northeast end of Missionary Ridge to Lookout Mountain southwest of the city, in full control of the road, the railroad, the Tennessee River, and Chattanooga itself. With losses of sixteen thousand killed, wounded, and missing, Rosecrans now found himself under siege, in practically the same predicament he had planned for Bragg.

On September 29, Halleck telegraphed Grant to send Rosecrans all the forces he could spare from his Department, suggesting Sherman or McPherson, "those good commanders"—and that Grant himself should go with the troops and supervise the movements personally.

"Rosecrans was in straits," wrote Captain S. H. M. Byers of the Fifth Iowa Volunteers, "and Sherman was called for, and we made the forced march of 400-miles from Memphis to Chattanooga."

In view of the Confederacy's military setbacks, a conference was held in Richmond in August of 1863 between President Davis and Confederate staff officers to decide on a new policy in the prosecution of the war—to change from a defensive to an offensive policy. The time had come to exert a maximum effort in a strategic place if the war were to be won. The final decision at this meeting was to reinforce Bragg's army facing Rosecrans's Army of the Cum-

Ruins of the Nashville & Chattanooga Railroad Bridge at Bridgeport, Alabama, August 1863.

Destroyed by the Confederates in their retreat on Chattanooga, the wrecked railroad bridge over the Tennessee River did not stop the Union Army's advance. Preparations *for such a contingency had already been anticipated, and the pontoon bridge was thrown across the river in record time.*

FROM A PHOTOGRAPH, PROBABLY BY GEORGE N. BARNARD,
AUTHOR'S COLLECTION.

berland since the two opposing armies were more or less evenly matched. Reinforcing Bragg would put the balance of force in his favor and give him the means for an overwhelming victory.

What led to this decision, among other considerations, was the fact that reinforcements could be sent to Bragg at Chattanooga in a few days by railroad via the Lynchburg route, down through the Tennessee Valley by way of the Virginia & Tennessee Railroad, a distance of about five hundred miles through Knoxville and Bristol. General James Longstreet, Lee's "Old Warhorse" and one of the most capable of Confederate commanders, with two divisions of his First Corps and a battalion of artillery, was selected for the railroad expedition. Quartermaster General Lawton was assigned the job of coordinating the rail movement; unfortunately for the Confederacy, he did not have the experience in railroad transportation that General Haupt or Colonel McCallum did.

While preparations were underway to move Longstreet's divisions over the Lynchburg, Knox-

ville and Chattanooga route, word was received that Burnside had captured Knoxville, thereby closing the direct route and creating some additional problems for General Lawton. Since the Knoxville route was out of the question, the only remaining option was to take the long way via Richmond, Wilmington, Augusta, and Atlanta, to Chattanooga. Since there were no east–west rail lines in Confederate military operations, this made the distance to be traveled about a thousand miles.

Moreover, it would now be necessary to make frequent train changes since no less than ten different rail lines would be involved in the transportation. Although he had no authority to operate like the U.S. Military Railroads system by commandeering the railroads for immediate priority in troop movements, Lawton somehow overcame the difficulties. Longstreet's first train pulled out on September 9, 1863, over the brokendown tracks of the Virginia Central Railroad.

When these trains rolled into the Richmond yards carrying Longstreet's seasoned veterans of Gettys-

The Battle of Missionary Ridge, Tennessee, November 23, 1863.

General Grant's assault on Missionary Ridge was something like the storming of a medieval castle stronghold. Grant's advance columns under Thomas drove back the Confederate skirmishers at the base of the mountain, followed by an all-out attack on the heights led by General Sheridan. The

Confederates, cannon barrels deflected, poured shot and shell, bombs, even stones and large rocks, down on their attackers from the heights; but the Union soldiers carried the summit.

FROM AN ORIGINAL DRAWING BY ALFRED R. WAUD,
LIBRARY OF CONGRESS.

Lieutenant General James Longstreet, CSA, 1864.

A classmate of Grant, Halleck, and Thomas at West Point, Longstreet conducted the rail expedition of his First Corps to reinforce Bragg at Chickamauga. An ideal corps commander, Longstreet was Lee's most trusted lieutenant.

FROM A PHOTOGRAPH BY GEORGE COOK, COURTESY THE VALENTINE MUSEUM, RICHMOND, VA.

burg, the entire expedition took on an air of exuberance and gaiety as the men were greeted by enthusiastic crowds. From then on, the rail expedition assumed the atmosphere of a hilarious summer outing; at each stop the troops were cheered by admiring crowds.

"Never before were so many troops moved over such worn-out railways," wrote G. Moxley Sorrel, Longstreet's chief of staff. "None first class from the beginning. Never before were such crazy cars—passenger, baggage, mail, coal, box, platform—all and every sort—wobbling on the jumping strap-iron—used for hauling good soldiers." The cars were jam-packed with troops, talking incessantly, laughing about the congestion inside and outside every car, even on the rooftops. Some soldiers even clung to hand-irons on the sides. When things became too uncomfortable the soldiers, in a spirit of adaptation,

got themselves some axes and chopped away the sides of the cars, leaving only the roof and the uprights and turning each passenger coach into a sightseeing car.

It was in this spirit that Longstreet and his men arrived at Catoosa Platform, a flag stop on the line near Chicamauga, on September 19, 1863, at three o'clock in the afternoon after a ten-day journey—within sound of the heavy firing from the battlefield. Bragg's battle at Chicamauga had already been underway a day, and Longstreet and his veterans arrived in time to turn the tide. Jumping from the train, Longstreet coaxed his horse out of the boxcar in which he had been riding and galloped off to find Bragg's headquarters, followed by two of his staff officers.

Sometime around ten o'clock that night they found Bragg asleep in an ambulance. The battle of

The Battle of Chickamauga, Tennessee, September 18–20, 1863.

The battle was indecisive for two days when Longstreet's columns arrived by train on September 19 in time to turn the tide. In the furious fighting that followed the Union right and center collapsed, but the left, under Thomas, held.

Thomas ordered his men to "aim carefully and make every shot count." Charles Dana wrote: "Chickamauga is as fatal a name in our history as Bull Run."

FROM A DRAWING BY ALFRED R. WAUD, LIBRARY OF CONGRESS.

Chicamauga resumed in all its intensity the next morning, September 20, and five brigades of Longstreet's corps, all that had arrived in time, were marched directly to the field to take part in the desperate engagement. Despite their rundown condition the Southern railroads had done their job, by the end of the day it was all over for Rosecrans. Only the generalship of George H. Thomas, and his corps' stubborn defense saved Rosecrans from losing his entire army, giving him time to withdraw to the defenses near Chattanooga.

A breakdown in communications delayed Grant's receipt of Halleck's telegram "to send all available forces to Memphis . . . along the Memphis & Charleston Railroad to cooperate with Rosecrans" until September 23, three days after the battle had ended with Rosecrans in full retreat on Chattanooga.

On the evening of that same day, Secretary Stanton received an urgent telegram from Assistant Secretary of War Charles A. Dana at Chattanooga. The telegram was dated September 19, and it read:

> No time should be lost in rushing twenty to twenty-five thousand efficient troops to Bridgeport [Alabama]. If such reinforcement can be got there in season, everything is safe and this place is indispensable alike to defense of Tennessee and as a base for future operations in Georgia will remain ours.

On the same day that Dana sent his telegram to Stanton, Longstreet and his two divisions were leaving Virginia by rail for Bragg's support at Chicamauga. Whether Stanton knew about Longstreet's rail expedition through the army's intelligence system in Virginia—and there is every reason to believe that he did—it is reasonable to suppose that he probably borrowed the idea of using the railroad to send reinforcements to Rosecrans.

Thus, when Stanton received Dana's wire, Rosecrans's position was desperate and relief was needed at once. Sherman was already on his way, as well as McPherson. But Bridgeport, Alabama, across the Tennessee River, Rosecrans's supply base, was twenty-six miles away, and under the circumstances getting supplies meant hauling them by wagon train over the mountain north of the Tennessee River and then ferrying them across to Rosecrans.

Rosecrans and the Army of the Cumberland were virtually besieged in the Chattanooga Valley. They had the Tennessee River behind them and Bragg commanding the heights to the east and west, running a strong line across the valley from mountain to mountain.

In response to Dana's telegram, Stanton called an urgent meeting at the War Department, with Halleck, President Lincoln, and the secretaries of state and the treasury, Seward and Chase. Stanton came right to the point, explaining Rosecrans's situation—Sherman was too far away to be of any assistance by marching to Bridgeport to relieve Rosecrans, and Burnside had his hands full trying to hold Knoxville and control eastern Tennessee.

Then Stanton, always a railroad supporter, having once been a railroad attorney, made a startling suggestion. Thirty thousand troops, he said, could be detached from the Army of the Potomac and sent to Chattanooga by rail to break the siege. The entire troop movement, he enthused, could be done in five days. Halleck, who had been wrong in most of his military decisions, was the first to object that it could not be done.

Even President Lincoln, an open-minded man eager for any kind of solution to the problem, had his doubts. "I will bet that if an order is given tonight," he said to Stanton, "the troops could not be got to Washington in five days." What Lincoln meant was that it would take that long to get them from the base in Virginia to Washington in that time, much less get them to Chattanooga.

But President Lincoln underestimated his war secretary. Adamant, and unshaken in his determination to give the idea a try, certain that with good planning the task of moving two fully equipped army corps to Chattanooga, almost a thousand miles away, was possible in the given time, Stanton argued until he won his point.

When it was finally agreed, Stanton wasted no time. For the rest of the night he kept the wires hot sending orders to railroad executives of the U.S. Military Railroads, the Baltimore & Ohio, and the Philadelphia, Wilmington & Baltimore railroads, and other directives to army officers in Virginia. Efficiency was the keynote of the railroad professionals Stanton contacted—Thomas Scott of the Pennsylvania Railroad, Samuel Felton of the Philadelphia, Wilmington & Baltimore, John W. Garrett of the Baltimore & Ohio, and W. P. Smith and Colonel Daniel McCallum of the USMRR system. Their combined knowledge and experience of the various lines involved in the venturesome enterprise would insure the success of the plan.

General Grant had no quarrel with the plan, but he did not agree with their ultimate destination.

Reinforcements for Rosecrans.

Alexandria Va Sept 25. 1863

Reinforcements for Rosecrans, September 25, 1863.

General Hooker's command boarding the USMRR's relief trains at the staging area at Alexandria, Virginia, for the run to Bridgeport, Alabama, to reinforce Rosecrans. William *Marshall Merrick, a photographer the military railroads, captured this scene faithfully in his on-the-spot drawing.*

FROM AN ORIGINAL DRAWING BY WILLIAM MARSHALL MERRICK, SKETCHBOOK III, COURTESY THE NEW YORK PUBLIC LIBRARY.

"Long before my coming into this new field," wrote Grant, "General Halleck had ordered parts of the Eleventh and Twelfth Corps, commanded respectively by Howard, Slocum, Hooker in command of the whole, from the Army of the Potomac, to reinforce Rosecrans. It would have been folly to have sent them to Chattanooga to help eat up the few rations there. They were consequently left on the railroad where supplies could be brought to them. Before my arrival, Thomas ordered their concentration at Bridgeport."

The route of this rail expedition began at Culpeper, Virginia, through Washington, D.C., where Hooker's troop trains would be picked up and carried by the Baltimore & Ohio's Washington branch line to Relay House, near Baltimore City. From there they would be transported over the B & O's main line to Benwood, on the Ohio River, and then ferried across to Bellaire, Ohio. Connecting lines would carry them to Jeffersonville, Indiana, where they would then recross the Ohio River to Louis-

ville, Kentucky. The Louisville & Nashville Railroad would carry them to Nashville and from there the important Nashville & Chattanooga Railroad would carry them over the last leg of the journey, through Stevenson, Alabama, to Bridgeport. When the route and train schedules had been agreed upon, President Lincoln issued a blanket order authorizing General Hooker to take military possession of all the railroads involved in the operations, which insured cooperation of the various companies.

By the night of September 24, Stanton, armed with presidential backing, selected Colonel Daniel McCallum to supervise the entire operation, including all car loadings and transportation from Culpeper, over the U.S. Military Railroads (Orange & Alexandria) to the army's base in Virginia and to Washington, D.C. John W. Garrett of the B & O would handle all train movements from Washington to Jeffersonville, Indiana. Tom Scott would take over from there and be in charge below Louisville.

Orange & Alexandria Yards and Sidings, Outskirts of Alexandria, 1862.

A section of the staging area for General Hooker's thousand-mile rail expedition to reinforce Rosecrans's army at Chat- *tanooga. Strings of USMRR "empties" stand on sidings alongside the O & A main line.*

FROM A PHOTOGRAPH BY CAPTAIN A. J. RUSSELL, USMRR, AUTHOR'S COLLECTION.

OFF TO THE WAR.

A Section of Hooker's Rail Expedition to Chattanooga, September 1863.

A trainload of Hooker's soldiers passes a local station on their expedition to support Rosecrans beseiged at Chat- *tanooga. Thirty trains of twenty cars each made up this spectacular military railroad expedition.*

FROM AN ORIGINAL DRAWING IN PEN AND INK BY WILLIAM TABOR, AUTHOR'S COLLECTION.

Stanton's directives were that McCallum would be in full charge—and no army officers, regardless of rank, were to contradict his orders.

For the rest, the troops were to be ready to board the moment the trains were ready to receive them. Each corps would travel with its own artillery. Cars would carry five days' forage for artillery horses and would join the trains at the Alexandria yards. Each artillery unit was to carry two hundred rounds of ammunition, and soldiers would be supplied with five days' cooked rations, with coffee and sugar to be furnished en route. Each soldier would carry forty rounds of rifle ammunition, and camp equippage would be kept to a bare minimum, without hospital tents. Only enough medical supplies would be carried for immediate use during the trip.

And so, by the afternoon of September 25, two days after Stanton had conceived the idea, the first two trains—made up of fifty-one passenger cars, and four cars carrying field guns—rolled into Washington. The rest of the trains followed behind at five-minute headways.

After the trains had cleared Washington, the efficiency of these railroad men manifested itself even further. When the first trains reached Relay House on the B & O's Washington branch, W. P. Smith wired Colonel McCallum asking that his trains be limited to twenty or twenty-two cars so that their engines would not be overloaded and the running speed reduced climbing the steep grades over the B & O's right-of-way through the mountainous country of western Virginia.

Stanton at the War Department was able to follow the progress of his rail expedition by the telegrams he received on an average of every two hours:

> 9:45 A.M. Three trains of more than sixty cars with more than 3,000 troops have passed Martinsburg in good order.
>
> 11:00 A.M. Twelve trains with 7,000 men have passed Relay, everything working smoothly. Transportation through Ohio all arranged.
>
> 4:00 P.M. First three trains have passed Cumberland.
>
> 6:00 P.M. Arrangements for transfer at Indianapolis and ferriage at Louisville all complete.

By 9:00 P.M. on September 27, it became plain that the plan was working, and very well. Trains carrying more than twelve thousand soldiers, thirty-three cars of artillery, and twenty-one cars of horses and baggage formed a great military support train, moving steadily between Washington, D.C., and Benwood, western Virginia.

Now that the plan was working, Halleck decided to cooperate. In a telegram to General B. F. Kelley, commanding in western Virginia, Halleck informed that officer what was coming his way and ordered him to take all precautions to protect the trains, adding that Kelley was to close all the saloons and drinking establishments in the neighborhood of Benwood.

The remarkable thing about the entire operation was the close cooperation between the army and the railroad men. It was a highly successful, harmonious operation from every standpoint—except one.

The only sour note came from Major General Carl Schurz, a former New York politician who thought a military career would help his political chances when the war was over. Irate that he had been relegated to a "rear position" in a train behind those carrying his own troops, Schurz telegraphed the station agent at Grafton, western Virginia, to hold the Third Division of the Eleventh Corps until its commanding officer arrived. The station agent flatly refused and Schurz was promptly told that the train operation was not to be interrupted by him or anybody else, that only a direct order from the War Department would permit changes in routine.

At this, Schurz lost his temper and wired Stanton at the War Department, furious that a mere station agent could defy a major general of the U.S. Army. Stanton's answer was not long in coming and was painfully explicit, threatening Schurz with arrest and removal from his command altogether if he interfered with the train movements. That settled the matter.

The expedition was an amazing railroad performance, encouraged by the efficiency, experience, and proper authority of both the government and the railroads, guided by professional men. It was this ingenuity and clearheaded management that brought the first contingent of Union troops to Bellaire on the morning of September 27, 1863.

Hooker's pageant of trains now stretched from the Rapidan River to the Ohio carrying more than twenty thousand troops; and all except thirty-three hundred members of the Twelfth Corps were on their way. By noon of September 28, the command moved on Bridgeport, Alabama, and by the fifth day at 3:30 P.M. the first trains passed through Columbus, Ohio. Two hours later, two two-

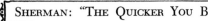

Relay House, on the Baltimore & Ohio Railroad, September 1863.

A contingent of Massachusetts volunteers is ready to board the train. Relay House was the checkpoint for all trains in the expedition. Here W. C. Smith, of the B & O wired McCallum to limit train loadings to twenty cars "so engines *would not be overloaded . . . climbing steep grades through Western Virginia." A very rare photograph from a "View-card."*

From View No. 819, E & H. T. Anthony & Company,
Loaned by John P. Hankey,
Baltimore & Ohio Railroad Museum and Archives.

hundred-car loads of troops had left Bellaire, and W. P. Smith telegraphed Stanton:

> So far not one of thirty trains of 600 cars has been delayed improperly. The only thing we have to regret is that the actual movement exceeds the requisitions by nearly 20% in men and more than 50% in horses.

The only delay in the passage of these trains took place at Jeffersonville, Indiana, where the difference in track gauges made it necessary to detrain and reload the entire force in trains of the Jeffersonville Railroad. At the same time, the five days of cooked rations of the soldiers had already been consumed and presented another temporary problem, but this was taken care of quickly. At Jeffersonville, on the bank of the White River, the Soldiers' Home provided the solution to the food problem. As each contingent was ready to board the Jeffersonville Railroad cars they were marched to the home and fed. Actually only six hours had elapsed during the transfer delay, and on September 29 when the long column passed through Louisville, Kentucky, the leading units were already on the banks of the Tennessee River, ready for action.

The entire operation from conception to conclusion had only taken eleven and a half days to transfer two army corps more than twelve hundred miles over some of the lines which had felt the wrath of enemy raiders. The first fifty miles of the Baltimore & Ohio Railroad had been completely disabled the previous autumn, while the final three hundred miles of the western leg, comprising two railroads, had undergone severe damage at the hands of Generals Morgan and Forrest during the summer of 1862.

But even so, it was all the more remarkable that twenty-five thousand men and their equipment, ten batteries of artillery with their horses, and a hundred cars of baggage, were brought safely to their destination without any mechanical difficulties. In the second section, trains carrying more than a thousand horses and mules, spare artillery, wagons, and equipment for field transportation, also arrived behind the first section without incident. When all these trains had delivered their men and equipment, the engines and cars were returned promptly to their owners and the railroads involved resumed normal operations.

Rosecrans was still under siege and getting discouraged. The only relief possible for him was by expelling the enemy from Missionary Ridge and about Chattanooga.

On or about October 17, Grant met with Secretary Stanton at the Galt House in Louisville, Kentucky, and they spent the day together comparing notes and exchanging news from the various war theaters. Later that evening, while Grant was visiting relatives with his wife, Stanton received another dispatch from Dana at Chattanooga, stating that "unless prevented Rosecrans would retreat." When Grant returned to the hotel, Stanton showed him Dana's wire.

"A retreat at that time would have been a terrible disaster," wrote Grant. "It would not only have been the loss of a most important strategic position to us, but it would have been attended with the loss of all the artillery still left with the Army of the Cumberland. . . ."

Rosecrans received his supplies from the base at Nashville. The railroad was under government control (USMRR) as far as Bridgeport, Alabama, to a point where it crossed to the south of the Tennessee River, but Bragg's position on Lookout and Raccoon mountains commanded the railroad, the wagon roads between Bridgeport and Chattanooga, and the Tennessee River, both north and south. By rail Bridgeport and Chattanooga are twenty-six miles apart, but Rosecrans's situation made it necessary to haul his supplies by wagon road over mountainous country a distance of about sixty miles.

Nearly ten thousand of Rosecrans's horses had already starved, with no horses to draw his artillery and ambulances. His soldiers had been on half rations of bread and few other supplies. Since only food could be transported by wagon, the men were without winter clothing or fuel—the trees had all been cut down.

When Stanton reported the situation to Grant, he immediately ordered Thomas to relieve Rosecrans and told him to "hold Chattanooga at all hazards." Thomas replied promptly: "We will hold the town till we starve."

On the morning of October 20, 1863, Grant and his staff set out for Chattanooga for a personal inspection of the situation facing General Thomas. Grant realized that at Chattanooga Thomas had "two courses open to him—to starve, or surrender and be captured," and he now made plans to break the siege.

Reaching Nashville, they stayed over, "it not being prudent to travel beyond that point at night." While at Nashville, Grant telegraphed Burnside at Knoxville that Sherman's advance had already passed Eastport, Mississippi, and that rations were on their way from St. Louis by boat under a naval escort. He then sent another telegram to Thomas to put a large working party on the roads leading to Bridgeport, from Chattanooga.

On the morning of October 26, Grant and his staff took the train for the front, reaching Stevenson, Alabama, where they stopped over for the night. The rest of the way was made on horseback by way of Waldron's Ridge and Jasper. Heavy rains had made the roads almost impassable, knee-deep in mud in some places and strewn with the debris of broken wagons and the carcasses of the thousands of dead mules and horses that had died of starvation.

On October 23, Grant reached Chattanooga and remained at Thomas's headquarters, later making a personal inspection of the Army of the Cumberland's position. "Chattanooga is on the south bank

Nashville & Chattanooga Railroad Station, Nashville, 1863.

Showing the effects of wartime wear, this station experienced a riot and the exigencies of military occupation. Confederate General A. S. Johnston's failure to seize military control of Nashville's railroads accounted for the Confederacy's enormous loss in stores and ammunition. Cabooses, converted *from boxcars, carried box-like lanterns on the car roofs. Front-end brakemen halted the train if the lamp was not visible. Gothic arches add a distinctive note to the round-house locomotive stalls.*

FROM A PHOTOGRAPH, PROBABLY BY GEORGE N. BARNARD, AUTHOR'S COLLECTION.

of the Tennessee River where the river runs nearly due west," wrote Grant. "Just below the town the river makes a turn to the south and runs to the base of Lookout Mountain, leaving no level ground between the river and the mountain. The Memphis & Charleston Railroad passes this point, where the mountain stands nearly perpendicular. East of Missionary Ridge flows the South Chicamauga River."

General Hooker had brought a full supply of land transportation by train from Virginia, and his animals were in good condition, never having been subjected to working on the roads without forage. Borrowing Hooker's animals, within five days of his arrival at Chattanooga Grant had the roads open to Bridgeport. Between Hooker's teams and the steamers on the river, the Army of the Cumberland was once again back on full rations; the supplies were brought in under the scrutiny of Bragg and his

officers, surprised by the reopening of the supply line. Therefore, Bragg's next move was to close the line.

"Having got the Army of the Cumberland in a comfortable position," wrote General Grant,

I now began to look after the remainder of my command. Burnside was in about as desperate a condition as the Army of the Cumberland had been, only he was not yet besieged. He was a hundred miles from the nearest possible base, Big South Fork of the Cumberland River, and much farther from any railroad we had possession of.

The roads back were over mountains, and all supplies along the line had long since been exhausted. His animals, too, had been starved, and their carcasses, lined the road from Cumberland Gap . . . toward Lexington, Kentucky. East Tennessee furnished supplies of beef, bread and forage, but it did not supply ammunition, clothing, medical supplies, or small rations, such as coffee, sugar, salt, and rice.

Sherman had started for Chattanooga on October 11, traveling from Memphis about three hundred thirty miles through hostile country. As with General Buell, Sherman's greatest handicap had been Halleck, whose antiquated military thinking had compelled Sherman to repair the broken railroad behind him as he marched. There was no possible way Sherman could have protected it, even with his entire army, and he had no possibility of maintaining it after it had been repaired. Among other damage, all the bridges had been blown up by the guerrilla bands that infested the country. Confederate cavalry units, such as they were, still prowled the west, and there were times that Sherman's work was destroyed as soon as it was completed—"though he was only a short distance away."

Knowing the futility of following Halleck's orders to repair the railroad, Grant ordered Sherman to discontinue the work and move on Stevenson, Alabama, with his whole force without delay. Sherman received this order by a messenger, who paddled down the Tennessee River in a canoe and delivered it to him at Iuka.

With his characteristic promptness, Sherman abandoned his railroad repairs and put his army in motion. He crossed the Tennessee River at Eastport and that same day entered Florence, Alabama, at the head of his column, while the rest of his army was still crossing the river at Eastport.

"Sherman's force made an additional army," wrote General Grant, "with cavalry and artillery and trains, all to be supplied by a single-track railroad from Nashville. All indicated pointed also to the probable necessity of supplying Burnside's command, in east Tennessee, 25,000 more, by the same road." Since the single-track line could not possibly handle the traffic that would be necessary to supply both armies daily, Grant decided to rebuild the line, and he ordered Sherman "to halt General Grenville Dodge's command of 8,000 men at Athens, Georgia." Grant directed Dodge to place his troops along the railroad from Decatur to Nashville and rebuild the railroad as quickly as possible.

Grant could not have selected a better man. Dodge was a railroad man, as competent, intelligent, and systematic as General Herman Haupt, and would later handle the affairs of the great Union Pacific. At the outset, Dodge had his work cut out for him. To rebuild the military railroad from Decatur, Georgia, to Nashville, Tennessee,

General Ulysses S. Grant, USA, 1864.
Commander of all the Union forces, east and west, Grant ordered General Grenville Dodge and his eight thousand men to rebuild the military railroad between Nashville, Tennessee and Decatur, Georgia, which had been badly damaged.
FROM A PHOTOGRAPH BY MATHEW BRADY, AUTHOR'S COLLECTION.

was an almost hopeless assignment. It ran over very rough country, broken by countless waterways and streams, many of them wider than the ordinary stream or brook. In many parts of the right-of-way, the tracks ran around mountains with valleys far below the roadbed. Every bridge had been destroyed by the Confederates and the rails had been taken up and twisted out of shape, making them useless. Locomotives and cars not carried off had been totally destroyed, as had every culvert and crossing from Nashville to Stevenson, Alabama, where the Memphis & Charleston and Nashville & Chattanooga railroads met. But rebuilding this road would give Grant's forces two railroads to carry supplies as far as Bridgeport, where the Tennessee River would supplement rails.

A capable and resourceful soldier and railroad builder, General Dodge set to work. To begin with he had no tools other than pioneer axes, picks, and spades. But the first thing he did was to entrench his men at various places along the line to protect them from the raiding parties sure to appear as soon as the word had been passed that the railroad was being repaired.

Since he had no base of supplies, Dodge's second

Major General Grenville Mellen Dodge, USA.

Dodge, like his counterpart General Haupt, was a brilliant railroad man. In forty days Dodge rebuilt 182 miles of track and 182 bridges, a bridge for every mile, and opened Sherman's supplementary rail supply line. Later, as chief engineer of the Union Pacific, Dodge built nine thousand miles of railroad in his lifetime.

FROM A PHOTOGRAPH BY MATHEW BRADY, NATIONAL ARCHIVES.

consideration was collecting grain, beef cattle, and any other food that could be found. Professional millers were detailed from the ranks to operate the grist mills along the line of the army. When it was found that some of these mills were too far away from the army's protection, they were dismantled and reassembled near the railroad.

Wherever a blacksmith's foundry was found it was moved to the line of the railroad, along with its iron and steel, and blacksmiths were recruited from the ranks to operate it and make the necessary specialized tools for railroad and bridge construction. Axemen were detailed to cut timber for the bridges, while others were detailed to cut wood for the locomotives when the road was ready for them.

The army provided the skilled car builders and mechanics, who set to work repairing the locomotives and cars. All this work was going on at once, but even so there were still not enough rails, except those in use at the moment, or cars and engines. To

supply these, Grant ordered that eight of the ten engineers General McPherson had at Vicksburg be sent to Nashville, along with all the cars that could be spared, except ten; in addition, he ordered that all the cars, locomotives, and rails from all the railroads in the region, except those of the Memphis & Charleston, be sent to Nashville. Grant then ordered all the troops in west Tennessee to points along the river and the Memphis & Charleston route.

The military manager of railroads, Daniel McCallum, was also directed to furnish more rolling stock and locomotives, along with bridging materials. The energetic General Dodge had the job finished in forty days, an enormous feat in view of the fact that he had to build 182 bridges, many over deep chasms, on a railroad 182 miles in length—one bridge for every mile of track repaired.

Grant's plan worked, and in November of 1863, following the hard-fought battles of Missionary Ridge and Chattanooga, the Confederate army fell back into Georgia. Grant and Sherman cleared the Tennessee and drove a deep wedge into the heart of the Confederacy.

The behind-the-front buildup for the war's final campaigns, east and west, was tremendous. All the federal armies were consolidated into three major striking forces under Grant, Sherman, and Thomas. At Nashville alone there were enough supplies for Sherman's forces to feed two hundred thousand men for four months, and enough grain and forage for his cavalry and draft animals to feed fifty thousand for a year.

Nor were the railroads neglected. The Nashville & Chattanooga, 151 miles long, "was the great main line," wrote Colonel Daniel McCallum, "over which passed all the supplies for the armies of the Cumberland, the Ohio and the Tennessee, through all the campaigns which terminated with the occupation of Atlanta.

Over this single line of railroad the provisions, clothing, and camp equippage for the men, forage for the animals, arms, ammunition, and ordnance stores, reinforcements, and all the varied miscellaneous supplies required for a great army in an active campaign. By it were returned the sick and wounded soldiers, captured prisoners.

About 115 miles of track were re-laid with new iron, cross-ties and ballast from February, 1864 to the close of the war. Sidings were put in at intervals . . . either miles apart, each capable of holding five to eight long freight trains . . . telegraph stations established at most of them. In all nineteen

Raccoon Gorge Bridge Near Chattanooga, Tennessee, 1863.

Colonel Herman Haupt's Potomac Creek Bridge in Virginia served as a model for the Raccoon Gorge railroad bridge and its larger counterpart, E. C. Smeed's trestle over the Chattahoochie River in Gergia, Smeed was Haupt's assistant in 1862.

FROM A PHOTOGRAPH, PROBABLY BY GEORGE N. BARNARD, AUTHOR'S COLLECTION.

miles of new sidings were added to this road, and forty-five new water tanks were erected. During the spring and summer of 1864, a few occasional guerrilla raids were made upon it, but they caused little damage or detention to transportation.

In March 1864, the Western & Atlantic Railroad, Sherman's main supply line into Georgia, 136 miles long, had been opened to Ringgold, twenty-one miles from Chattanooga, and kept pace with the movements of Sherman's army in its advance on Atlanta.

Sherman began his advance into Georgia on May 4, 1864, at the head of an army numbering 98,789 men and 254 guns, with a determination "to make Georgia howl." His railroad men were Adna B. Anderson, E. C. Smeed, and W. W. Wright, all of whom had served under Herman Haupt and all with distinguished service records. Colonel Daniel McCallum was in overall charge of the entire U.S. Military Railroads operations in Sherman's campaign.

The big problem, however, was the delivery of supplies over the single line of railroad when Sherman's advance got underway, and keeping the Confederate raiders and guerrillas away from it. To insure its safety, a series of blockhouses and small forts was established at stategic points and the military guard strongly reinforced.

Sherman and his army reached Cassville to find that Johnston had fallen back to Allatoona Mountain and fortified it, believing that Sherman would attack and dash himself to pieces against his

Allatoona Pass, Georgia, on the Western & Atlantic Railroad, 1864.

The main line of the W & A Railroad as it looked at the time of Sherman's advance into Georgia in 1864.

PHOTOGRAPH PROBABLY BY GEORGE N. BARNARD, USMRR,
AUTHOR'S COLLECTION.

Allatoona Mountain, Georgia, 1864.

General Johnston fortified this mountain (on left) and waited for General Sherman to attack him. But Sherman, unwilling to waste his soldiers in a frontal assault, maneuvered Johns- *ton out of his stronghold by threatening his rail supply line behind him.*

FROM A PHOTOGRAPH BY GEORGE N. BARNARD,
AUTHOR'S COLLECTION.

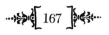

Military Railroad Bridge over the Chattahoochie River, Georgia.

Regarded by General Sherman as the "most important single structure, 780 feet long and 92 feet high, to the success of his campaign," the amazing bridge was built by E. C. *Smeed, an engineer under Herman Haupt in 1862. General Dodge supervised the work. Smeed built the Chattahoochie Bridge in four and a half days.*

entrenchments. But Sherman was too wily for that. Instead, he began a series of flanking moves which compelled Johnston to evacuate his strongholds and fall back to protect his railroad supply line.

At New Hope Church and Resaca, Sherman met the Confederate army head-on, which precipitated a week of ferocious fighting in which Johnston was again compelled to fall back to prearranged fortifications on Kenesaw, Pine, and Lost mountains, eight miles north of Marietta.

The battle of Kenesaw Mountain was a bloody affair, and Sherman admitted that his assault "inflicted comparatively little loss to the enemy, who lay behind his well-formed breast-works. Fail-

ure as it was, and for which I assume the entire responsibility, I yet claim it produced good fruits, as it demonstrated to General Johnston that I would assault and that boldly." Wrote a Confederate, "In three-fourths of an hour the attack was over and the Federals were gone, leaving large numbers of their dead lying at the bottom of the hill."

Sherman now resorted to his flanking tactics once again, and threw his forces across the Western & Atlantic Railroad at Big Shanty, where two years before the *General* had started on its great locomotive race. Johnston retreated across the Chattahoochie River, and on July 5, Sherman came in sight of Atlanta.

FROM A PHOTOGRAPH BY GEORGE N. BARNARD, NATIONAL ARCHIVES.

Sherman now ordered W. W. Wright and the U.S. Military Railroad Construction Corps to reopen the supply line and to reconstruct the Chattahoochie Bridge, "the most important single structure, 780 feet long and 92 feet high." To solve the engineering problems involved in building a bridge similar to Haupt's "bean and cornstalk" bridge over Potomac Creek in Virginia, E. C. Smeed, the engineer who had worked under Haupt, was put to work. Using the original stone piers, which the Confederates had failed to destroy, with timber cut from the woods nearby and plenty of tools and materials, Smeed had the enormous bridge built in four and a half days. Haupt, his former mentor, applauded, calling it "the greatest feat of the kind that the world has ever seen." In a few days supply

trains from Nashville were rolling over the incredible structure and into Sherman's camps every day.

The Western & Atlantic Railroad, "while occupied as a military road," wrote Colonel McCallum, "was more infested by guerrillas than any other during the war. Every device possible to apply was used to throw trains from the track, and though occasionally successful, the preparations to guard against such attempts was so complete that few of them caused loss of life or more than a few hours' detention."

When Sherman's siege of Atlanta began, General Joe Johnston was replaced by John Bell Hood. Hood, a fighter who had lost an arm and a leg in the war, and who had to be strapped to a horse, planned a massive retaliation.

The change in Southern generals did not displease Sherman, for he held a wholesome respect for his former antagonist, whom he regarded as one of the country's great soldiers. Facing Johnston, Sherman knew he had to watch his step. But Sherman knew that young Hood, an impetuous, brave man, would not stay in his entrenchments and would look for an opportunity to fight—and this was precisely what Sherman wanted him to do. The battles were fought and Hood lost; Atlanta fell to Sherman in September. (Later, Sherman had a few ideas of his own, and the march to Savannah was one of them.)

In retrospect, Sherman's campaign for Atlanta was a remarkable undertaking, and the military railroad played an important role in it. Moreover, Sherman's railroad construction corps had been the despair of the Confederate raiders, whose job it was to cut Sherman's railroad behind him. To them, the prowess of the railroad men at rebuilding the damage so quickly was nothing short of miraculous. Why march for miles to put a section of railroad out of commission only to have it rebuilt in record time? Even the rank and file of the Confederate army joked about it. When General Joseph Wheeler, Johnston's cavalry commander dynamited the railroad tunnel at Dalton, Georgia, a rebel soldier thought it was a waste of time. When he was told about the dynamiting of the tunnel by a friend, he made the remark, "Oh, hell, didn't you know that Sherman carries a duplicate tunnel?"

Sherman's men loved him and were always in awe of his sagacity, but they sometimes felt the sting of his tongue. When Sherman's railroad had been temporarily cut behind him and the supply trains were delayed, there was some grumbling

Major General William Tecumseh Sherman, USA.

Sherman's campaign in Georgia was a remarkable undertaking. His USMRR Construction Corps' extraordinary ability to rebuild wrecked railroads in record time became the despair of the Confederate generals. In the course of the campaign, when supply trains could not get through because of a break, Sherman told his men, "The quicker you build the railroad, the quicker you'll get something to eat!"

FROM A PHOTOGRAPH BY MATHEW BRADY, AUTHOR'S COLLECTION.

Lieutenant General John Bell Hood, CSA, 1864.

A former lieutenant in the U.S. Second Cavalry, Hood led the "Texas Brigade" in the first two years of the war. He lost a leg at Chickamauga, but recovered in time to replace Johnston before Atlanta. Hood directed the battle of Atlanta "strapped to a horse," but lost the battle to Sherman's superior forces.

FROM A PHOTOGRAPH BY GEORGE COOK, COURTESY THE VALENTINE MUSEUM, RICHMOND, VA.

from his hungry men. "The quicker you build the railroad," he told them, "the quicker you'll get something to eat!"

General Sherman was lavish in his praise of the railroad men who had kept his army supplied under the most trying circumstances. "The Atlanta campaign would have surely been impossible," he wrote, "without the use of the railroad from Louisville to Nashville—from one hundred and eighty-five miles—and from Nashville to Chattanooga—one hundred and fifty miles—and from Chattanooga to Atlanta—one hundred and thirty-seven miles—Every

mile of this single track was so delicate that one man could in a minute have broken or removed a rail!"

Early in October of 1864, General Hood executed a surprise move around Sherman's army and attacked the railroad at several locations in his rear. Hood destroyed thirty-five miles of track and 455 linear feet of bridgework. But it was a useless move, since the damage was repaired thirteen days after Hood left it and trains again ran over its entire length.

The Battle for Atlanta, 1863–1864.

This furious battle, fought with desperation on both sides, was an enormous military engagement. Sherman's superior numbers and equipment were the deciding factors when Hood tried to break out of Sherman's encirclement. Hood was defeated with heavy losses and soon after Sherman occupied Atlanta, wrecking all the railroads and military facilities left to the Confederacy. Sherman then moved on to Savannah and the sea.

FROM AN ORIGINAL DRAWING BY ALFRED R. WAUD,
AUTHOR'S COLLECTION.

The Men Who Followed Sherman, Murfreesboro, Tennessee, 1864.

Of the veterans of Stone's River, Sherman had this to say: "As to the rank and file, they seemed so full of confidence in themselves . . . whether to build bridges or tear up a railroad, they did it with alacrity."

FROM A PHOTOGRAPH, PROBABLY BY CAPTAIN A. J. RUSSELL, USMRR, AUTHOR'S COLLECTION.

CHAPTER 10

"Like a Fly Crawling over a Corrugated Washboard"

THE YEAR 1864 was to be momentous. Shortly before the opening of General Ulysses S. Grant's spring campaign in Virginia, the U.S. Military Railroads underwent some operational changes consistent with the rapidly shifting military emphasis, according to Colonel Daniel C. McCallum's report. The first U.S. Military Railroad to be abandoned by the army command, since it "ceased to bear any important part" in the campaign, was the Alexandria, Loudon & Hampshire Railroad. And as the campaign developed, other changes in operations would follow.

That year saw some of the bloodiest, most furious military actions ever witnessed. Grant had taken command of all the Union armies, and personal command of the Army of the Potomac, with the conviction that he would fight Lee on the line of the Rapidan River "if it took all summer."

On May 4, 1864, General Grant and the Army of the Potomac, one hundred twenty thousand strong, crossed the Rapidan River into the Wilderness of Spottsylvania, and by midnight, to all intents and purposes, had vanished into thin air.

And while Grant's army fought its way through the thickets and swamps President Lincoln and members of the War Department, having received no word from Grant by May 6, had grave concern for the nation's new commander. The only word they had received as to Grant's progress and condition came from Henry Wing, a *New York Tribune* correspondent who had reached Union Mills on the Orange & Alexandria Railroad. Wing had told an army telegrapher that "everything is pushing along favorably." Otherwise all was silent. Eager to learn what had happened to Grant and his army, Secretary of War Stanton telegraphed Wing that unless he released his information to the War Department he would be subject to arrest as a spy.

Another, more temperate, wire was then sent to the reporter, asking if he would be willing to tell the president in person where Grant's army was. The reporter's reply was conditional. Wing said he would tell the president everything he knew if he would be permitted to transmit a one-hundred-word dispatch to his paper, the *New York Tribune*. President Lincoln accepted Wing's offer, and also agreed that Wing's dispatch could run over a hundred words if necessary. The president then made arrangements with the *New York Tribune* to share the reporter's story with the Associated Press. Mr. Lincoln then placed a military locomotive at the disposal of the reporter, who traveled to Washington for the meeting with President Lincoln at 2 A.M. Wing's interview with Lincoln was short. He informed the president that Grant had given the order for an all-out dawn offensive against the enemy, and said that General Grant had told him: "If you see the president, see him alone and tell him that General Grant says there will be no turning back."

Grant's battle of the Wilderness was a blazing holocaust of forty-eight hours of some of the most sanguinary fighting of the entire war. When it had ended, fourteen thousand men were listed as killed or missing in action. "The battle of the Wilderness," wrote General Grant, "was renewed by us at 5 o'clock on the morning of May 6th, and continued with unabated fury until darkness set in, each army holding substantially the same positions that they had on the evening of the 5th. After dark the enemy made a feeble attempt to turn our right flank, capturing several hundred prisoners and creating considerable confusion, but the promptness of General Sedgewick . . . soon reformed it and restored order. . . ."

Two days later, on May 7, seeing that Lee was

Culpeper, Virginia, Site of the Army of the Potomac's Base Camps.

Culpeper, Virginia, was the little town where the Army of the Potomac prepared for the last campaigns of the war. Grant marched out of this camp, crossed the Rapidan River unopposed, and entered the "Wilderness" to bring a series of battles unsurpassed for ferocity. Although heavily dam- *aged from Manassas Junction to Brandy Station, the Orange & Alexandria served this base from November 16, 1863, to May 4, 1864, when the road was abandoned from Burkes Station, fourteen miles from Alexandria.*

FROM A PHOTOGRAPH BY MATHEW BRADY, AUTHOR'S COLLECTION.

Culpeper, Virginia, Site of the Army of the Potomac's Base Camps.

Grant opened his campaign in the swamps and thickets of the Virginia wilderness, a flaming furnace of forty-eight hours after which fourteen thousand men failed to report for roll call. "If you see the president," Grant told Henry *Wing, a New York Tribune reporter, "see him alone and tell him that General Grant says there will be no turning back."*

FROM A PAINTING BY WINSLOW HOMER, COURTESY ROBERT C. VOSE GALLERIES, BOSTON.

Where Grant Crossed the North Anna, June 1864.

In a third attempt to get his army between Lee and Richmond, Grant crossed the North Anna and met Lee in *another bloody battle at Cold Harbor.*

FROM A PHOTOGRAPH BY MATHEW BRADY, AUTHOR'S COLLECTION.

determined to wait for him behind entrenchments, Grant made a rapid "shift to the left" movement to Spottsylvania Courthouse with the Fifth Corps, to get between Lee and Richmond. Lee divined Grant's strategem and General Richard Anderson's division reached Spottsylvania first, precipitating a battle which lasted three days.

The construction corps, which had first been organized by General Haupt in 1861 and 1862, and which now numbered "in the east and west, nearly 10,000," consisting of skilled workmen in railroad building and repair, directed by competent engineers, and furnished with materials, tools, and mechanized equipment, began the repair of the Aquia Creek & Fredericksburg Railroad. The work started on May 9, 1864, the crews opening the line to Falmouth, a distance of fourteen miles, in a record two days. This was the same line that General Haupt had first rebuilt after it had been destroyed by the Confederates in 1861–62. The Potomac Creek Bridge, seven miles from Aquia Creek, rebuilt by Haupt and unnecessarily

destroyed by General Burnside in 1862, the new crews completed in forty hours, using the same methods Haupt had used two years before.

Grant's campaign now increased in intensity as the Army of the Potomac advanced to Cold Harbor, using the Aquia Creek Railroad for the removal of wounded from the battles of Spottsylvania, and later Cold Harbor, operating until May 22, when it was largely abandoned, only occasionally being used as a military supply line.

The remarkable thing was that all the innovations and methods of railroad reconstruction and military use that General Haupt had introduced two years before were now operating with precision. Even the generals had learned the use of railroads in warfare, especially when a man like Grant was directing them; and there was no doubt as to who was the commander-in-chief.

On May 29 and 30, the two opposing armies clashed at Cold Harbor, where twenty-two hundred men were killed in the first twenty minutes of action. Even Grant said that Cold Harbor "was the

The Battle of Spottsylvania Courthouse, May 8, 1864.

Almost unsurpassed for its ferocity and killing, Spottsylvania was the result of Grant's masterly maneuver of slipping around Lee's army and cutting it off from Richmond by getting between it and the Confederate capital. Lee divined the move and won the race to Spottsylvania, precipitating ten days of almost continuous fighting and slaughter.

FROM A PAINTING BY DE THULSTRUP, AUTHOR'S COLLECTION.

only general attack made from the Rapidan to the James which did not inflict upon the enemy losses to compensate for our own losses. . . ."

On or about the first of June, the U.S. Military Railroads opened the Richmond & York River Railroad from White House Landing on the Pamunkey to Despatch Station, a distance of fourteen miles. The USMRR operated the line until June 10, when General Grant ordered the line abandoned and the tracks, materials, and equipment removed to Alexandria. To equip the Aquia Creek and York River railroads, rolling stock was transported from Alexandria on special barges equipped with tracks, to Aquia Station where it was used until it was no longer needed. And when the road was abandoned, the cars and locomotives and other equipment were removed to Alexandria "in the same manner without loss or injury."

Executing a skillful maneuver, Grant now brought the Army of the Potomac to the south bank of the James River in an effort to capture Petersburg and the Petersburg & Richmond Railroad, and thereby cut Lee's Richmond supply artery. As Grant set his sights on Petersburg, Lee determined with equal tenacity to defend it to the last ditch. Both men knew full well that if Petersburg fell, Richmond, only twenty miles away, would fall with it. Thus began almost a year of trench warfare, both armies constructing a vast network of trenches and redoubts, forts, and salients, which ran for almost twenty miles parallel to each other, encircling the city of Petersburg.

Grant established his base at City Point on the James River, eastern terminal of the South Side Railroad, the Confederate railroad which Grant now used to a point where it reached his army and where the City Point Railroad was hastily constructed to meet it.

The City Point & Petersburg Railroad, its full name, was an unusual military railroad which ran parallel to Grant's entrenched lines before Petersburg, touching at the camps, forts, and redoubts, from one end of Grant's line to the other.

Lieutenant Colonel Horace Porter, a former railroad executive and a graduate of Harvard University and West Point, who was awarded the Con-

The Soldiers' Winter Quarters at Grant's City Point Base, 1864.

Situated on high ground above the tracks of the City Point Railroad, the rank and file of the Army of the Potomac spent *their off time in these log and canvas huts. At the left of the picture soldiers are hanging up their wash.*

FROM A PHOTOGRAPH BY CAPTAIN A. J. RUSSELL, USMRR, AUTHOR'S COLLECTION.

gressional Medal of Honor for bravery at the Battle of Chicamauga, was Grant's twenty-eight-year-old aide-de-camp. An acute observer and delightful writer, Colonel Porter described Grant's City Point Railroad with humor and grudging affection:

The military railroad connecting headquarters with the camps south of Petersburg was about thirteen miles long, or would have been if it had been constructed on a horizontal plane; but as the portion of it built by the army was a surface road, up hill and down dale, if the rise and fall had been counted in, its length would have defied all ordinary means of measurement. Its undulations were so striking that a train moving along it looked in the distance like a fly crawling along a corrugated washboard.

When Grant's investment of Petersburg began at the close of June 1864, the U.S. Military Railroads operated the line as far as Pitkin Station, eight miles from Grant's base and headquarters at City Point. A month later the line was extended to eighteen miles.

For the first two years of the war the use of railroads for military operations was in the swaddling stage. General Haupt had performed miracles of bridge building, track laying, and military train movements against the almost insurmountable obstacle of enemy actions which destroyed his handiwork and military and political stupidities which, to the detriment of the Union cause, caused more problems for U.S. Military Railroad function-

U.S. Military Railroads Construction Corps at City Point, 1864.

Amid the Sibley tents lining both sides of the tracks, soldiers of the USMRR construction crews try to make things "homey" by covering their mess tents with pine boughs for shade. A lone track worker shovels ballast. In the background is the USMRR locomotive General Dix, *a Baldwin built in 1862 with sixty-inch drivers and sixteen- by twenty-four-inch cylinders. The locomotive on the right is believed to be No. 92,* General Sherman, (*USMRR Northern Light*).

FROM A PHOTOGRAPH, PROBABLY BY CAPTAIN A. J. RUSSELL, USMRR, AUTHOR'S COLLECTION.

Troop Staging Area at City Point, Virginia, 1864.

U.S. Military Railroads locomotive No. 162 stands with steam up in the staging area at the Army of the Potomac base headquarters. A regiment stands in the background. No. 162 was built by Baldwin in 1862, with sixteen- by twenty-two-inch cylinders and sixty-inch drivers. The wheel pants over drivers are similar to USMRR locomotive No. 156, another Baldwin.

FROM A PHOTOGRAPH BY CAPTAIN A. J. RUSSELL, USMRR, 1864, AUTHOR'S COLLECTION.

Busy Yards and Roundhouse of the City Point Railroad, 1864.

Unglamorous yard locomotives, workhorses of the military railroad, shunt flatcars loaded with track ballast and move a freight train headed for the lines before Petersburg. The third engine has just dropped "empties" at the wharf.

FROM A PHOTOGRAPH, PROBABLY BY CAPTAIN A. J. RUSSELL, USMRR, AUTHOR'S COLLECTION.

President Lincoln's Private Car at City Point, 1864.

Typical of the open-end coaches of the Civil War period, this passenger car differed in one respect—it was reputed to have bulletproof lead sides. Apparently, it was only used a few times, once when President Lincoln visited Grant's headquarters, and later to carry General Grant and his staff to the Petersburg front. The same train also carried their horses.

FROM A PHOTOGRAPH BY MATHEW BRADY, AUTHOR'S COLLECTION.

Men of the U.S. Military Railroads Construction Corps, 1864.

The work crew waits for a train at a way station, probably Humphrey's, on the City Point Railroad. The photographic wagon stands on the right.

FROM A PHOTOGRAPH BY CAPTAIN A. J. RUSSELL, USMRR, AUTHOR'S COLLECTION.

USMRR Construction Corps, City Point R.R., 1864.

Taking time out from their work on the trestles, the construction corps constantly checked the trestles for damage and weakness. Supporting locomotives weighing from fifty-six to sixty thousand pounds required substantial support. Although the trestles looked rickety, they were nevertheless quite strong. Upright head frames (prefabricated) were made of six-by-ten-inch logs. Cross members were usually the same size. Parallel timbers, supporting the crossties and rails, measured ten by ten inches. Oddly enough, crossties were only three inches thick by six inches wide. The gauge was the standard four feet, eight and one half inches.

FROM A PHOTOGRAPH BY CAPTAIN A. J. RUSSELL, USMRR, AUTHOR'S COLLECTION.

The Long, Long Trestle to the Petersburg Front, 1864.

Receding into the distance, the City Point Railroad right-of-way was dotted with trestles of varying lengths, bridging dry streambeds, gullys, creeks, and uneven terrain. This is one of the longer ones. Since bulldozers were not available it was quicker to trestle a gully than grade, and the surrounding woods supplied the timber.

FROM A PHOTOGRAPH BY CAPTAIN A. J. RUSSELL, USMRR, AUTHOR'S COLLECTION.

One of the Short Trestles on the City Point Railroad, 1864.

Looking as if it might collapse at any given moment, this "scratch-built" trestle could support sixty-thousand-pound locomotive, providing it crossed at about ten miles per hour.

There is no record of any of these military railroad trestles collapsing under normal operating conditions—other than damage by the enemy.

FROM A PHOTOGRAPH BY CAPTAIN A. J. RUSSELL, USMRR,
AUTHOR'S COLLECTION.

Where the City Point Tracks and Trestles Led in 1864.

The City Point Railroad kept these frontline combat troops well supplied and fed during the year-long siege of Peters-

burg. The line also transported the wounded and disabled from the field hospital to the base hospital at City Point.

FROM A PHOTOGRAPH BY CAPTAIN A. J. RUSSELL, USMRR,
AUTHOR'S COLLECTION.

ing than any Confederate action ever could. But in 1864, with the coming of Grant, matters took a turn for the better. Two years of learning how to operate the railroads under wartime dangers and conditions gave the U.S. Military Railroads an advantage over any like operation the Confederate Army command could muster. Haupt had taught them well, and in the final years of the conflict exceptional feats in military railroad operation became commonplace, everyday functions. This railroad construction efficiency did not go unnoticed by the Confederate soldiers ordered to destroy a bridge, since there was no point in it—the Yankees could build them faster than they could burn them down.

Trains of the City Point & Petersburg Railroad transported enough military provisions and supplies to feed and equip more than one hundred thousand men daily. Food, forage for horses and draft animals, military hardware and cannon, ammunition, and medical supplies for the field hospitals were distributed to the various camps, forts, and redoubts along the twenty-mile trench line at regular intervals. Once the cars were unloaded, they were immediately prepared for the removal of the wounded and disabled soldiers from the field hospitals to the larger City Point base hospital. This military railroad efficiency was due in no small measure to the direct thinking and systematic decision-making of one, clear-headed, quiet man—Grant—who had no patience with inefficiency or incompetence. For example, among other things the record shows that the moment an arterial railway was no longer important to a campaign, Grant ordered it abandoned, and its equipment, locomotives, cars, and rails transferred to those military railroads needing that equipment. Grant's orders were peremptory, and in the long run this saved the federal government millions of dollars in expensive railroad equipment that would otherwise have stood on sidings unused for long periods of time, if at all.

The long stalemate in the trenches before Petersburg was underscored by many actions in various sectors of the line, determined assaults designed for a breakthrough, and the strangulation of the Confederate Army by destruction of the railroads that kept it supplied and fed.

Ever since the investment of Petersburg, both sides appreciated the importance of the Weldon and South Side railroads. In June, the Virginia Central Railroad remained partially operative, despite the extensive damage done it by Sheridan at Beaver Dam Station and by Grant's advance to the North Anna, where the Union right hammered the Con-

federates unmercifully. Sheridan had started for Richmond on May 9, and had reached Beaver Dam Station on the tenth, destroying two trains that just happened to be there with a large amount of food rations and medical supplies for Lee's army. Sheridan then tore up the track and telegraph lines for several miles in both directions.

In June, with Sheridan moving into the Shenandoah Valley, Lee had to defend the Virginia Central, his main rail connection with his food supply, at all costs, so Lee sent Major General Wade Hampton's cavalry to protect it. Lee also dispatched General Jubal A. Early to the Shenandoah Valley to threaten Washington by his presence, and to rid the valley of Sheridan's depredations. After Early ran head-on into Sheridan's forces at Winchester and was defeated, Sheridan laid waste to the valley to such an extent that "a crow flying over it couldn't find enough food to feed on."

Sheridan returned to White House, the terminal of the York River Railroad and a large Union supply depot, on June 19 in time to break up an attempt to wreck the depot, after which he moved to the James River. After some heavy fighting, he crossed the river near Fort Powhatan on June 25 and rejoined the Army of the Potomac.

During the course of his raid against the Virginia Central, Sheridan sent a detachment to damage the Richmond, Fredericksburg & Potomac Railroad, tearing up track and pulling down telegraph lines. In so doing, he came within six miles of Richmond, where he ran into Jeb Stuart's cavalry, which had made a long, circling ride around Sheridan's force to head it off. A furious cavalry fight took place at Yellow Tavern, in which Stuart took a bullet in the abdomen (from an unknown Union trooper, it is said), and fell off his horse mortally wounded.

As the war for the railroads in Virginia continued, on June 22, Major General James Harrison Wilson and his cavalry division of the Army of the Potomac, and Major General A. W. Kautz's division of cavalry of the Army of the James, set out together to move against the Confederate railroads south of Richmond. Under orders from General Meade, Wilson started for the Weldon and South Side railroads "to destroy the lines until driven from it by attacks of the enemy as you can no longer resist."

Wilson carried out his part of the assignment to the letter, his cavalry preceded by Kautz's cavalry division from Prince George's Court House to the Weldon Railroad at Reams's Station and "thence via Dinwiddie Court House, to a point on the South Side Railroad, fourteen miles from Petersburg."

Major General Philip Henry Sheridan and Staff, 1864.

Sheridan, Grant's highly competent cavalry commander, brought General Jubal Early to battle at Cedar Creek, or Winchester, in the Shenandoah Valley. A railroad raider of exceptional talent, Sheridan destroyed the Virginia Central Railroad and devastated the valley "so a crow flying over it couldn't find enough to feed on." (Left to right, standing: Generals H. E. Davis, Sheridan, Alfred Torbert. Seated: Generals David McMaxy Gregg, Wesley Merritt, James Harrison Wilson.)

FROM A PHOTOGRAPH BY MATHEW BRADY, AUTHOR'S COLLECTION.

Then Fitzhugh Lee's Confederate cavalry attacked Wilson's leading division under Kautz, but did not interrupt the march of Wilson's own division, under MacIntosh. Meanwhile, Wilson, despite a loss of seventy-five men, continued on to destroy the South Side Railroad. "At Burkeville," wrote General Orlando Willcox, "on the 26th June, Kautz inflicted great damage. Wilson found the bridge over the Staunton River in the enemy's possession and impassable. He [Wilson] then turned eastward, and moved on Stony Creek Station on the Weldon Railroad. Here he had a sharp fight, and learned from the prisoners, that in addition to a small infantry garrison, Hampton had just returned from Trevillian Station and was in his front!"

This was bad news for Wilson, who withdrew during the night of June 26 and headed for Reams's Station, where he had good reason to believe he would find Meade's infantry. On the way, he was mauled severely.

Meanwhile, Kautz, reaching Reams's Station with Wilson's advance troopers, found the enemy infantry in possession of the station. Thus, when Wilson came up he found himself surrounded. Destroying his wagons and caissons, Wilson tried to retire via the Double Bridges over the Nottoway River, but was forced to abandon all his artillery. Then his troopers stampeded. Kautz managed to return with "a fragment of his command by one route. Wilson, with all the troopers he could rally, by another." Finally, on July 2, Wilson and what remained of his command rejoined the Cavalry Corps of the Army of the Potomac at Lighthouse Point.

Even though Wilson had been defeated, he had accomplished his mission. In ten days he had marched three hundred miles and destroyed sixty miles of railroad and much valuable rolling stock—all at the price of the loss of a thousand men and sixteen guns in the raid. But Grant understood: "The damage inflicted on the enemy," he said,

White House Landing on the Pamunkey, 1864.

This was the terminal of the Richmond & York River Railroad. Grant ordered the line abandoned, as no longer useful to the campaign, and the tracks, rolling stock, and loco- *motives returned to Alexandria and the government yards. From here they were transferred to the Aquia Creek Railroad by railroad barge.*

FROM A PHOTOGRAPH BY MATHEW BRADY, AUTHOR'S COLLECTION.

"more than compensated for any that had been received."

In August, in a diversionary strike against the Weldon Railroad timed to coincide with General Winfield S. Hancock's and General Ben Butler's movements north of the James River, Grant set up an operation to cut off one more rail supply line into Petersburg. The movement, a reconnaissance in force, was designed to effect a lodgment on the railroad "as near to the enemy's fortifications as possible, and to destroy the railroad as far as possible." "The track had already been pretty badly cut up by our cavalry," wrote General Willcox, "but only in spots and not beyond speedy repair. General G. K. Warren started out early on the morning of August 18th, with his own Fifth Corps and a brigade of General A. V. Kautz's cavalry, under Colonel Samuel Spear. The heat was intense, and the country so drenched with rain that the fields were well-nigh impassable for artillery. Griffin's division, in the lead, and Spear's cavalry, met the enemy's pickets a mile from the railroad, which was guarded by General James Dearing's brigade of cavalry—de-

ployed in skirmish line, and advancing rapidly on the railroad in column of brigades, and then turned to the south and west." In a rough fight with General Henry Heth's division, Warren drove Heth from the ground, but with heavy losses. Another action followed, with Warren's and Potter's divisions from the Ninth Corps. Coming up fast was General Maxcy Gregg's cavalry brigade and two hundred railroad men to destroy the tracks toward Reams's Station. Willcox's division, being nearest, was the first to arrive the next morning, and was ordered to bivouac near Globe Tavern, Warren's headquarters.

Meanwhile, General W. S. Hancock was ordered in support. Moving from Deep Bottom with two divisions, Hancock arrived at Reams's Station on August 22 and set to work with energy. Finding the station house already burnt, "and some sorry entrenchments in a flat, woody country, which had been hastily thrown up during the June operations," on the evening of August 24, Hancock, in the midst of tearing up some miles of track, received a message from Meade to the effect that large bodies of

Confederate troops estimated at ten thousand men were observed by Union signalmen moving within the Confederate lines toward the Union left. Meade thought that the Confederate troops moving down the Halifax–Vaughn road were probably headed for Reams's Station, and Meade was right. Before long a bitter fight developed and for a time it seemed to be going well for Hancock's troops. However, Hancock's men included some new recruits who froze in their tracks before the oncoming Confederates: "Suddenly our recruits gave way, and a break occurred between two regiments on the right," wrote General Willcox, "and although General Miles, ordered up what little reserves he had, these men [the recruits] would neither move forward nor fire."

The fight for the railroad was won when the Sixty-first New York formed a line at right angles, rapidly moved down the line recapturing most of the ground lost, including MacKnight's battery, and threw two hundred men across the railroad, threatening the enemy's rear. But even this did not inspire the recruits. "They could not be got up," said

a veteran officer who with his staff had tried his best "with sword and expostulation" to get them to fight. It was some dismounted regiments of Gregg's and Spear's cavalry, "fighting with bravery that shamed the infantry," who saved the railroad from the enemy.

While the cavalry raids were being conducted against the railroads, the long stalemate in the Petersburg trenches was further underscored by a new development when Lieutenant Colonel Henry Pleasants, a former mining engineer from Pennsylvania, devised a mine that could be run under the enemy's trenches and exploded. The plan, approved by General A. E. Burnside, was executed, and for a month the spade took the place of the musket.

An underground tunnel was dug from the Union lines under the shell-scarred "no man's land" to the Confederate trenches, where it joined two lateral galleries beneath them. When the galleries were ready, eight magazines of powder were placed in them and fused. Shortly before dawn on July 30, 1864, the mine was exploded. "It was a magnificent

The Battle of "The Crater," July 1864.

Characterized as "a magnificent spectacle," the Petersburg mine explosion opened a breach in the Confederate lines but the Union charge into the breach failed. The operation, *which Grant called "a stupendous failure," cost his army four thousand casualties.*

A Section of the Wharves of the City Point Railroad, 1864.

Cargoes of military supplies and ordnance arrived at this wharf, and were later distributed to the front-line troops in *the trenches at Petersburg. A lone USMRR locomotive works on a track leading to the loading docks.*

FROM A PHOTOGRAPH BY CAPTAIN A. J. RUSSELL, USMRR, AUTHOR'S COLLECTION.

spectacle," wrote Major William Powell, "and as the earth went up in the air, carrying with it, men, guns, carriages, and timbers, and spread out like an immense cloud as it reached its altitude, so close were the Union lines that the mass appeared as if it would descend immediately upon the troops awaiting the charge."

The charge that was to follow after the explosion breached the line failed, being misdirected, and the Confederates reformed and restored their line. General Grant, who had voiced skepticism from the beginning, characteristically described "the magnificent spectacle," as "a stupendous failure," and the war went on from there.

The bitter siege continued throughout the rest of the hot summer, each side feeling for a weakness in the other's armor, which led to bloody, sporadic actions and skirmishes all along the line. It was during one of the bloodiest phases of these operations, in October, that news of a new and devastating weapon soon to make its appearance began to circulate in the Northern press—stories about a fear-

some mortar, capable of hurling a three-hundred-pound shell five miles with cataclysmic effect.

Stories about the terrors of this new military devilment were allowed to "leak" to the Southern press, and in Petersburg the news created a nervous curiosity and anticipation among the citizens, as well as among the soldiers in the trenches defending the beleaguered city.

It all came to pass one hot, sultry day in October, when a puffing USMRR locomotive was seen rolling down the track of the City Point Railroad pushing a flatcar upon which was mounted a strange-looking object of gigantic proportions. Down the uneven track rolled the monster, finally coming to a squeaking stop some four miles from the Confederate lines. Seeing the huge mortar for the first time, the soldiers immediately dubbed it "The Dictator," and its train, "The Petersburg Express," saying that it "would dictate the terms of surrender to the rebels."

The advance publicity given this enormous gun had not been an exaggeration. Cast in Pittsburgh, by the Knapp, Rudd & Company Foundries, the Dictator weighed in at seventeen thousand pounds.

The Mortar "Dictator" and the "Petersburg Express," 1864.

Despite its capability of lobbing a three-hundred-pound shell five miles with horrendous effect, its first round frightened *a pack of nervous, hungry, stray cats the Confederate officers had been trying to get rid of.*

FROM A PHOTOGRAPH BY DAVID WOODBURY, AUTHOR'S COLLECTION.

It had a bore of thirteen inches and a depth of bore of thirty-five inches, and was capable of firing a three-hundred-pound shell approximately five miles with a maximum charge of seventy-five pounds of powder as a propellant.

The Dictator's gunners, men of the First Connecticut Heavy Artillery, busily made preparations for its debut, and by evening everything was ready to fire the first of the Dictator's forty-five rounds. Preparations completed, the gun was loaded and the elevation and range corrected with a crowbar, and locked in position. The command to fire was given by Colonel Henry L. Abbott.

Suddenly came a blinding flash which lit up the night sky, followed by a deafening report that increased in successive stages as the Dictator hurled its first shell skyward.

At that moment of the evening, Colonel William Willis Blackford, in his tent poring over a map with his officers by the light of lanterns, suddenly became alert to a strange sound. "The first of these 300-pounders," he wrote, "was connected with such an amusing scene at my quarters, that I must relate it:

My camp was back of Old Blanchard Church, dug into the slope of a hill. From the camp to the church was open, a closely-grazed field called "the common," sloping down towards the camp, and a favorite resort for the cats from town at night.

My fly was pitched in a dugout about ten feet wide dug back into a hill. A working party was to be sent out to start a mine in an exposed place, and the officers who were to go with it, four or five in number, were sitting around a table in my tent examining a plan of the work I had made and was explaining to them. We were all intently engaged on this when we heard approaching through the air what sounded like an express train. We all knew what it was. It was the long-expected 300-pounder, but no one spoke, all pretending unawareness, and I went on with my explanation. It must have been three miles off when it started [it was actually four] and by a computation I made, it must have reached an elevation of at least five thousand feet.

It seemed hours that we were in suspense, though I suppose it was not really more than two or three minutes. Presently the sound came from right over our heads, apparently, and increased to a terrific roar, becoming louder and louder every second, and I was sure it was going to fall right on my table. Just then a young lieutenant sitting at the end of the table—not over eighteen or twenty, got so nervous that he slipped under the table; this started a titter among the others, which an instant later burst into an irrepressible roar of laughter from the most unexpected event.

As I have said, the common above the fly was a resort for cats from the town at night, and these cats, hearing the fearful noise above them, and seeing the long stream of fire shooting towards them from the heavens, became completely demoralized and went scampering by as fast as they could run, back to the deserted houses where they had made their homes.

One huge tomcat, however, came tearing down the hill with eyes flaming and claws out, and hair on end, directly toward my tent. He was going so fast that he could not avoid the pit in which the fly stood, but came dashing, spitting and sputtering with one bound flop on the table, and with another clear out at the front and away. The effect was irresistible. If we were all to go to kingdom come the next instant, laugh we must, and laugh we did until the tears ran down our cheeks.

Even the young fellow under the table was relieved and came out crawling and looking very crestfallen, and this convulsed us the more. But still that horrid sound became fiercer and fiercer, and nearer and nearer, and more and more directly above us. The laugh cooled down as suddenly as it all began and we looked around at each other very gravely. Then to our intense relief came a tremendous blow nearby; the earth shook like an earthquake as the great shell struck the ground twenty paces away. Then we waited and waited for the explosion, but it never came. The fuse had been extinguished by the blow. . . .

The Dictator, and its train the Petersburg Express, were later run closer to the Confederate fortifications to a "Y" in the tracks, where it could be aimed in three directions—left, right, or straight ahead—simply by pushing the flatcar to either curve of the "Y" switch. Because of its mobility, the army photographers who made pictures of it likened the Dictator to the "Irishman's Flea" to describe its elusiveness. For as soon as the enemy got its range and started shelling, the Dictator was hauled to another position along the track and then, "like the 'Irishman's Flea,' when they put their hands on it, it wasn't there."

Shortly thereafter, the Dictator was hauled to the vicinity of the Jordan House where it was placed in a permanent position at the end of a special siding. "The mortar shells are thrown to a great height," wrote a Confederate soldier, "and fall down in the trenches like a ball thrown over a house. We have become perfect at dodging them, and unless they are thrown over too thick, I think we can escape them, at least at night. It was easy to trace their burning fuses as they hurled themselves against the darkened sky."

With the Weldon and Virginia Central railroads to all intents and purposes lost, Lee still had the four railway lines that met at Petersburg under the protection of his extensive fortifications: the Norfolk & Petersburg; the South Side, from Lynchburg into southwestern Virginia; part of the Petersburg & Weldon, which ran to Weldon, North Carolina, and Wilmington on the Atlantic Coast; and the Richmond & Danville crossed the South Side Railroad at Burkeville, fifty-five miles from Petersburg. Of course, then there was Grant's City Point military railroad.

"By September 12th," wrote General Grant, "a branch railroad was completed from the City Point Railroad to the Weldon Railroad, enabling us to supply, without difficulty, in all weather, the army in front of Petersburg. The extension of our lines across the Weldon Railroad compelled the enemy to extend his, and it seemed he could have but few troops north of the James for the defense of Richmond." The City Point Railroad, roughly following the contour of Grant's fortifications and originally about thirteen miles long, was extended to eighteen miles of track.

Lee had always contended that Petersburg was the key to the defense of Richmond, capital of the Confederacy; and should Petersburg fall, there was nothing to prevent Grant from destroying the Richmond & Danville and South Side railroads. If such were the case, Richmond would fall as well. Sometime in October, a Union commando unit attempted to wreck the South Side Railroad, Lee's supply line west of Petersburg, but the attack failed. Thus ended operations on the Petersburg–Richmond front for the winter.

The armies spent the Christmas holidays in their respective trenches watching each other warily, the soldiers of both sides suffering from boredom, fatigue, and the cold of a barren Virginia winter. But "Johnny Reb" suffered far worse. The City Point Railroad kept Grant's army amply supplied throughout the long winter of 1864–65, but Lee's

The "Y" Track at Devereaux Station, City Point Railroad, 1864.

Used for moving supply trains to either the right or left flanks of the Petersburg trenches, the "Y" was also used to change the firing direction of the great mortar Dictator. By *pushing the mortar's car to either leg of the "Y," the mortar had a wide range of fire.*

FROM A PHOTOGRAPH BY CAPTAIN A. J. RUSSELL, USMRR, NATIONAL ARCHIVES.

Burnside's Wharf, Army of the Potomac Base at City Point, 1864.

Army river steamers and transports unloaded supplies, food, provisions, and ammunition at this wharf is an almost endless procession. Materials were later transported by Grant's City Point Railroad to camps and forts along the front line. *"Empties" brought out the wounded and disabled from the field hospitals to the base hospital at City Point, to be transported by boat to hospitals in Washington, Baltimore, and New York.*

FROM A PHOTOGRAPH, PROBABLY BY CAPTAIN A. J. RUSSELL, USMRR, NATIONAL ARCHIVES.

men starved and went cold and ragged, many without shoes or warm clothing, while Richmond's army warehouses bulged to the rafters with ample food, grain, hams—enough to last for the winter.

There was no excuse for this condition. General L. B. Northrop, commissary general of the army, knowing full well the desperate condition of Lee's men, refused every requisition for food and supplies, acting as if it were all his personal property. Under these circumstances Lee could have had this officer court-martialed, but Lee was too much the gentleman to resort to this measure. Instead, he went to plead his case with President Davis, who assuaged his leading general with promises he had no intention of keeping. When word of the army's desperate condition became public, resentment and outrage finally caught up with Davis and his personal friend and former classmate Northrop, and Davis was compelled to relieve that officer of his command.

For a short time afterward, food became available to Lee and his soldiers, but the damage had been done. As usual, Davis's decisions were either wrong or too late. After more than three years of Davis's bungling and ineptitude, the attitude of the Confederate soldier was summed up in a statement by one of Lee's captured veterans. When asked by a kindly Union officer why he continued to fight, knowing the Confederate cause was hopeless, the soldier replied, "I guess we're fighting for General Lee."

Throughout the winter Grant's artillery battered the Confederate lines at almost regular intervals, while the extension of Grant's lines grew longer and longer to the south and southwest of Petersburg. Less the depletions by desertion, sickness, and battle casualties, Lee's army numbered about fifty thousand men, while Grant's army, with constant replacements, still numbered about one hundred twenty thousand.

Although there was not an officer on Lee's staff who did not believe that the end of the great adventure was at hand, their misgivings were never voiced. The Army of Northern Virginia was still putting up a formidable defense, and though it was outmanned, outgunned, hungry, ragged, and disheartened, a lot of fight still remained in the ranks. But no one knew better than Lee that should Grant capture the South Side Railroad, the Richmond & Danville would be indefensible and subject to capture.

Meanwhile, General Sherman, with his army of sixty thousand advancing from Savannah, Georgia, to the North Carolina border, had all but devastated South Carolina, leaving a trail of railroad wreckage in his wake, not to mention the destruction he visited on Columbia and Charleston. Sherman was advancing up behind Lee, placing Lee in the precarious position of being caught between Grant's and Sherman's forces.

A decision had to be made and quickly. General Joseph E. Johnston, with no more than fifteen thousand men, the only military force between Lee and Sherman, was no match for Sherman's veterans. With the prospect of almost certain defeat if he remained in the Petersburg trenches, Lee came to Richmond to see Jefferson Davis. Lee carefully explained to the recalcitrant Confederate president that unless he agreed to the abandonment of Richmond, there was no way the army could possibly be saved. Supplies and forage, he informed Davis, would have to be stored at various locations along the line of the army's retreat, and his remaining railroads protected while his supplies and munitions were being gathered. These supply depots would be located at Greensboro, Lynchburg, and Danville. Since Lee left him with little alternative, Davis finally agreed to evacuate Richmond.

At Grant's City Point headquarters a day or two before the final advance on Petersburg, Captain A. J. Russell, the Army of the Potomac's chief photographer, while preparing his equipment, had a visitor—Thomas C. Roche, one of the army's excellent photographers, who had been busy making pictures of the military railroad's operations. Entering Captain Russell's quarters, he said: "Cap, I am in for repairs and want to get things ready for the grand move, for the army is surely to move tonight or tomorrow night. The negatives on hand I wish to send north with some letters, prepare my glass and chemicals; in fact, get everything ready, for this is the final one, and the rebellion is broken, or we go home and commence all over again."

"I sat up with Mr. Roche until the 'wee sma' hours," wrote Captain Russell. "He had everything in A No. 1 order for the morrow, and we sat smoking and talking of our adventures, and among others of Dutch Gap Canal, and of the pictures taken there under difficulties a few days before, of which a friend of mine had been an eye-witness:

The enemy was bombarding Howlett's Point, throwing immense shells every few minutes, tearing up the ground and raising a small earthquake every time one of them exploded. He had taken a number of views, and had but one more to make to finish up the most interesting points, and this one

U.S. Military Railroads Photographic Headquarters at City Point, June–July 1864.

The photographic quarters tent, situated in a tree-shaded area, is shielded by an awning. Captain Russell (standing second from right), his hand on a "twelve by sixteen" plate camera, stands in the entrance. The man leaning against *the tree is believed to be Thomas Roche, a photographer for the Topographical Engineers. The officer on the right is unidentified. An army teamster leans against the photographic wagon.*

FROM A PHOTOGRAPH BY MATHEW BRADY, AUTHOR'S COLLECTION.

was to be from the most exposed position. He was within a few rods of the place, when down came with a roar of a whirlwind a ten-inch shell, which exploded and threw dirt in all directions.

But nothing daunted and shaking the dust from his head and camera he quickly exposed his plate as cooly as if there was no danger, and as if working in a country barnyard. The work finished, he quickly folded his tripod and returned to cover. I asked him if he was scared. "Scared?" he said. "Two shots never fell in the same place!" At this moment, the heavy boom of a cannon at Howlett's Point dropped another ten-inch shell precisely over the spot he just left.

Roche's prophecy proved to be correct. Lee had to defend the South Side Railroad while he prepared for the evacuation of the Army of Northern Virginia from its fortifications before Petersburg. If the rail line was lost, it meant the loss of the Richmond & Danville and an enforced surrender.

One day near the war's close, at City Point headquarters one of Grant's officers asked him why he had not invited the president down for a visit. Grant replied that Mr. Lincoln, as commander-in-chief, could visit him whenever he wished to. Someone then mentioned that the main reason for Lincoln's reluctance to come to City Point was the idle talk that would be generated about his interference with his generals in the field, and he did not want to impose himself on them.

Grant took the cue, telegraphed Washington, and invited Lincoln to visit the army at City Point. "He came at once," wrote Grant. "He was really most anxious to be with it in its final struggle. It was an immense relief to him to be away from Washington. He remained at my headquarters until Richmond was taken. He entered Richmond, and I went after Lee."

Richmond, Virginia in 1864–1865.

The capital of the Confederacy, Richmond was also an important railroad center to Lee. Petersburg controlled the Weldon, Richmond & Danville and South Side railroads, Richmond's supply lines. If Petersburg fell, Richmond would also fall.

FROM A PHOTOGRAPH BY MATHEW BRADY, AUTHOR'S COLLECTION.

The Illustrious Americans

The *William Mason*—"A Thing of Beauty."

Named for her designer and builder, William Mason of Taunton, Massachusetts, No. 25, built in 1856, was the turning point in locomotive design. Mason's locomotives were described by an engineers who drove them as "the neatest, best-proportioned, trimmest engines ever built by anybody." Efficient and elegant in appearance, No. 25

measured forty-eight feet four inches overall, and weighed one hundred five thousand pounds. "A thing of beauty," the color livery was standard Indian red originally, which was changed to conventional color. No. 25 saw long Civil War service.

COURTESY BALTIMORE & OHIO RAILROAD ARCHIVES.

A Typical William Mason "American 4–4–0" of 1860.

Flying two American flags, her safety valve blowing off steam, B & O No. 232 poses for her picture at Cumberland, Maryland, in 1861. A B & O Class 2, there were six of her type. Characteristic were her sixteen by twenty-two-inch cylinders and sixty-inch drivers, and an estimated weight of 54,760 pounds. No. 232 was retired in 1893.

COURTESY BALTIMORE & OHIO RAILROAD ARCHIVES AND MUSEUM.

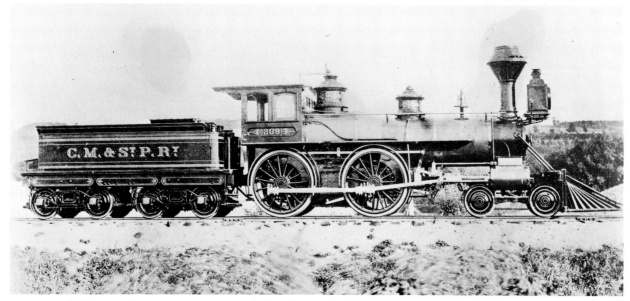

A Famous American Locomotive of the Chicago, Milwaukee & St. Paul Railway, 1865–1866.

No. 209, of the Chicago, Milwaukee & St. Paul Railway, broke a speed record carrying General Ulysses S. Grant from Chicago to Alton, Illinois, in 1870. No statistical, performance, or mechanical data are available.

COURTESY CHICAGO, MILWAUKEE & ST. PAUL RAILWAY.

The *Memnon*, Another War Veteran of the Baltimore & Ohio, 1861–1865.

Affectionately called the "Old Warhorse," the Baldwin-designed No. 57 was built in 1848 by the New Castle Manufacturing Company of New Castle, Delaware. The *Memnon* had seventeen-by-twenty-two-inch cylinders and forty-three-inch drivers. Both the *Memnon* and the Saturn, her counterpart, saw long military service hauling troop and supply trains of the Union Army.

COURTESY BALTIMORE & OHIO RAILROAD MUSEUM AND ARCHIVES.

An Inveterate Old Warhorse of the Civil War.

Antebellum Louisville & Nashville Locomotive No. 8, an 0–6 wood-burner, saw long military service in the Southern Department of the war. Extended driving rods attached to the rear wheels deliver power to the front four by her side rods. No other data are available.

COURTESY LOUISVILLE & NASHVILLE RAILROAD.

A Famous Confederate

Engine No. 14 of the Richmond & Danville Railroad, a sturdy-looking American 4-4-0, was the locomotive that hauled President Jefferson Davis, General Braxton Bragg,

Locomotive, 1865.

and members of the Confederate cabinet to Danville in their flight to escape capture. Davis was finally arrested, tried, and sentenced to Fortress Monroe military prison.

PHOTOGRAPH BY GEORGE COOK,
COURTESY THE VALENTINE MUSEUM, RICHMOND, VA.

A Ten-Wheel "Camel" of the Baltimore & Ohio.

Designed by Samuel Hayes, the B & O's master of machinery, and built by the New Castle Manufacturing Company of Delaware, in May 1853, No. 139 saw long war service. Designed for negotiating steep grades, No. 139 had nineteen-by-twenty-inch cylinders and fifty-inch drivers. Seventeen of these effective locomotives were built between 1853 and 1854.

COURTESY BALTIMORE & OHIO RAILROAD MUSEUM AND ARCHIVES.

A Conventional Long Furnace Camel

Ponderous, looking like some prehistoric metallic monster out of the past, No. 199 of the Baltimore & Ohio nevertheless saw long war service and had the distinction of being captured. Built by Denmeade & Son in May 1853, her firebox length compelled the fireman to stand on the upper platform of the tender and feed coal into the chute so it fell in front of the grate. Captured by the Confederates, she was recovered in Greensboro, North Carolina, in 1865, but could not be run because of her war damage. She was retired in 1884.

COURTESY BALTIMORE & OHIO RAILROAD MUSEUM AND ARCHIVES.

A "Saddle Tank" Locomotive of the Chicago & Northwestern Railway in Civil War Days.

A distinctive Civil War locomotive, the Iowa had a unique 4–0 wheel arrangement, an extended frame and long piston rods, and a water tank that straddled the boiler. Her tiny fuel box apparently precluded long runs.

COURTESY CHICAGO & NORTHWESTERN RAILWAY.

CHAPTER 11

Grant Ends the War on the Weldon Railroad

On November 16, 1864, General William Tecumseh Sherman had decided that the time had come "to make Georgia howl . . . and make short work out of what was left of the Confederate Government and Cause." For two months Sherman and his army had fought its way through the Mississippi Valley to the very doorsteps of Atlanta where, following a series of skillful battles and flanking movements against the forces of General Joseph E. Johnston, he threw a ring around the city and settled down to a seventy-five-day siege.

Then, in a stroke of genius, Sherman conceived the idea of marching his army to Savannah on the Atlantic Coast, two hundred fifty miles away, "to establish a new base upon the sea." Such a move would separate the Carolinas from the Gulf States and split the Confederacy in two, but could only be accomplished by the thorough destruction of the railway lines in Georgia.

Sherman's main problem was General John Bell Hood, who had managed to extricate his army from Atlanta before Sherman had completely invested the city. Hood had wired Richmond for reinforcements after Atlanta had fallen, but was informed that there were none left, that "no other source remains."

There was a lot of opposition to Sherman's plan to march his army eastward to Savannah, but he was adamant in his judgment that his plan would be successful. He had wired his plan to Grant at City Point, and had awaited comments and approval. In his judgment, should Hood follow him and cross the Tennessee somewhere near him, he could deal with him. On the other hand, should Hood head for Tennessee, General George H. Thomas, "The Rock of Chicamauga," in addition to troops already stationed there had an army large enough to handle the situation.

There is a story told by Mark Twain long after the war about a controversy in the newspapers concerning who it was who conceived the "March to the Sea." Twain, Grant's friend and publisher, came to visit the general at his cottage at Mount MacGregor, New York, to ask that very question. When Twain asked Grant whose idea it was,—his or Sherman's—the general replied, "Neither. It was the enemy's!" Twain then asked Grant what he meant. Grant went on to explain that in war the enemy makes a move and his adversary makes a countermove, and that Sherman's march to Savannah was the logical and brilliant move to make, in response to General Hood's move to Decatur.

Grant then told Twain that when Stanton at the War Department heard what Sherman contemplated, he telegraphed Grant to stop Sherman. Twain then asked Grant what he did after he received Stanton's telegram. Grant replied laconically, "Out of deference to the Government, I waited an hour. Then, since that was enough deference to the Government, I wired Sherman to go ahead!"

Sherman received Grant's consent on November 2, 1864, and preparations began in earnest. First, Sherman and his army would travel light, and in the first week in November he concentrated his forces at Rome and Kingston. He then "put all the capacity of the railroad, now repaired to the utmost strain to remove the surplus stores and war materials from Atlanta and other posts in Georgia, to Nashville."

Sherman then ordered Schofield to march to Resaca and Dalton, where he could transport his troops to Nashville by rail. The problem of removing the surplus stores from Atlanta to Nashville and bringing in the stores he intended taking with him overtaxed the railway, and it was not until Novem-

Hood's Fortifications Outside Atlanta, 1864.

Hood's veterans once held these now abandoned trenches until almost encircled by Sherman's forces. A few of "Sher- *man's Bummers" in full marching uniform pose for the photographer.*

FROM A PHOTOGRAPH BY GEORGE N. BARNARD, AUTHOR'S COLLECTION.

Nashville & Chattanooga Railroad at Atlanta, Georgia, 1864.

USMRR boxcars (empties) stand on a siding, probably await-ing the removal of General Sherman's surplus supplies. A military railroad locomotive works is to the right. The *buildings housing the Atlanta Lard Factory and Wholesale Grocers are burned out shells.*

PROBABLY PHOTOGRAPHED BY CAPTAIN A. J. RUSSELL OR GEORGE N. BARNARD, ATLANTA CAMPAIGN, NATIONAL ARCHIVES.

The Atlantic & West Point Railroad's Roundhouse at Atlanta, Destroyed by Sherman in 1864.

With only part of the walls left standing, this roundhouse still functions—under handicaps. The locomotive in the center of the picture carries the nameplate Texas, *identifying it as the hero of the Great Railroad Chase of 1862. The* Texas *captured the* General *near Ringgold, Georgia, after running in reverse for forty-eight miles.*

FROM A PHOTOGRAPH, PROBABLY BY GEORGE N. BARNARD, AUTHOR'S COLLECTION.

ber 7 that Schofield's command received transportation.

"The one chance left," wrote General Jacob Cox, "would be if Lee were to break away from Grant, and reestablish the Confederate power in a central position by the abandonment of Virginia. But this implied that Lee could break away from Grant who, on the south side of Petersburg, was as near to Columbia, and Lee would be on his heels the moment he abandoned the lines about Richmond." Facing Lee at Petersburg, Grant entertained the same worry.

However, as far as Sherman was concerned, the army was ready:

The condition of the army was all that could be desired. As to the rank and file, they seemed so full of confidence in themselves that I doubt if they want a compliment from me; but I must do them justice to say that whether called on to fight, to march, to wade streams, to make roads, clear out obstructions, build bridges, make corduroy, or tear up railroads, they have done it with alacrity and a degree of cheerfullness unsurpassed. . . . A little loose foraging, they did somethings they ought not to have done. Yet, on the whole they supplied the army with as little violence as could be expected, and as little loss as I calculated.

A few days before Sherman's troops left Atlanta for the March, Captain A. J. Russell, chief of the U.S. Military Railroads Photographic Department, arrived in Nashville for the purpose of making photographs of all bridges, trestles, buildings, boats that were under Sherman's control, or built, or operated by the Quartermaster's Department. As Russell later wrote:

The rear guard and engineer corps were still at Nashville, but left for Atlanta the day of my arrival. I there met many former friends and

The Macon & Western Central Railroad at Atlanta, 1864.

In this rare photograph, an Adams Express Company box-car stands in the foreground; behind it is a military rail-road personnel car with rifle ports above the windows. The unique-looking car in the lower right is a self-propelled steam rail car, complete with handpainted headlight, bell,

short stack, and whistle. Small locomotive pistons mounted on the forward truck drive the wheels. Screened louvres on the sides relieve the boiler heat inside the car. The car was employed as an army pay car, as well as for transportation.

FROM A PHOTOGRAPH, PROBABLY BY GEORGE N. BARNARD, NATIONAL ARCHIVES.

acquaintances, among whom was Mr. George N. Barnard, then Chief Photographer for the Topographical Engineers. We had but a short time together, as he, with the rear guard, were ordered to report at Atlanta and left immediately. The next news was that the army would leave Atlanta marching east, its destination then being unknown, no one being aware of its destination except the officers of the command.

As the work I had to do extended over a large tract of territory, a special train for my exclusive use and a car were fitted up for me and the work in hand. This was done by using a boxcar and making a darkroom at one end, with a barrell fastened up for a tank to hold water, of which we required considerable, as the plates used were 12 × 16-inches in size. The rest of the space of the car was utilized as a kitchen, where all the cooking was done; and in one corner berths were arranged for sleeping, with a stove, mess chest, cooking utensils, and all the implements and paraphernalia

necessary for making pictures. Frequently, four or five men were also domiciled in this space, and it is easy to see that there were no rooms "to let." Nevertheless, sometimes we had a boarder for a day or two at a time. The territory covered was from Nashville to Chattanooga, to Atlanta, Georgia; thence to Knoxville; also from Chattanooga to Atlanta; from Nashville to Huntsville, Alabama, to Decatur, to Johnsonville, Tennessee, and Louisville, Kentucky.

(George N. Barnard did all the photography of Sherman's campaign to the Carolinas.)

Prior to Sherman's March, the railroad south of the Etowah had not been completely demolished. So, under the efficient direction of Colonel Orlando Metcalf Poe, the army's chief engineer officer, "all that was of a public nature in Atlanta which could aid the enemy was destroyed," wrote General

Atlanta Railroad Terminal and "Old Car Shed" in 1864.

Built in 1864, the "Old Car Shed" survived the battle for Atlanta, only to be destroyed by General Sherman be-fore the March to the Sea. Army wagons are part of Sher-man's wagon train.

FROM A PHOTOGRAPH, PROBABLY BY GEORGE N. BARNARD, AUTHOR'S COLLECTION.

Hood's Lines Before Atlanta in 1864.

Running parallel to the railroad tracks which were torn up for some distance in both directions, Hood's lines follow the tracks in many places. A disabled locomotive stands in the center of the picture, while car wheels and trucks lie scattered about.

FROM A PHOTOGRAPH, PROBABLY BY GEORGE N. BARNARD, NATIONAL ARCHIVES.

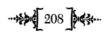

A Thorough Job of Railroad Execution at Atlanta, 1864.

Under the personal supervision of General Sherman's very efficient engineer Colonel Orlando Metcalf Poe, "all that was of a public nature in Atlanta which could aid the enemy was destroyed, . . . nothing was left of the railroad for a hundred miles . . . the destruction was complete."

FROM A PHOTOGRAPH, PROBABLY BY GEORGE N. BARNARD, AUTHOR'S COLLECTION.

How to Make "Sherman Hairpins," Atlanta, 1864.

Wrecking, as well as building, railroads was an art in the Civil War, and one way to destroy a railroad was to twist the rails out of shape. Rails were piled on top of a mound of crossties, fired, and heated red hot. They were then bent around trees into useless "hairpin" shapes.

FROM A PHOTOGRAPH, PROBABLY BY GEORGE N. BARNARD, AUTHOR'S COLLECTION.

The Remains of Hood's Ordnance Train, Atlanta, 1864.

Before Hood's army evacuated Atlanta to escape Sherman's encirclement, Hood burned his own ammunition train to *keep it out of Sherman's hands. When the fire reached the ammunition and powder, the explosions rocked the city. All*

that remains of the train are its iron wheels. Wrote General Howard, "The blackened ruins and lonesome chimneys saddened the hearts of the peaceful people."

FROM A PHOTOGRAPH, PROBABLY BY GEORGE N. BARNARD, AUTHOR'S COLLECTION.

Sherman's Occupation of Atlanta, 1864.

Prior to the March to the Sea, Sherman's troops all but laid waste to Atlanta's rail and industrial facilities. Here, some of *those troops pose for the camera.*

FROM A PHOTOGRAPH BY GEORGE N. BARNARD,
AUTHOR'S COLLECTION.

Oliver Otis Howard. "Wrecked engines, bent and twisted iron rails, blackened ruins, and lonesome chimneys saddened the hearts of the peaceful few citizens who remained there."

On November 12, 1864, communication with the rear was broken. The railway bridge at Alatoona was taken to pieces and carried to the rear to be stored, but from the crossing of the Etowah northward to Atlanta the entire rail line was destroyed. To complete the process, the railroad between Atlanta and Dalton, about a hundred miles of it, was abandoned, the forty-six miles of track from the Etowah torn up and destroyed; and from Resaca to Dalton, the sixteen miles of rails were torn up and carried to Chattanooga for use elsewhere. The U.S. Military Railroads system was becoming efficient under two soldiers who knew how to use railroads or to destroy them, whichever the occasion called for. Sherman's General Henry W. Slocum, commander of the Army of Georgia's left-wing force (which had its share of railroad wrecking on the advance to Savannah), wrote: "A knowledge of the art of building railroads is certain of more value to a country than that of the best means of destroying

them; but at this particular time the destruction seemed necessary. . . ."

Sherman's great march to Savannah and the Atlantic Coast was unique in the annals of warfare of the time. It was perhaps not as lengthy as Hannibal's crossing of the Alps or Alexander the Great's march across the middle East, but it was certainly the most devastating. However one considers the morality of such tactics, the overall practical effect was to save many lives by hastening the end of a hopeless war. "Pierce the shell of the C.S.A., and it's all hollow inside," Sherman had once said, and this time he meant to prove it.

He divided his army into two wings, the Fifteenth and Seventeenth Corps comprised the right wing under Major General Oliver Otis Howard, The left wing was comprised of the Fourteenth and Twentieth Corps under Major General Henry W. Slocum. A cavalry brigade led the vanguard of each wing, and a five-thousand-man cavalry unit, under Major General Hugh Judson Kilpatrick, who made a reputation for himself as "one of the chief spoilers" on the famous march, made an aggregate of sixty-eight thousand men of all arms.

Stripped down to the essentials of food, forage, and ammunition so as not to have his movement delayed by weak and insufficient horses, Sherman reduced his field artillery to one battery per thousand men, in batteries of four guns each, with eight good horses to each gun and caisson. Twenty days' rations and two hundred rounds of ammunition of all types were in the wagons, and a herd of beef cattle accompanied the army to provide the meat ration.

Thus the march began. "Behold now this veteran army thus organized and equipped with moderate baggage and a few days supply of small rations, but with plenty of ammunication, ready to march anywhere Sherman might lead," wrote General Howard. "Sherman explained in detail what he proposed and pointed significantly to Goldsboro, North Carolina, on his map saying: 'I hope to get there!'"

"On November 15, 1864, we set forth in good earnest," General Howard continued. "Slocum, Sherman accompanying him, went by the Augusta Railroad, and passed on through Milledgeville. I followed the Macon Railroad, and for the first seven days had Kilpatrick with me."

Sherman accompanied the left wing, which applied itself in earnest to the destruction of the railway from Atlanta to Augusta, making a thorough work of it at Madison, seventy miles from Atlanta, and destroying the bridge over the Oconee River ten or twelve miles farther on. The Twentieth Corps passed Saudersville, reached the line of the Central of Georgia Railroad at Tennille, and marched to Davisboro, destroying the tracks as they went. The right wing began destroying the railroad at Griswoldeville and ended a hundred miles later. Between that station and Milledgeville there was very little of the railroad left. Major General Francis Blair's corps reached Millen, Georgia, on December 3 and cut the closest railroad communication between Savannah and Augusta.

While this railway execution was being attended to, cavalry detachments with advance infantry scouts were sent out to cut the Gulf & Mobile Railway, severing the last connection between Savannah and the South, and opening communication with the fleet.

The extent of this railway destruction was almost indescribable. It was not unusual for a corps marching along a railway to destroy ten to fifteen miles of track in a day, and Sherman himself "gave close watch to the work to see that it was not slighted." All mechanical shops, railway stations, bridges, and roundhouses were destroyed, culverts and other masonry blown up.

From the Etowah River through Atlanta, and south to Lovejoy, nothing was left of the railroad for a hundred miles, the destruction complete. From Fairlawn through Georgia eastward to Madison and the Oconee River, and another hundred miles beyond, the destruction was equally devastating. From Gordon, the ruin of the Central of Georgia Railroad was continued southwestward to the very suburbs of Savannah, one hundred and sixty miles away.

"Here, at Gordon," wrote General O. O. Howard, "Sherman, from Milledgeville, came across to me. Slocum had enjoyed a fine march, having had but little resistance. The stories of the mock legislature at the State Capitol, of the luxurious supplies enjoyed all along, and the constant fun and pranks of 'Sherman's Bummers,' rather belonged to that unit than ours."

Such great destruction in the North would have caused serious interruptions, but the U.S. Navy blockade of Southern ports and the meager facilities for manufacturing in the Confederacy made the repair of Sherman's damage practically impossible under wartime conditions. The railways which were wrecked were the only ones then connecting the Gulf States with the Carolinas. And even had Sherman not marched north from Savannah, the food and other reserves of the Confederacy, meager at best, had already been crippled.

As with invading armies, Sherman's force had its following of displaced persons and refugees, the backwash of the army's advance. Throngs of escaped slaves, "from a baby in arms to the old negro hobbling painfully along the line of march—negroes of all sizes, in all sorts of patched costumes, with carts, and broken-down horses and mules to match, fell in behind the army."

"We brought along our wounded, I believe two hundred, in ambulances," wrote General Howard, "and though they were jolted over corduroy roads and were much exposed to hardships, and participated in the excitements of the march, they all marched to Savannah without the loss of a life. Our system of foraging was sufficiently good for the army; but the few citizens, women and children, who remained at home, suffered greatly. We marched our divisions on parallel roads when we could find them, but sometimes we used rails or evenly-cut poles and made our way through the swamps and soft ground, employing thousands of men. Arriving at the Oconee River, General Osterhause found a wooded valley, with log bridges and a narrow causeway on his road."

Now, as Sherman's army ground its way on

Savannah, leaving havoc in his wake, Lieutenant General William Hardee and a "scratch" army prepared to defend Savannah. Sherman had fixed an appointed time on which his army would assemble, in a line running from Ogeechee Church on the river of that name to Halley's Ferry on the Savannah River. As General Howard later described the march:

> General Hardee had assumed to defend the city with about eighteen thousand troops. Trees had been felled where Sherman's road crossed creeks, swamps, or narrow causeways. But his pioneer companies were well organized and removed the obstructions quickly. So, no opposition from Hardee worth mentioning was encountered till the heads of the columns were within fifteen miles of the city.
>
> Here the roads were systematically obstructed by felled trees, earthworks and artillery. These obstructions were easily turned. And Hardee was driven from his line. This followed first a swampy creek that emptied into the Savannah River about three miles above the city, and thence across the divide to the head of the corresponding stream which emptied into the Little Ogeechee. These streams were generally favorable to Hardee as a cover, because very marshy ground, bordered by rice fields, were flooded either by tide water or inland ponds.

From the standpoint of terrain, Savannah was admirably suited for a defensive battle. Fort McAllister was the main point of defense in Sherman's advance, but even this did not prove to be much of a deterrent. A strong, brick fortress, Fort McAllister had twenty-three heavy-caliber guns manned by two companies of artillery and three companies of infantry, two hundred men in all, but they were no match for an attack by a division.

At first, Sherman had sent Kilpatrick to try and take Fort McAllister, but it had been too much for the cavalry. General Howard "asked Sherman to allow me to take that fort with infantry. Hazen's division was selected. My chief engineer, Reese, with engineers and pioneers and plenty of men, in three days repaired the burnt bridge, then marched over and took the fort by assault, which Sherman and I watched from a rice mill some miles away, on the other bank of the Ogeechee. Now we connected with the Navy, and our supplies flowed in abundantly. Slocum soon put a force beyond the Savannah. Hardee, fearing to be penned up, abandoned his works, and fled during the night, before Slocum seized his last road to the east."

Sherman had been expecting the federal fleet to support him, and while watching Hazen's attack he saw the smokestack of a warship. A signal from the ship's captain read, "Has Fort McAllister been taken?" "Not yet," signalled Sherman, "but it will be in a minute." The final attack on Fort McAllister lasted exactly fifteen minutes, with a loss of 134 Union men and 48 defenders.

General Sherman moved into Savannah with his army on December 21, 1864, and remained there a month, and then moved his army across the river to advance on Charleston, South Carolina. In a telegram to President Lincoln at Washington, which was received on Christmas Eve, Sherman said: "I beg to present to you, as a Christmas gift, the City of Savannah, with one hundred and fifty heavy guns and plenty of ammunition, and also about twenty-five thousand bales of cotton."

Thus ended the Savannah campaign, in which the railroads of the Confederacy were virtually eliminated. On February 1, General Sherman and his elated army advanced toward Columbia, South Carolina, another march which made the recently ended march through Georgia seem like child's play. Columbia, the capital of South Carolina, was burned to the ground. (Sherman was charged with the burning, but later evidence proved that stored cotton was put to the torch by the retreating Confederate army under Johnston, who had taken over the command from Hardee. Fanned by a high wind and assisted by "citizens who distributed liquor too liberally to the released Union prisoners" and Negroes "itching for revenge," the city was virtually a total loss.)

At City Point, Grant's headquarters in Virginia, at nine o'clock on the morning of March 29, 1865, General Grant and the officers of his command bid good-bye to President Lincoln, who had been visiting the general at his headquarters, and boarded the special passenger coach of the train that would carry them from City Point to the Petersburg front. Thus began the final campaign in the eastern theater of the war. As the brilliant Colonel Horace Porter, aide-de-camp to General Grant later wrote:

> Since three o'clock that morning, the columns had been in motion, and the Union Army and the Army of Northern Virginia would soon be locked in another death grapple. The general sat down near the end of the car, drew from his pocket the flint and slow match that he always carried, which, unlike a match, never missed fire in a gale of wind, and was soon wreathed in the smoke of his inevitable cigar.
>
> I took a seat near him with several other officers

Five Forks, Virginia, April 1865.

The South Side Railroad Bridge, over the Appomattox River, and the trains of cars, water tanks, burned by the rebels, as seen by Alfred R. Waud, combat artist with Grant's army.

Colonel Oliver Wendel Holmes, Jr. reported that "Waud was quite a truthful draughtsman."
FROM A DRAWING BY ALFRED R. WAUD, AUTHOR'S COLLECTION.

of the staff, and he at once began to talk over his plans in detail. It was his custom, when commencing an advance, to have his staff officers understand fully what objects he wished to accomplish, and what each corps of the army was expected to do in different emergencies, so that these officers when sent on to distant points in the line, might have a full comprehension of the general's intentions . . . when communication with him was impossible. . . .

Such was the inauspicious beginning of the campaign which would bring to an end the conflict in Virginia. Lee had lost the Weldon Railroad and the Virginia Central, and in the first weeks of the campaign Lee's army was wholly dependent upon the Richmond & Danville and the South Side railroads. The Piedmont Railroad, worn out, with antiquated rolling stock, and subject to frequent wrecks, was a poor means of transporting supplies from North Carolina, when and if it were needed. But the two main rail arteries Lee now needed were the Richmond & Danville and the South Side, lines which cross at Burkeville, fifty-five miles west of Petersburg.

The end was not far away. On April 2, 1865, in Richmond, President Jefferson Davis was attending St. Paul's Episcopal Church when a mud-spattered officer strode meaningfully up the aisle and handed Davis a message from General Lee. The urgent message read: "I advise that all preparations be made for leaving Richmond tonight. I will advise you later according to circumstances." Picking up his hat, President Davis left the church, his face showing his anger. He hurried to the War Department where he telegraphed Lee to the effect that it was impossible to evacuate the Confederate government, "as it would involve the loss of many valuables, both for want of time to pack and of transportation."

When Lee received Davis's message at Petersburg, he tore it into small pieces, saying to his officers: "I am sure I gave him sufficient notice." Lee then telegraphed Davis that it "was absolutely imperative" that the Confederate Army move out of their positions that night; that he would inform Davis of the army's retreat route so that Davis could move with it; and that he would be furnished with a guide. But Davis ignored the warning. After

The "Displaced" Slave Population, 1864.

Displaced Negro slaves, living in tents supplied by the Union Army, live alongside the tracks of the remains of the Weldon Railroad, in Petersburg, Virginia, awaiting disposition.

FROM A PHOTOGRAPH BY MATHEW BRADY, AUTHOR'S COLLECTION.

Richmond, Virginia, in April 1865.

Following Lee's evacuation of Petersburg and Richmond, the Great Fire gutted an entire section of town. Nothing but bare, blackened walls remained. Spared by the conflagration were St. Paul's Episcopal Church (first left), two other churches, and the Greek-style Confederate Capitol, seen on the skyline. The fire was started by vandals, not by the Union Army.

FROM A PHOTOGRAPH BY MATHEW BRADY, AUTHOR'S COLLECTION.

Ruins of High Bridge, the Richmond, Fredericksburg & Potomac Railroad's Viaduct into Richmond, 1865.

All that Lee's forces left of this bridge in their retreat are the end and middle granite piers, broken tracks, and switch stands.

From a photograph by Mathew Brady, Author's Collection.

leaving instructions with his subordinates for the removal of Confederate funds and archives, Davis boarded the eleven o'clock train on the Richmond & Danville Railroad, still open, and with his cabinet members headed for Danville, North Carolina, arriving there safely at noon the next day.

As news of Lee's evacuation of Petersburg and the threat to the Confederate capital itself spread across Richmond, pandemonium broke loose. "Dismay reigned supreme," reported Captain Clement Sullivane, the officer in charge of Richmond's evacuation. "Battalions melted away as fast as they were formed . . . partly, no doubt, from desertions."

Meanwhile, at City Point, on April 1, 1865, President Lincoln had telegraphed Secretary of War Stanton that Grant's dispatches reported that "Sheridan had pretty hot work yesterday [at Five Forks], that infantry was sent to his support during the night." Sheridan, who had never let his commander down, had performed at his best at Five Forks. Incongruous as it was, his battle, a masterpiece of maneuver, had been fought to marching music

played by his regimental band mounted on gray horses.

On April 2, as soon as Lee and his veterans were in full retreat toward Danville, out of the Richmond cellars came predatory bands to loot and pillage while the ammunition dumps went up in thunder and flames roared through the abandoned city. With the retreat of Lee's army went the last semblance of law and order. Panic had taken hold of the populace, breaking out in bloody riots. Crazed men with guns and torches went on a rampage, running amok through the dark streets. The remaining railroad bridges entering Richmond were dynamited. Arsenals were put to the torch, with great flashes of flame and roar of exploding shells, their fragments spreading into the night sky. Across the stricken city, gangs of hoodlums, murderers, thieves, and deserters roamed the city's streets, their felonious activities lit by the flames from burning warehouses and buildings.

Explosions from the vicinity of the James River told of the sinking of the last of the Confederacy's

Ruins of the Richmond, Fredericksburg & Potomac Roundhouse, 1865.

Destroyed by both Lee's army and the Great Fire, this once busy roundhouse is now nothing but a mass of twisted *metal with a wrecked locomotive on a broken turntable and turntable machinery.*

FROM A PHOTOGRAPH BY MATHEW BRADY, AUTHOR'S COLLECTION.

gunboats, and before dawn thousands of starving citizens—men, women, and children—stormed the army's last supply depot, ransacking its contents for sugar, molasses, hams, bacon, barrels of whiskey, and coffee, while fights broke out among the raging individuals struggling to see who would get the best of the spoils.

The three high-arched bridges leading into Richmond were on fire and blazing fiercely. Only the last bridge between Richmond and Manchester remained intact—but not for long. While the looters cleaned out the military warehouses and supply depots, Captain Sullivane and two officers watched the last contingents of cavalry, led by General Gary, gallop over. As the last gray horseman crossed the bridge, General Gary saluted Captain Sullivane and ordered: "All over! Goodbye, blow her to Hell!"

Five days before Lee's formal surrender on April 9, the U.S. Military Railroads Construction Corps was already at work restoring the wrecked Richmond & Petersburg Railroad from Petersburg to the south bank of the James River, opposite Richmond,

twenty-one miles away. The Petersburg & Lynchburg Railroad, under repair between April 4 and 11, was opened as far as Burkeville, sixty-two miles from City Point. For a short time thereafter the line was used by General George G. Meade to supply his armies and the paroled soldiers of Lee's army. During this period four short-line railroads in the Carolinas were opened. Between April 4 and April 19, 1865, the USMRR repaired and reopened a total of 293 miles of rail lines. General Daniel McCallum wrote in his report:

When it was ascertained to what point of the coast General Sherman was directing his march from Atlanta, preparations were at once made to furnish him with railroad facilities. A portion of the construction corps from the Division of the Mississippi, that had rebuilt the railroads during the Atlanta campaign, were ordered in December, 1864, to proceed to Baltimore by railroad from Nashville and embark for Savannah. Upon reaching Hilton Head, information was received that General Sherman would not use the railroads, and

A Confederate Locomotive That Didn't Weather the Storm, Richmond, 1865.

In plain view of the Confederate Capitol on the upper right of the picture, this locomotive of the South Side Railroad stands a total wreck. Three of General Godfrey Weit- *zel's troops and a civilian, probably the photographer's assistant, survey the damage.*

FROM A PHOTOGRAPH BY MATHEW BRADY, AUTHOR'S COLLECTION.

The Devastation of War, Richmond, 1865.

The Richmond Canal provides a serene setting for the war- *blackened walls and chimneys of the Richmond Flour Mills.*

FROM A PHOTOGRAPH BY MATHEW BRADY. AUTHOR'S COLLECTION.

orders were received to proceed to New Bern, North Carolina, and open the railroad to Goldsboro. Eleven miles for the Savannah & Gulf Railroad were opened and operated, with rolling stock captured at Savannah for local military purposes and supply citizens of the town with fuel. The tracks and buildings of the Georgia Central Railroad within the city's limits were also used. Five serviceable and nine unserviceable locomotives, and two hundred and thirteen cars, about one half damaged and unfit for service, were captured at Savannah.

On that fateful day, April 9, 1865, almost four years to the day after it began at Fort Sumter, the War of the Southern Confederacy quietly ended at Appomattox Court House, Virginia, at the house of Wilmer MacLean, amid an atmosphere of dignity and respect between two of the nation's leading soldiers. There was no rancor or gloating, but a meeting between distinguished soldiers who respected each other's gallantry and ability.

The Last Days of the City Point Railroad, April 1865.

Its military usefulness come to an end, the USMRR City Point Yards are empty except for a lonely flatcar and a single locomotive standing over an ash pit in the shed. Some *railroad yard workers gaze at the once thriving military railroad base, which for a year and a half kept an army in the field.*

From a photograph, probably by Captain A. J. Russell, USMRR, Author's Collection.

CHAPTER 12

The Long Silent Journey into History

THE WEATHER was raw and cold on the evening of Good Friday, April 14, 1865. President and Mrs. Lincoln, and their guests Major Henry Rathbone, a War Department attaché, and his fiancée Clara Harris, arrived late at Ford's Theatre on Tenth Street in Washington, and entered the flag-draped presidential box. On stage, Tom Taylor's comedy *Our American Cousin*, starring Laura Keene, was well into the first act. Outside the door of the president's box, John F. Parker, an ex-policeman, cashiered from the Washington police force for drunkenness, dereliction of duty, and consorting with prostitutes, was serving as the presidential bodyguard.

The rest happened very suddenly, and without warning. Parker, having left his post of trust to watch the performance, had unwittingly allowed the crazed actor John Wilkes Booth to enter the box unobserved by anyone in the theater. In his pocket, Booth's hand gripped a Derringer pistol, a small-caliber weapon, fatal at close range. His left hand held a steel dagger.

Once inside the box, Booth raised his pistol, took careful aim at the back of the president's head less than five feet away and pulled the trigger, sending a lead ball crashing into the head of the man he hated more than anyone else in the world.

The unconscious president was carried to the Petersen House, opposite the theater, where he lingered in life until twenty-one minutes and fifty-five seconds past 7 A.M. It then remained for Secretary of War Edwin M. Stanton to pronounce the first eulogy, "Now he belongs to the ages." Abraham Lincoln, sixteenth president of the United States, was dead.

On Friday morning, April 21, 1865, a special seven-car train of the U.S. Military Railroads, headended by the locomotive *Union*, backed into the Washington Station of the Baltimore & Ohio Railroad and slowly rolled to a stop. Six days after Mr. Lincoln's tragic death at the Petersen House, this last train of the U.S. Military Railroads, with its special sixteen-wheel coach, would perform its last official duty—transporting the mortal remains of the man whose official order had brought the military railroads into existence four years before.

Later that morning, at the B & O depot, President Andrew Johnson, General Ulysses S. Grant, Secretary of War Edwin M. Stanton, and members of the Lincoln cabinet walked down the platform to the center of the train where the special coach stood on the tracks, and gazed on sadly as the casket bearing the body of Abraham Lincoln was carried on board. Moments later, a second, smaller casket, bearing the remains of Willie Lincoln, the late president's young son, was also placed on board. The boy's body had been disinterred for reburial with his father at Springfield, Illinois.

Before long the train pulled slowly out of the station, preceded by a pilot locomotive running twenty minutes ahead to test the rails. As the Lincoln funeral train eased itself through the Washington yards, engineers of the busy yard locomotives tolled their bells in a final farewell, while crowds of silent mourners with uncovered heads sadly watched the passing train bearing the man who would never pass their way again.

Once clear of the yard limits, the train gathered speed for the forty-five-mile run to Baltimore. Thus began the tragic, seventeen-hundred-mile return journey to Springfield, Illinois, over the same route and same rail lines which had carried Lincoln to Washington as president-elect four years before. Yet, things were not precisely the same as they

Abraham Lincoln, Sixteenth President of the United States.

FROM A PHOTOGRAPH BY MATHEW BRADY, AUTHOR'S COLLECTION.

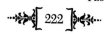

President Lincoln's Remains Lying in State, April 1865.

The rotunda of the United States Capitol provides the setting for the nation's obsequies. A statue of the late sixteenth president stands on a pedestal at the head of the casket. Colonel John Trumbull's painting of Cornwallis's Surrender at Yorktown and the Declaration of Independence provide fitting reminders of the nation's beginnings.

FROM A PHOTOGRAPH BY MATHEW BRADY, AUTHOR'S COLLECTION.

President Lincoln's Private Sixteen-Wheel Railroad Coach.

Built in the shops of the Orange & Alexandria and Manassas Gap railroads, a part of the U.S. Military Railroads, this luxurious, though ornate, passenger coach of the period, was never used by President Lincoln during his term in office.

The car's only official journey was carrying the mortal remains of the man whose official order brought the railroads of the United States into military service.

COURTESY SOUTHERN RAILWAY.

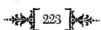

Official Seven-Car Funeral Train of the U.S. Military Railroads, April 1865.

This was the beginning of the official, pageant-like progress of the martyred president's body through the great northern cities, to its final resting place at Springfield, Illinois. The scene is the Washington Station and yards of the Baltimore & Ohio Railroad. The entire train is decked in mourning.

PHOTOGRAPHER UNKNOWN,
COURTESY BALTIMORE & OHIO RAILROAD MUSEUM AND ARCHIVES.

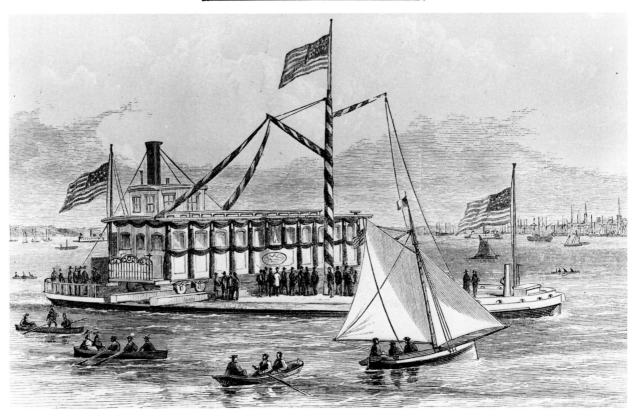

Railroad Car-Ferry *Jersey City*, April 24, 1865.

The Jersey City, *decorated in mourning, flags at half-mast, carries the Lincoln funeral car and cortege across the Hud-* son River to the New York & Hudson River Railroad Terminal at Thirtieth Street.

COURTESY MUSEUM OF THE CITY OF NEW YORK.

were that cruel winter of 1861. Only four of the five men who had accompanied Lincoln on that previous occasion were aboard this train. The deeply saddened Colonel Ward Lamon, Judge David Davis, General David Hunter, and former presidential secretary John Hay, were the only remaining members of the original party. Members of Congress Isaac Arnold and Elihu Washburne of Illinois, George Julian of Indiana, and Senator James Harlan of Iowa, lifelong friends of the late president, completed the party. Mrs. Mary Todd Lincoln, with her eldest son Robert, and her youngest son Tad, accompanied by a relative, Ninian W. Edwards, were the only members of the immediate family.

The run to Baltimore was uneventful. The Maryland city, draped in mourning, now presented a vastly different attitude from the one it had shown in 1861 when Lincoln's life was threatened during the stopover of the inaugural train four years before. Now the body of the late president lay in state beneath the rotunda of the Exchange Building, where thousands of citizens passed the bier to pay reverence to the memory of the gentle man who had saved them from themselves.

Across the beautiful rolling Pennsylvania countryside, from Baltimore to Harrisburg, wherever country roads crossed the railroad right-of-way, farmers and their wives and children watched with saddened faces and uncovered heads until the funeral train became a speck of smoke on the horizon.

That night the train arrived in Harrisburg in a drenching downpour, but more than thirty thousand persons viewed the open coffin until the early hours of the morning. At York, Pennsylvania, while the locomotive refueled and took on water, a group of young ladies placed a three-foot wreath of red and white roses on the coffin.

On the way to Philadelphia, as the train passed through Lancaster, Senator Thaddeus Stevens, the man known as the "thorn in Lincoln's side" for his vitriolic opposition to Lincoln's amnesty policy toward the defeated South, lifted his hat in tribute, tears streaming down his face. Also at Lancaster, Lincoln's predecessor, the infirm James Buchanan, seated in a carriage in the midst of a crowd of mourners, stared at the train and wept openly.

At noon on Saturday, April 22, the funeral train pulled into Philadelphia. At Independence Hall, on the spot where the Declaration of Independence

Arrival of the Lincoln Funeral Cortege at Desbrosses Street Ferry House in New York City, April 24, 1865.

The plate-glass hearse and the funeral procession moves through the "hollow square" formed by soldiers of the *Seventh Regiment of New York. Somber crowds packed the route from the ferry to New York's City Hall.*

Courtesy Museum of the City of New York.

was signed eighty-five years before, the coffin rested in state before the Liberty Bell. Here the line of mourners stretched for more than three miles.

In Jersey City, on April 24, banners stretched across the tracks at each end of the platform. One banner read "Be Still, and Know That I am God." Even the decks and fore and aft pilothouses of the ferryboat *Jersey City*, which carried the cortege across the Hudson River to New York, were dressed in mourning, the vessel's flags at half-mast. Huge crowds lined the edge of the dock as the *Jersey City* entered her Desbrosses Street slip, while New York's famed Seventh Regiment formed an impressive hollow square through which the funeral procession moved.

Somber crowds packed the route from the ferry, staring in wonder at the enormous plate-glass hearse, topped and cornered with eight plumes of black and white feathers, and drawn by six gray horses, each horse led by a groom dressed in black.

It was left to New York City to outdo itself in official mourning. Private businesses were "advised" to close for the mourning period. All ships in the harbor flew their flags at half-mast. Throughout the city, the windows of nearly every store and private home displayed copper and bronze plaques with

Lincoln's face engraved in relief, and plaster busts of the late president were everywhere.

And there were banners. One such banner stretching across a Broadway storefront spelled out a truism, "We Shall Not Look upon His Like Again." Another banner on the Bowery Savings Bank carried the single word "Lincoln," while the Old Bowery banner read "We Mourn the Loss of an Honest Man." At Cooper Union, where Lincoln had delivered his first presidential campaign speech, a large banner stated simply "A.L."

From noon Monday, April 24, through the night until noon the following day the body of Abraham Lincoln lay in state at City Hall as thousands of mourners moved past the bier to view the familiar face. Attending also were the dissidents, the unreconcilables of the lunatic fringe, the Lincoln haters, those directly responsible for New York's Draft Riots which had taken the lives of so many policemen and Negroes. They, and the faceless monsters who had looted and killed and committed arson at the time, now gloated in empty triumph. One of those wretches was overheard to say, "I went down to City Hall to see with my own eyes and be sure he was dead." But from midnight to daybreak, long double lines of grief-stricken men and women

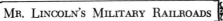

Midnight, under the Dome of New York's City Hall, April 24, 1865.

From noon Monday to noon the following day the body of Abraham Lincoln was viewed by thousands of mourners in the rotunda of New York's City Hall. *"New York never saw such a day,"* commented the New York Herald.

New York & Hudson River Railroad Terminal at Thirtieth Street.
The departure of the Lincoln funeral train for Chicago, Springfield, and the west.

COURTESY MUSEUM OF THE CITY OF NEW YORK.

passed in front of the bier at the rate of eighty persons a minute, totalling one hundred twenty-five thousand mourners.

At noon on Tuesday, April 25, the giant canopied hearse drawn by six gray horses moved from City Hall, crossed Broad Street to Fourteenth Street, and turned up Fifth Avenue to Thirty-Fourth Street and Ninth Avenue to the Hudson River Railroad Terminal, followed by thousands of marchers, people from every walk of life and every nationality. At one point during the procession word was received that a race riot element, bent on making trouble, threatened "to never let the damn niggers march." Nothing came of it, and two thousand Negroes, many wearing blue service uniforms of the Army of the Potomac, joined the mourners. Later, the *New York Herald* commented:

> New York never saw such a day. . . . Four years ago Abraham Lincoln passed through the city armed with authority as the nation's leader . . . which scoffed and scowled him a doubtful welcome. Yesterday he was a great martyr of a nation united, and these same people, inspired with a universal sorrow, sadly followed his body, crowned with more honors as the nation's saviour. The test of his success and his greatness can never be doubted or disputed.

The locomotive *Union* and its seven-car train now traveled along the east bank of the Hudson River to Albany, the New York State capital, over what is now called the "Water Level Route." At Yonkers hundreds of people gathered to stare with tear-stained eyes. A banner read "YONKERS MOURNS WITH THE NATION."

Farther along, at Irvington, the pretty little settlement named after Washington Irving, one of America's greatest writers, seven thousand persons paid their last respects. A little station banner read: "WE MOURN THE NATION'S LOSS." As the train passed through Tarrytown and Peekskill, those on board saw the people's faces in the glow from hundreds of torch lights and heard the sounds of church bells and cannon in tribute.

Below the U.S. Military Academy at West Point, at Garrison's Landing, an officer of the teaching staff and a thousand uniformed cadets in gray capes stood silently at attention until the train rolled out of sight. At Fishkill crowds lined both sides of the track while flags of General George Washington's Old Continental Army Headquarters, across the river, flew at half-staff.

At Poughkeepsie, Newburgh, Rhinebeck, and Catskill, through the majestic Hudson River Valley, many sections of the route were lit by bonfires built by ex-soldiers and others carrying torches. At Albany, the terminal of the New York and Hudson River Railroad, a ferryboat carried the cortege across the river, where a corps of firemen and soldiers met and escorted the procession up the hill to the Assembly Chamber of the New York State Capitol, moving through long lines of somber crowds.

As elsewhere, public buildings, factories, and shops displayed the black drapes of mourning, and every private home and stately mansion bore some kind of tribute to the late war president.

In the Assembly Chamber, four thousand mourners passed the open coffin throughout the night and morning, and the return to the train was followed by a procession of sixty thousand persons. Services at Albany were followed by those in Buffalo and Ohio. When the train stopped at Toledo, the late president's favorite humorist David R. Locke, who wrote satirical commentary on the times under the pen name of Petroleum V. Nasby, said of his friend Lincoln:

> I saw him, or what was mortal of him, on the mournful progress to his last resting place. . . . the face was the same in life. Death had not changed the kindly countenance in any line. There was upon it the same sad look he had always worn, though not so intensely sad as it had been in life. It was as if the spirit had come back to the poor clay, reshaped the wonderfully sweet face and given expression of gladness, that he finally gone "where the wicked cease to be troubling, and the weary are at rest" . . . the look of a man suddenly relieved.
>
> Wilkes Booth did Abraham Lincoln the greatest service a man could possibly do for him . . . he gave him peace.

The locomotive *Union* had thus far hauled the train over the same railroad divisions, with the same crew that had hauled the inaugural train four years before. But now, the locomotive *William Jones* was coupled onto the train at Erie, Pennsylvania, for the run to Cleveland, Ohio, over the tracks of the Cleveland, Columbus & Cincinnati Railroad. It had fallen to the road's superintendent, Henry Nottingham, to direct the presidential funeral train movement as he had the inaugural train in 1861.

On April 25, 1865, from a high bank along Lake Erie's shore, an enormous crowd of people gathered to watch the train come up the lake shore and pull into Cleveland's Union Station. Here the road engines were uncoupled and replaced with a switch engine, which hauled the train to the Euclid Street Station.

One reporter noted that as the train "came up the lake shore track, a Miss Field, of Wilson Street had erected an arch of evergreens on the bank of the lake near the track, and as the train passed she appeared in the arch as the Goddess of Liberty in Mourning."

At Cleveland, a group called the Committee on the Location of the Remains decided the crowds were too large to be accommodated by any of the city's available buildings, and authorized the construction of an ingenious pagoda in the city park. Open on two sides, the structure enabled two columns of people to view the coffin at the same time. The floor, set on an incline, allowed the visitors to view the late president from the time they entered until the time they left. Major General Joseph Hooker, the soldier whom the late president had removed from command of the Army of the Potomac for his failure at the Battle of Chancellorsville, led the military contingent that escorted the hearse drawn by six white horses, accoutered in crepe rosettes and silver stars.

The somberness of the occasion became more pronounced when a soft rain began to fall, which soon developed into a drenching downpour. Bishop Charles Petitt McElvaine read the Episcopal church service to a crowd of nine thousand. Despite the rain, by ten o'clock that night the mourners had swelled into almost half a million, undismayed by the weather. The same torrential downpour stayed with the cortege from Cleveland to Crestline, where mourners carrying torches and banners stood with uncovered heads while veterans of the Grand Army of the Republic nursed bonfires, the light from the flames plames piercing the black night sky. By morning of April 30, the rain had stopped and the body of the martyred president lay in state in the rotunda. From half-past nine in the morning, until four o'clock in the afternoon, eight thousand more persons viewed the bier.

"Lincoln performed greatly . . . supported by a great people," extolled the orator, J. E. Stevenson. "Peace and prosperity would yet roll along the railways, blossom on the Great Lakes, and whiten the seas, while over and above all shall rise . . . the great dome of his fame."

Again, bonfires lighted the slow night run to Indianapolis, throngs of people lining the tracks at various intervals. At New Milford, some four thousand people assembled bonfires and waved handker-

The Lincoln Funeral Train at Cleveland.

The Cleveland, Columbus & Cincinnati's Locomotive No. 113, the Nashville *is bedecked with a Brady portrait of the late president, flags, and black bunting for her somber jour-* ney *in April 1865. The* Nashville *was built in 1852 by the Cuyahoga Locomotive Works.*

COURTESY THE PENN CENTRAL RAILROAD.

chiefs, while at Urbana ten young women boarded the train and dropped roses on the coffin.

At Indianapolis, Governor Oliver P. Morton and U.S. Senator Thomas Hendricks headed a committee of a hundred public officials who took charge of the train during its stay in their state. Accompanied by ringing bells and falling rain, the coffin was brought to the State House and viewed by one hundred fifty persons a minute until the doors were closed at ten o'clock that night. The casket was then taken to the waiting hearse, which rolled through a column of soldiers and torch-bearers to the west end of the Union Depot, where the casket was placed aboard the funeral train readied by the Lafayette Railroad Company.

The run to Chicago was slow. As before, thousands lined the tracks, some waiting all night to see the train pass at daylight. At Michigan City the train pulled up under a canopy of evergreen arches and flowers, carrying banners ambiguous in their implications. "OUR GUIDING STAR HAS FALLEN" and "THE PURPOSES OF THE ALMIGHTY ARE PERFECT AND MUST PREVAIL" they read.

Around the shore of Lake Michigan, with its pine trees and sand dunes, rolled the train, arriving in Chicago on Monday, May 1. Here, more than a hundred thousand persons had come from across the Midwest, to pay their final respects. The train slowly rolled to a stop at Twelfth Street and Michigan Avenue. Under a canopy of evergreen columns and Gothic windows in Lake Shore Park, eight sergeants carried the coffin from the train and placed it on a dais encircled by a guard of honor and pall-bearers. "The Lincoln Requiem," written especially for the occasion, was played by the band as thirty-six high school students walked past the coffin and placed garlands of white and red roses upon it. The coffin was then carried at the head of a procession

The Locomotive *William Jones.*

One of the locomotives that shared the honor of hauling the Lincoln funeral train to Chicago and the west.

COURTESY BALTIMORE & OHIO MUSEUM AND ARCHIVES.

of fifty thousand people representing every nationality and class in America.

A light rain fell over Chicago, creating muddy potholes in the unpaved streets. Every so often an improvised wood-planked sidewalk would collapse and crash down under the weight of the spectators. Many fainted, and horse-drawn ambulances carried off the injured to the hospitals.

As always, the lunatic fringe, which manifested itself without regard to the nature or solemnity of the occasion, was on hand. Saloons did a land-office business, and Chicago's police stations were soon filled with large assortments of petty thieves, crooks, and pickpockets rounded up during the procession.

During the night hours of Monday and Tuesday, one hundred fifty thousand people moved past the bier until the services were over. A German chorus of three hundred voices sang an accompaniment to a thousand torch-carrying men who escorted the

bier from the courthouse to the Chicago & Alton Railroad Depot for the final run to Springfield.

At Springfield, the casket, which had traveled seventeen hundred miles and had been viewed by more than seven million people, was placed temporarily in the Lower House of the State Capitol, which the prophetic warnings of the famous "House Divided" speech had once echoed. Throughout the day and night, an unbroken line of friends and mourners, numbering seventy-five thousand, passed the coffin—a hometown saying farewell to an old and cherished friend. Among these was William "Billy" Herndon, Lincoln's former law partner. "We," he later wrote, "who had known the illustrious dead in other days . . . before the nation lay its claim on him, moved sadly through and looked for the last time on the silent, upturned face of our departed friend."

On May 4, 1865, the long, silent journey into history ended at Oakridge Cemetery, where, on the green, sloping hillside, mourning thousands heard Bishop Mathew Simpson read aloud the lines of the Second Inaugural Address:

With malice toward none; with charity for all; with firmness in the right, as God gives us to see

the right, let us strive on to finish the work we are in, to bind up the nation's wounds, to care for him who shall have borne the battle, and for his widow and orphan—to all which may achieve a just and lasting peace among ourselves and with all nations.

The Lincoln Funeral Train on Chicago's Lake Shore, May 1, 1865.

The train poses for a history-making photograph following its arrival in Chicago on May 1, 1865, its last run and final official service of the U.S. Military Railroads. A procession *of fifty thousand people, representing every nationality and class in America, accompanied the casket from the station.*

COURTESY ILLINOIS CENTRAL RAILROAD.

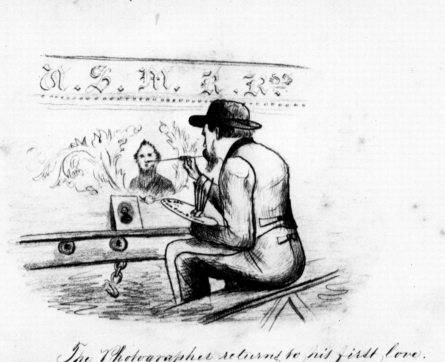

The Photographer returns to his first love.

Alexandria Jan. 12th 1864.

Civil War Railroads by States

Of the 30,000 miles of railroads in operation in America at the outset of the Civil War, only about 9,000 miles of these lines lay within the Confederacy. In all of Texas, Arkansas, and Louisiana, only 700 miles of trackage were in operation.

RAILROADS OPERATING IN THE SECEDED AND LOYAL STATES DURING THE CIVIL WAR, 1861–1865

(Asterisk indicates lines crossing state boundaries)

Alabama
    Alabama & Florida R.R.
    Alabama & Tennessee River R.R.
    *Memphis & Charleston R.R.
    Mobile & Girard R.R.
    Montgomery & West Point R.R.

Arkansas
    *Memphis & Little Rock Railroad

California
    Central Pacific R.R. (operative to Reno, Nevada, by 1863)
    Sacramento Valley R.R.

Delaware
    The Peninsula R.R. (short line)

Florida
    Florida, Atlantic & Gulf R.R.
    Florida R.R.
    *Pensacola & Georgia R.R.

Georgia
    *Atlantic & West Point R.R.
    Augusta & Savannah R.R.
    Georgia R.R.
    Georgia Central R.R. (now Central Railroad of Ga.)
    Macon & Western R.R.
    Marion & Western Central R.R.
    Savannah, Albany & Gulf R.R.
    *South Carolina R.R.
    Southwestern & Muscogee R.R.
    *Western & Atlantic R.R.

Idaho
    None

Illinois
    *Chicago, Alton & St. Louis R.R.
    *Chicago, Burlington & Quincy R.R.
    *Great Western of Illinois R.R.
    *Illinois Central R.R.
    *Chicago Branch, Illinois Central
    *St. Louis, Jacksonville & Chicago R.R.
    *Toledo & Wabash Railway
    *Chicago & Northwestern Railway
    *Rock Island R.R.
    Aurora Branch, Peoria & Oquanika R.R.
    Central Military Tract Railroad (Became C B & Q in March 1855)
    Galena & Union Railway

Iowa
    *Mississippi & Missouri R.R. (formerly the Northern Cross Railroad)

Indiana
    Cincinnati & Chicago R.R.
    Evansville & Crawfordsville R.R.
    *Indianapolis & Madison R.R.
    *Indianapolis, Peru & Chicago R.R.
    Lafayette & Indianapolis R.R.
    Ohio & Mississippi R.R.

Kansas
    None

Kentucky
  *Lexington & Ohio R.R.
   Lexington & Frankford Railway
   Kentucky Central Railway
  *Louisville & Nashville R.R.

Louisiana
  *New Orleans, Opelousas & Great Northern R.R.
   Ponchartrain Railroad of Louisiana
  *Vicksburg, Shreveport & Texas R.R.

Maine
  *Boston & Maine R.R.
   Old Town Railway
   Whitneyville & Machiasport R.R. (abandoned in
     1890)

Maryland
   Annapolis & Elk Ridge R.R.
  *Baltimore & Ohio R.R.
  *Pennsylvania Central R.R.
   Western Maryland R.R.
  *Philadelphia, Wilmington & Baltimore R.R.

Massachusetts
   Granite Railway of Massachusetts (the first railroad
     in America)
  *Providence & Boston R.R. (Fall River)
  *New York, New Haven & Hartford R.R.
   Western Railway of Massachusetts

Michigan
   Detroit & St. Joseph Railway
   Michigan Central R.R.

Minnesota
   None

Mississippi
  *Alabama & Mississippi R.R.
   Mississippi Central R.R.
  *Mississippi & Tennessee Railway
  *Mississippi & Missouri R.R.
   Natchez & Hamburg Railway
  *Mobile & Ohio Railroad
  *New Orleans, Jackson & Great Northern R.R.
   Southern Mississippi Railroad (Southern Railway of
     Mississippi)

Missouri
   Hannibal & St. Joseph R.R.
   Northern Missouri R.R.
   Pacific R.R. (Southern Branch)
   Pacific R.R.
   St. Louis & Iron Mountain Railway

Montana
   None

Nebraska
   None before 1863

Nevada
   Carson & Colorado R.R. (narrow gauge)
   Central Pacific R.R. (begun 1862; operative to Reno,
     1863; now the Southern Pacific)

New Hampshire
   None

New Jersey
  *Central Railroad of New Jersey
  *Pennsylvania R.R.
  *(Lehigh Valley R.R.)

New Mexico Territory
   None

New York
   Albany & West Stockbridge R.R.
  *Delaware & Hudson R.R.
  *Cayuga & Susquehanna R.R.
  *Delaware, Lackawanna & Western R.R.
   New York Central & Hudson River R.R.
   Mohawk & Hudson R.R.
  *New York & Erie R.R.
  *New York, Ontario & Western R.R.
   Utica & Buffalo R.R.
   Utica & Schenectady R.R.
   New York & Harlem River R.R.
   Saratoga & Schenectady R.R.

North Carolina
   North Carolina R.R.
   Raleigh & Gaston R.R.
   Western R.R.
  *Wilmington & Weldon R.R.
   Wilmington, Charlotte & Rutherford R.R.

North Dakota Territory
   None

South Dakota Territory
   None

Ohio
  *Baltimore & Ohio R.R.
   Central of Ohio R.R.
   Cincinnati & Zanesville R.R.
   Marietta & Cincinnati R.R.
   Little Miami, Columbus & Xenia R.R.
  *Dayton & Michigan R.R.
   The Bellfonte Line

Oklahoma Territory
   None

Oregon Territory
None

Pennsylvania
Cumberland Valley R.R.
Gettysburg & Hanover R.R.
Huntington & Broadtop R.R.
*Lehigh Valley R.R.
Northern Central R.R.
*Pennsylvania Central R.R.
*Pennsylvania R.R.
*Philadelphia, Wilmington & Baltimore R.R.

South Carolina
Greenville & Columbia R.R.
Northeastern R.R.
South Carolina R.R.
Spartanburg & Union R.R.
Wilmington & Manchester R.R.

Tennessee
*East Tennessee & Georgia R.R.
*East Tennessee & Virginia R.R.
*Memphis & Ohio R.R.
*Nashville & Decatur R.R.
*Nashville & Chattanooga R.R.

Vermont
Rutland R.R.
Central of Vermont R.R.
Washington & Rutland R.R.

Virginia
Alexandria, Loudon & Hampshire R.R.
*Baltimore & Ohio R.R.
Manassas Gap R.R.
Norfolk & Petersburg R.R.
North Eastern Virginia R.R.
*Orange & Alexandria R.R.
Piedmont R.R.
Petersburg & Lynchburg R.R.
Richmond, Fredericksburg & Potomac R.R.
Richmond & Danville R.R.
Seaboard & Roanoake R.R.
Virginia Central R.R.
Virginia & Tennessee R.R.
York River R.R.
York & Cumberland R.R.
Weldon & Petersburg R.R. (The Weldon)
Winchester & Potomac R.R.
Northwestern Virginia R.R.

Railroads in Virginia, Maryland, and Pennsylvania Conscripted as Military Lines by the War Department and the U.S. Military Railroads

NAME OF RAILROAD	TERMINAL STATIONS		LENGTH IN MILES
	FROM	TO	
Alexandria & Washington	Alexandria	Washington	7
Alexandria, Loudon & Hampshire	Alexandria	Vienna	15
Orange & Alexandria	Alexandria	Mitchell's Station	68
Warrenton Branch	Warrenton Junction	Warrenton	9
Manassas Gap	Manassas	Strasburg	62
Richmond, Fredericksburg & Potomac	Aquia Creek	Fredericksburg	15
Richmond & York River	White House	Fair Oaks	20
Richmond & Petersburg	Manchester	Petersburg	22
Clover Hill Branch	Clover Hill	Coal Mines	18
Richmond & Danville	Manchester	Danville	140
South Side	City Point	Burkesville	62
Army Line & Branches	Pitkin	Humphrey	18
Norfolk & Petersburg	Norfolk	Blackwater	44
Seaboard & Roanoake	Portsmouth	Suffolk	17
Winchester & Potomac	Harper's Ferry	Stevenson	28
Hanover Branch & Gettysburg	Hanover Junction	Gettysburg	30

WHEN the Civil War began, the federal government possessed only one railroad, seven miles in length, which connected Washington, D.C., with the Alexandria, Virginia, training camps of the Army of the Potomac. The first U.S. Military Railroad was under the control of the U.S. Army Quartermaster Department, and commanded by Captain R. F. Morley, assistant quartermaster. The Alexandria & Washington Railroad was in continuous operation from February 11, 1862, until August 7, 1865—three years, five months, and twenty-eight days. Until the army began operations, both passengers and freight were transferred across the Long Bridge by horsepower.

Number of trips made between Alexandria and Washington, February 11, 1862, to August 7, 1865

Locomotives	8,983
Number of loaded cars	30,457
Number of empties	20,699
Total number of cars employed	51,156

These trains ran without interruption until after the close of the war. On August 7, 1865, the line was turned over to the Washington & Georgetown Railway Company.

Restoration of the USMRR

THE RESTORATION of the railroads taken over by the War Department and U.S. Military Railroads under the Congressional Railway & Telegraphs Act of 1862 began almost at once. Beginning in April 1865, tracks and bridges destroyed during the conflict were repaired and restored to their former owners. In Tennessee, for example, reconstruction work began as early as January 1865 (according to Colonel McCallum's report in 1866), and completed in a little over a month. Some twenty-two hundred linear feet of bridges were rebuilt, only to be carried away by regional floods in February, March, and April. By May and June of 1865, all these trestles were replaced by permanent truss bridges.

Colonel McCallum reported in 1866 that "railroads leading south to Nashville were kept in active operation for some months, transporting paroled prisoners to their homes, also returning those that had been confined in camps north of the Ohio River; together with the movement of Union troops to be mustered out, or to take up new positions in Tennessee and Georgia."

RAILROADS REOPENED BY THE USMRR IN 1865

RAILROAD	TERMINALS	MILES	RETURNED TO OWNER
Wilmington & Weldon	Wilmington–Goldsboro	95	August 27, 1865
North Carolina	Goldsboro–Hillsboro	88	October 22, 1865
Raleigh & Gaston	Raleigh–Cedar Creek	25	May 3, 1865
Atlantic & North Carolina	Moorhead City–Goldsboro	95	October 25, 1865

RAILROADS IN VIRGINIA, MARYLAND, AND PENNSYLVANIA UNDER USMRR AUTHORITY

RAILROAD	TERMINALS	MILES
Alexandria & Washington	Alexandria–Washington	7
Alexandria, Loudon & Hampshire	Alexandria–Vienna	15
Orange & Alexandria	Alexandria–Mitchell's Station	68
Warrenton Branch	Warrenton Junction–Warrenton	9
Manassas Gap	Manassas–Strasburg	62
Richmond, Fredericksburg & Potomac	Aquia Creek–Fredericksburg	15
Richmond & York River	White House–Fair Oaks	20
Richmond & Petersburg	Manchester–Petersburg	22
Clover Hill Branch	Clover Hill–Coal Mines	18
Richmond & Danville	Manchester–Danville	140
South Side Railroad	City Point–Burkesville	62
Army Line & Branches	Pitkin–Humphrey (etc.)	18
Norfolk & Petersburg	Norfolk–Blackwater	44
Seaboard & Roanoke	Portsmouth–Suffolk	17
Winchester & Potomac	Harper's Ferry–Stevenson	28
Western Maryland	Baltimore–Westminster	36
Hanover Branch–Gettysburg	Hanover Junction–Gettysburg	30

RAILROADS IN TENNESSEE, MISSISSIPPI, AND
GEORGIA OPERATED BY THE USMRR

RAILROAD	MILES OPERATED	RETURNED TO OWNER
Nashville & Chattanooga	151	September 25, 1865
Nashville, Decatur & Stevenson	200	September 15, 1865
Nashville & Northwestern	78	September 1, 1865
Nashville & Clarksville	62	September 23, 1865
Shelbyville Branch	9	September 15, 1865
McMinnville & Manchester	35	
Mount Pleasant Branch	12	September 15, 1865
Chattanooga & Knoxville	112	August 28, 1865
Cleveland & Dalton	27	August 28, 1865
Knoxville & Bristol	110	August 28, 1865
Rogersville & Jefferson	12	
Chattanooga & Atlanta	136	September 25, 1865
Rome Branch	17	
Atlanta & Macon	11	
Memphis & Charleston	75	September 12, 1865
Mississippi Central	68	September 12, 1865
Memphis & Ohio	35	August 25, 1865
Memphis & Little Rock	49	August 25, 1865
Louisville City	2	November 1, 1865

Between 1862 and 1865, 21,783 tons of rails were purchased by the federal government for the U.S. Military Railroads, removed from the following railroads: Seaboard & Roanoke, Norfolk & Petersburg, Manassas Gap, Richmond & York River, Winchester & Fayettsville, McMinnville & Manchester, Mount Pleasant Branch,—for a total of 155 miles of rails.

Finally, a list of all the locomotives purchased and operated by the USMRR, and their disposition during the war and after, would take many pages. Those readers interested in the subject will find such a listing, an exhaustive study, in Bulletin No. 108 of the Railway & Locomotive Historical Society, Inc.; or in the Smithsonian Institution, Washington, D.C.

Maps

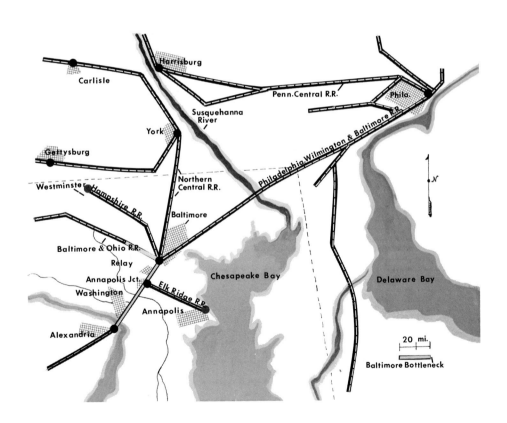

The Washington – B & O Bottleneck from Relay House
to Washington, D.C., in 1861.

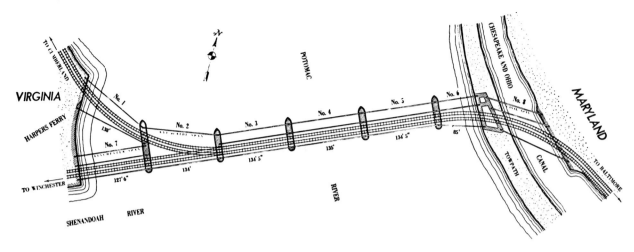

Diagram and Plan of the Latrobe Harper's Ferry Railroad Bridge over the Potomac River in 1862, Showing the Track Arrangement.

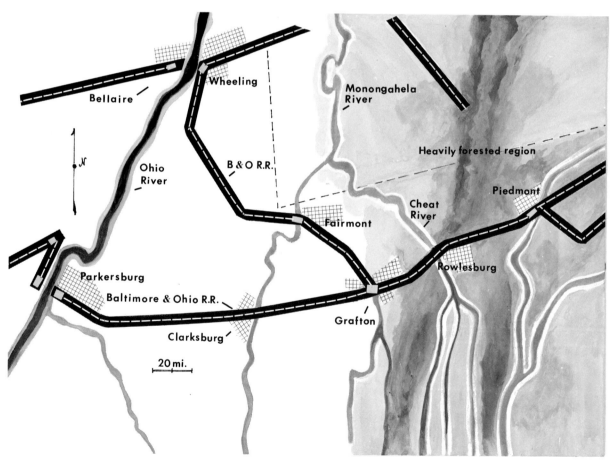

The Baltimore & Ohio's Parkersburg Cutoff and Track to Grafton, Rowlesburg, and Piedmont in Western Virginia, ca. 1861.

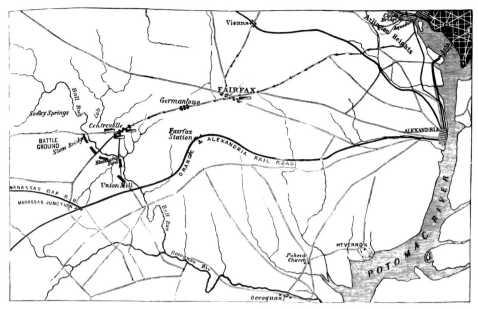

The Route of the Orange & Alexandria Railroad (U.S. Military Railroads) Between Alexandria and Manassas Junction, Virginia, 1862.

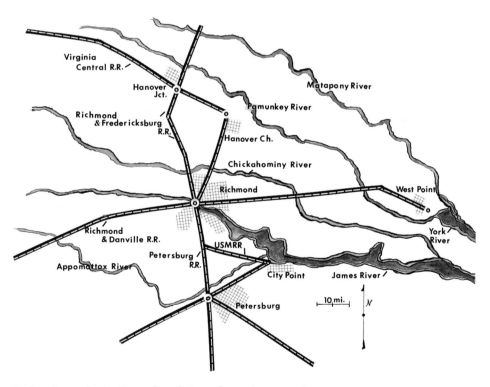

Railroads in the Richmond and Petersburg Areas, and the USMRR City Point Railroad. The City Point Military Line Came into Being in 1864.

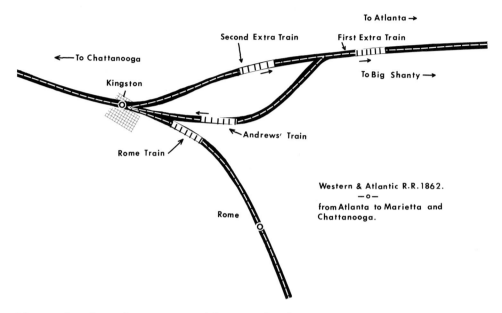

The Bottleneck on the Western & Atlantic Railroad in
1862, and the Position of Andrews's Train at Kingston,
Georgia, During the Great Locomotive Chase.

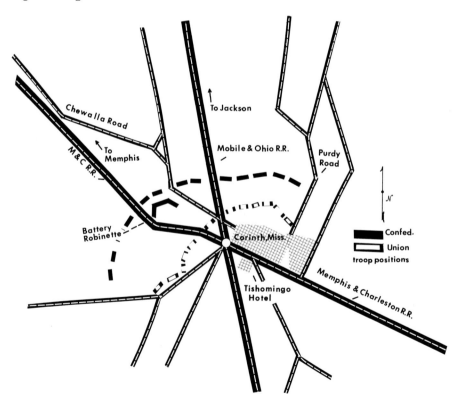

Corinth, Mississippi, in 1862, Showing the Railroad
Junction of the Memphis & Charleston and Mobile &
Ohio Railroads. Troop Positions Are Shown as They
Were on the Last Day.

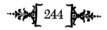

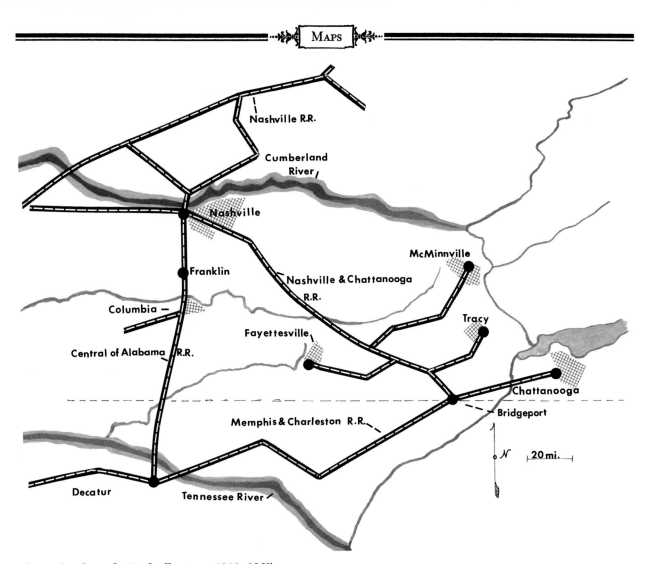

The Railroads in the Nashville Area, 1863–1865.

Acknowledgments

ON BEHALF of my late son and myself, I want to express our grateful appreciation to a number of generous people who have graciously given of their time and assistance in locating important sources of information and long-forgotten photographs essential to this book:

John B. Hankey, historical consultant of the Baltimore & Ohio Railroad Museum and Archives, for his untiring efforts in directing me to important pictorial and historical material in the B & O archives, invaluable to the relationship of that road with the federal government throughout the war.

Richard T. Eltzroth, archivist of the Atlanta Historical Society, for his aid in the use of the historical materials and Wilbur G. Kurtz watercolor paintings of the Great Locomotive Chase; and Ralph Righton, owner of the original paintings, who commissioned the artist-historian to paint a lasting memorial to the participants of that great historical event, for his permission to use them.

Michael Savedra, librarian and photographic archivist of The Valentine Museum, Richmond, Va., for his kind assistance in locating some long-forgotten pictorial material in the midst of moving the archives.

Elizabeth Roth, keeper of prints, the New York Public Library Rare Print Division; I extend my thanks and appreciation for calling to my attention the little-known William Marshall Merrick sketchbooks, on-the-spot drawings of incidents during the operations of the U.S. Military Railroads not found in USMRR official photographs. Acknowledgement is due also to Leon Weidman, first assistant, American History Division, New York Public Library, an old friend, for his aid in locating long-out-of-print books on a specialized subject.

Josephine Berti; I am deeply indebted for her assistance in assembling the pictures and research material, and her patient aid throughout the project.

I am indebted to John White, curator of transportation, Smithsonian Institution, and editor of the Railway & Locomotive Historical Society, Washington, D.C., for allowing me the use of the McCallum Report of the U.S. Military Railroads, in the Society's Bulletin No. 108, a journal indispensable to the subject. Grateful appreciation is also due to Glenwood Publishers of Felton, California, for permission to quote from J. Snowden Bell's book, *Early Motive Power of the Baltimore & Ohio Railroad*, originally published in 1912, a specialized work.

Acknowledgement is also made for assistance provided by the following railway companies: Baltimore & Ohio Railroad; Gulf, Mobile & Ohio Railway Company; Chicago & Northwestern Railway; Chicago, Milwaukee, St. Paul & Pacific Railway (The Milwaukee Road); Louisville & Nashville Railroad; Southern Railway; Illinois Central Railroad; Southern Pacific Company; Wabash Railroad Company; Chicago, Burlington & Quincy; and Chicago, Rock Island & Pacific.

Contributing historical institutions include the Illinois State Historical Society, Maryland Historical Society, Baltimore & Ohio Museum and Archives, National Archives, Washington D.C., Atlanta Historical Society, and the Library of Congress. I have taken all possible care to make full acknowledgement for the use of material and illustrations in this book where it is due, and I hope that no errors or oversights have occurred.

Roy Meredith

Sources

THE long-standing *Official Records of the War of the Rebellion*, an indispensable source of official reports, have been consulted. Also indispensable as a source is *Battles and Leaders of the Civil War*, the original version, of papers written by the participants. The *U.S. Grant Memoirs*, and the *W. T. Sherman Memoirs*, both valuable sources, are a wealth of information, as experienced by two of the North's most important general officers, and absolutely reliable. General Horace Porter's description of the City Point Railroad, by a distinguished officer and Congressional Medal of Honor winner, is about as accurate and firsthand as can be found anywhere.

Brigadier-General Herman Haupt's *Reminiscences* as superintendent and director of construction of the U.S. Military Railroads is also indispensable, particularly in the early organization and operations of the USMRR from Bull Run to Gettysburg, and is a wealth of information. Also invaluable as a source is the report of Colonel D. C. McCallum, general manager of the U.S. Military Railroads, written in 1866, and recorded in Bulletin No. 108 of the Railway and Locomotive Historical Society; and the John W. Garrett papers in the Baltimore & Ohio Archives. *B & O Power*, a pictorial history of that road's motive power, by Laurence W. Sagle, is a mine of information of locomotives of the B & O Civil War period.

Index

Page references in bold type refer to illustrations.

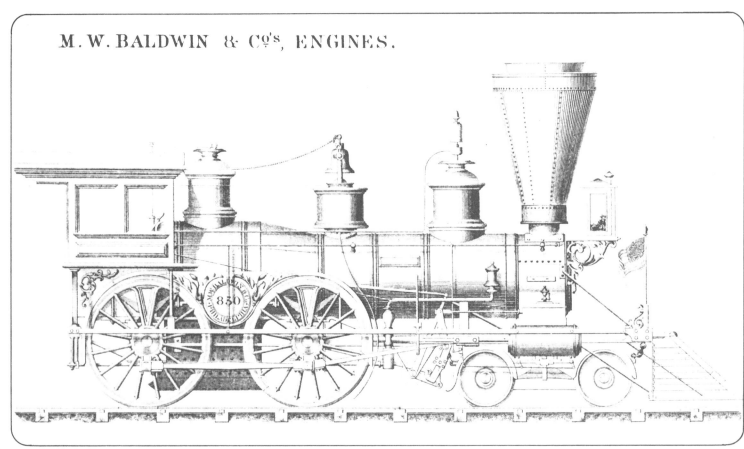